Object
Relations
Therapy

Object Relations Therapy

USING THE RELATIONSHIP

Sheldon Cashdan, PhD

University of Massachusetts

W. W. Norton & Company • *New York* • *London*

Published simultaneously in Canada by Penguin Books Canada Ltd.,
2801 John Street, Markham, Ontario L3R 1B4.

Printed in the United States of America.

First Edition

Library of Congress Cataloging-in-Publication Data

Cashdan, Sheldon.
  Object relations therapy.

  ''A Norton professional book.''
  Bibliography: p.
  Includes index.
  1. Object relations (Psychoanalysis) 2. Psycho-
therapy. I. Title.
RC455.4.023C37   1988   616.89'17   88-12415

ISBN 0-393-70059-3

W. W. Norton & Company, Inc., 500 Fifth Avenue, New York, N.Y. 10110
W. W. Norton & Company Ltd., 37 Great Russell Street, London WC1B 3NU

1 2 3 4 5 6 7 8 9 0

To the memory of Dora and Joseph,
my parents and first objects

Contents

Acknowledgments

Although this book deals with psychotherapy and object relations, it also is about internalizations and the way significant others are incorporated into the self. Included among these "others" in my case are teachers and supervisors. It would be difficult to list them all but the contributions of a few stand out. Hans Strupp, for example, taught me that psychotherapy is a systematic process and that there is order beneath the complexity of the therapist-patient relationship. Bob Carson sensitized me to the nuances of human interaction and their potential for understanding the nature of change. I suspect that the influence of the rest was conveyed through a word of encouragement or a specific recommendation that occurred during supervision. However it came about, their influence has coalesced into an "inner supervisor" that guides much of the clinical work I do.

I also owe a debt to my patients. They must necessarily go unnamed but each and every one has contributed to whatever skills and clinical acumen I possess. I am especially indebted to those I saw in the early years of my work as a clinician for I suspect that many of them helped me more than I helped them. But I am thankful to all of them. They are a part of me and though they may not know it, each has contributed in no small way to my work as a therapist.

My family has contributed to this book in a number of ways. My children, David and Jessica, have put up with my foibles, irritability, and unavailability on more occasions than I would like to admit. For this as well as other reasons, they share some of the credit for this book. I also wish to thank Steve Kraft for reading portions of the manuscript and making valuable suggestions.

My wife Eva has been a constant source of support and inspiration. I don't know how many times she has stopped whatever she was doing to help me thrash out a conceptual point or go over my writing for style and continuity. She is the "hidden partner" in my writing enterprises and my debt to her in this regard is just a small part of a greater debt I owe her.

Finally, I want to express my appreciation to my editor, Susan Barrows, who brought much more to this book than I had reason to expect. Throughout the project she constantly impressed me with her knowledge of psychology and her ability to help me say what I wanted to say clearly and forcefully. She is a dedicated and sensitive person, and working with her has been a delight.

Preface

Object relations theory is fast becoming one of the dominant perspectives in contemporary clinical work. Its influence ranges from work with borderline patients to new ways of understanding early childhood development. One can hardly attend a clinical meeting nowadays without finding papers and presentations on splitting, projective identification, and the use of the countertransference. There is change in the air and object relations theory is leading the way.

An interesting question about this development is why it is taking place now. Melanie Klein first began writing about object relations as far back as the 1930s. One explanation may be that object relations theory is particularly useful in understanding "contemporary" psychiatric disturbances. Interest in hysterical conversions and dissociations has over the years given way to interest in narcissistic disturbances and borderline states. It also may be that influential writers like Winnicott, Fairbairn, and Kohut have helped to bring the theory more in line with mainstream clinical thought.

A more profound explanation is that object relations theory reflects deeper changes in how we go about viewing human beings. Within object relations theory, the mind and the psychic structures that comprise it are thought to evolve out of human interactions rather than out of biologically derived tensions. Instead of being motivated by tension reduction, human beings are motivated by the need to establish and maintain relationships. It is the need for human contact, in other words, that constitutes the primary motive within an object relations perspective.

What implications, if any, does this have for the practice of therapy? Is there a unique psychotherapy associated with object relations theory? Are there different ways of working with people that are suggested by an object relations approach? Until recently the answers to these questions have been locked behind psychoanalytic doors. Whatever impact object relations theory has had on treatment has been confined mainly to alterations in traditional psychoanalytic technique.

This book describes a treatment approach that places maximum emphasis on the therapist-patient relationship. Instead of focusing on transference, defense mechanisms, and insight, the therapy focuses on the way that the "relationship-in-the-room" is used to treat the patient's pathology. The ultimate goal of the therapy is to use the therapist-patient relationship as a stepping stone to healthier object relationships and to promote positive changes in the patient's sense of self.

The first section of the book sets down the theoretical foundations for an object relations approach. Chapter 1 offers an overview of some of the major writings in the area. Beginning with the work of Melanie Klein, the chapter reviews the contributions of Mahler, Kernberg, and other contemporary object relation theorists. The purpose of the chapter is to identify some of the basic themes inherent in object relations thinking and to consider how they might form a conceptual scaffolding for a theory of therapy.

Chapter 2 examines the developmental origins of object relations with a special focus on "splitting." The chapter begins with the infant's first object relationship—that between mother and child—and describes how the interactions that make up this relationship play an important role in both normal and abnormal development. Drawing on the work of Mahler and recent findings on the nature of the infant-mother relationship, the chapter follows the developing child through different self-object experiences and shows how these experiences affect adult identity.

Chapter 3 describes the different forms of interpersonal psychopathology as they are expressed through "projective identifications." Drawing on case material, a number of these identifications are described, along with the interpersonal implications of each. An appreciation of the different projective identifications and the communications that comprise them provides a basis for understanding why patients behave the way they do and what kinds of interventions are required to enact change.

The next section of the book is devoted to a description of the object relations treatment process. Chapters 4 through 7 outline the four stages of the therapy process, beginning with engagement and continuing through projective identification, confrontation, and termination. Contained in each of the chapters is a set of relatively discrete interventions designed to bring about the changes needed for the therapy to succeed.

A major focus in these chapters is the use of the countertransference in object relations work and the way this differs from other therapies. Case studies and clinical vignettes are provided to demonstrate how the therapist's personal reaction to what is taking place can be used to further the treatment process. The overall process describes how the patient's pathology emerges in the relationship and how the therapist uses the countertransference to deal with it.

An underlying theme in this section is that psychotherapy follows an orderly course and can meaningfully be described by means of stage-related interventions. The assumption is that most questions regarding therapeutic technique are more satisfactorily addressed when viewed in the context of specific stages. This does not mean that object relations therapy is practiced in lock-step fashion. There is plenty of room for innovation and improvisation. But for a system of therapy to be effective, it must contain relatively invariant "principles of practice" for a therapist to follow and rely upon.

In addition to the more technical side of object relations therapy, one needs to consider personal factors which affect one's work. The last section of the book, accordingly, examines issues having to do with the personal side of object relations work. What does it mean for a therapist to be the target of the patient's projective identifications? How does the therapist distinguish between countertransference responses that are therapy-related and those that are not? Chapter 8 attempts to answer some of these questions.

Chapter 9 extends the personal emphasis in Chapter 8 to consider ways in which the therapist's work interfaces with interests outside of therapy. In this, the last chapter, we examine how literary and cinematic sources can, under certain circumstances, enrich an object relations therapist's approach to his work.

The overall goal of *Object Relations Therapy* is to provide the reader with a means of translating object relations concepts into effective psychotherapy. The therapy that emerges is one which focuses largely on the therapeutic relationship. Rather than seeing the relationship as a means of facilitating intrapsychic change, be it insight, emotional catharsis, or self-actualization, object relations views the relationship *itself* as the focus of treatment. It is the centrality of the "relationship" both in treatment and outside of it that forms the keystone of object relations therapy.

Object Relations Therapy

SECTION I
The Theory

CHAPTER 1

Object Relations Theory: An Overview

In recent years, object relations theory has been gaining prominence as a unique point of view in the mental health field. The concepts associated with the theory have been used to look at psychopathology in new ways, as well to analyze what takes place in therapy. This has been accompanied by a shift in the way early childhood events are construed. The central role of the oedipus complex, for example, has been reexamined with a keener eye to the role that preoedipal events play in the life of the child. In a number of different ways and in a variety of contexts, object relations theory is reshaping much of contemporary clinical thought.

What precisely is meant by object relations? What kind of "objects" are we talking about? The answer to that is relatively straightforward. The "objects" in object relations are human beings. To quote Kernberg, "The term 'object' in object relations theory should more properly be 'human object' since it reflects the traditional use of this term for . . . relations with others" (1976, p. 58). These relations may be internal or external, fantasied or real, but they essentially center around interactions with other human beings.

This is very different from the way the term is used in traditional psychoanalysis. In Freudian theory, an object is the target of a libidinal drive. It consequently is "created" by dint of the fact that psychic energy becomes attached to it. An object does not necessarily have to be human or even animate. It can be a piece of clothing or a work of art. An object needs only to possess a potential for discharging energy. Thus, the term "object" as it is used in "object relations," is nothing more than a vestigial byproduct of traditional psychoanalysis. It probably would clarify matters if the term "human" could be substituted for "object" wherever it occurred. But catchwords, being what they are, catch on.

What, then, is "object relations theory"? The answer to this question is a bit more complex. A survey of the various theoretical positions that fall under the rubric of object relations fails to reveal a unified object relations theory. Greenberg and Mitchell, two highly regarded observers in the field, write, "Discussion of theories of object relations is complicated by the fact that the term has been used in many different contexts and with any number of different connotations and denotations . . . " (1983, p. 12). This does not mean that an object relations theory does not exist, only that pinning it down may require some detective work.

Examination of various theories with an object relational bent reveals that each tends to focus on a particular aspect of object relations. Some highlight the operation of mechanisms such as splitting and projective identification; others direct their attention to clinical entities such as narcissism and borderline states; and yet others focus on the way that object relations affect development. To determine whether common threads exist among these different approaches, it is necessary to briefly review the work of some of the major object relationists. Only by identifying the basic ingredients in their approaches to object relations *theory* can we hope to make informed statements about an object relations *therapy*.

MELANIE KLEIN

Melanie Klein, an English psychiatrist and a contemporary of Freud, became interested in psychoanalysis very early in her clinical career. In order to learn more about the new discipline, she entered analysis with one of Freud's most brilliant students, Sandor Ferenczi. Somewhere in the course of the analysis, Ferenczi suggested that Klein consider applying psychoanalytic techniques to work with children. In following his suggestion, Melanie Klein almost single-handedly opened up an entire new realm of clinical investigation.

Up until then, little psychoanalytic work had been done with children. Freud himself had never directly treated a child. His famous case of Little Hans, for example, was conducted solely on the basis of interviews held with the child's father. Most of his writings on hysteria, moreover, came out of work with young women in their twenties. One by one, they provided him with the clinical material upon which he would build his psychosexual vision of the world. As elegant as Freud's formulations were, they were constructed almost entirely out of the childhood reminiscences of adult patients (Breuer and Freud, 1895).

Melanie Klein sought to remedy this. She began to incorporate psycho-analytic techniques into her therapies in the hope of clarifying the connections between childhood experiences and adult personality. The futility of this quickly became apparent. Children, particularly very young ones, were not very verbal. It also was difficult for them to meaningfully relate what was currently going on in their lives to events from their past. Because of their limited conceptual skills, children simply were unprepared, if not unable, to make use of psychoanalytic techniques.

Klein consequently turned to play therapy, hoping to use dolls, clay, drawings, and other relatively nonverbal techniques to gain access to the inner world of the child. What she discovered contrasted sharply with Freud's findings. Klein's observations revealed that children devoted more energy to constructing their interpersonal worlds than to trying to control libidinal impulses. Her findings led her to contend that children were driven less by a compulsive need to control erotic impulses than by a need to control feelings directed at significant figures in their lives. For Klein, the internal representations of these figures—what she termed "the internal object world" of the child—were the stuff of which the psyche was made. The inner world of the child was a world of human relationships.

Of all the relationships that make up the life of the child, it was the mother-child relationship that interested Klein the most. Because it is so intense, and because it subsumes so many of the infant's interactions with the world, the mother-child relationship forms the prototype for all subsequent relationships. A basic tenet of Klein's, if not of object relations theory in general, is that the core of selfhood is inextricably tied to the infant's first and most fundamental object relationship—the relationship with the mother. This relationship more than any other forms the foundation for the construction of the child's inner world.

One of the more unique and controversial aspects of Klein's work, particularly her early writings, has to do with the origins of this relationship. For Klein, the mother exists for the child before the child is even born. Existing as an innate endogenous presence, she constitutes a form of unconscious inner knowing that is part of the infant's genetic makeup. Along with other innate images (breasts, explosions, penises, etc.), the "innate mother" determines the way the child responds to the external world.

One does not need to examine this very deeply to realize that Klein is describing what amounts to a collective unconscious. Though Klein does not actually use the term, the mother exists as an "archetype" in the mind of the child. It is the primal maternal image of the mother that guides the child's interaction with a flesh and blood caretaker, i.e., the real mother, rather than the other way round.

Another unique feature of Klein's early thinking centers about the death instinct. Like Freud, Klein believed in the existence of a destructive inner force that, if left unchecked, would lead to self-annihilation. Freud felt that this destructive inner force became expressed through either sadism or self-directed masochism. In his later thinking, he largely abandoned the notion, analyzing depression, for example, in relational rather than instinctual terms (Freud, 1917). Klein, on the other hand, continued to subscribe to the notion of a death instinct and proposed that an inner struggle between the forces of life and death ultimately was projected onto the outer world.

In Klein's view, this development is responsible for the child's early division of the world into good and bad. A large part of the death instinct, for example, is projected onto external objects. This leads to a world filled with malevolent and destructive figures, i.e., bad objects. So that the child's world not be exclusively populated with bad objects, some of the child's libidinal energy is projected outward to create good objects. All these objects, in turn, are reintrojected to produce an inner representational world that is split into destructive (bad) and benevolent (good) components.

It is the dynamic interplay of good objects and bad objects that makes up Klein's view of the infant psyche. The child constantly projects and introjects hateful feelings in an attempt to deal with innate destructive impulses. Though Klein became increasingly interested in the child's "real" interactions as her career progressed, she never abandoned her belief in the existence of a death instinct. For Klein, life was dominated by a "mighty and mysterious inner struggle between the forces of creation and destruction" (Guntrip, 1971, p. 58).

The basic conflict for Klein, consequently, revolved about preservative (loving) and destructive (hateful) feelings, between a desire to protect those close to the child and the malicious wish to destroy them. She conceived of this conflict in terms of what she called "positions," types of interpersonal stances along which the child organized experience. Each position represents a developmental stepping stone along a continuum of love and hate, and describes the way that object relations originate and mature.

The first of these positions, the "paranoid" position, spans the first three or four months of life and characterizes the infant's first encounters with the world. Klein felt that the pain of birth coupled with the loss of intrauterine security led the child to feel persecuted and attacked, hence the term "paranoid." She later changed the name to "paranoid-schizoid," drawing upon Fairbairn's writings to describe the splitting which is an integral part of this stage.

It is during the "paranoid-schizoid" period that the child comes into contact with his first object, the breast. The child's interactions with this object (more correctly a "part-object") constitutes the infant's first real object relation. It also is the first opportunity the child has to deal with his or her destructive urges.

Klein is very graphic about the nature of these urges and the way they are expressed in fantasy. She talks about "vampire-like sucking" and the child's "scooping out of the breast." Describing the infant's aggressive impulses, she writes, "In his destructive phantasies [the child] bites and tears up the breast, devours it, annihilates it; and he feels that the breast will attack him in the same way" (1952, p. 63). Though the child undoubtedly also experiences positive feelings toward its only source of sustenance, the negative responses it inspires are truly awesome.

It is no wonder that the introjection of these images creates a great deal of inner turmoil and apprehension. The child responds by splitting off the images from one another, i.e., by mentally separating images that are frightening and malignant from those that are comforting and benign. This early division of the inner world into frustrating and destructive (bad) elements and gratifying, loving (good) ones, represents the infant's primitive way of reconciling inner impulses.

The "depressive" position begins in the second quarter of the first year and extends almost until the beginning of the second year. This is a period of rapid psychological growth, during which splitting is reversed and the mother established as a whole object. Interacting with the mother as an object rather than part-object, the child comes to appreciate that good and bad flow from the same person. Now the mother is experienced more realistically, as a fallible human being who can be good *and* bad, instead of good *or* bad. And to the extent that this happens, the child is forced to acknowledge negative, often hateful, feelings toward the mother.

But while this development, the reversal of splitting, marks a move in the direction of maturity, it is not without its costs. The child can come to feel that he has harmed—even destroyed—the parent. Such feelings are very intense, even though they are generated by events that have occurred only in fantasy; the line between fantasy and reality is still a very thin one for the infant. The result is the onset of what Klein calls "depressive anxiety." For the moment, it seems that all the child has done is trade one type of anxiety (persecutory anxiety) for another (depressive anxiety), thereby replacing destructive urges with guilt.

This is to an extent true, but there is a positive side to it. To subjectively experience the pain brought upon the mother and simultaneously feel sorry about it means that the child has begun to develop the capacity for empathy. This and the human desire to make reparation to the injured object signify that a higher level of object relations has been achieved. As this process develops, good internal objects become more firmly established and feelings of security come to increasingly replace feelings of persecution.

The depressive position constitutes a significant maturational advance over the paranoid-schizoid position. For one, the child is able to integrate split perceptions of the mother and combine them into a whole. Depressive anxiety, though unpleasant, comes to replace persecutory anxiety and paves the way for more mature interrelating. Finally, the capacity for reparation comes to the fore, suggesting the potential for establishing relationships based more on caring and preservation than on destruction and loss.

Klein's "positions" are her way of depicting the significant developmental stages through which the child passes. Instead of emphasizing psychosexual stages with their focus on libidinal dominance, she describes the psychological growth of the child in terms of the way the child deals with love-hate relationships. It is unfortunate that Klein chose psychiatric terms to describe the various "positions" the child adopts since they are essentially normal developmental progressions. Stripped of their pathological connotations, they describe the child's attempts to deal with significant figures (real and representational) rather than with biological impulses.

Klein's contribution to object relations theory can be summarized by the fact that she pioneered the study of early personality development as it evolved out of primitive object relations. As a result, she was instrumental in promoting a shift from oedipal to preoedipal concerns, from an analysis of the way children gratified their psychosexual drives to the way they constructed their representational worlds. Not only was Klein one of the first to propose the existence of early introjects, but she also championed the idea that the internal object world formed the basis for the human psyche.

Though many of her notions, such as the innate origins of maternal experience and the apocalyptic struggle between the inner forces of good and evil, have been superseded, her ideas regarding the operation of splitting and other unconscious mechanisms have influenced a whole generation of object relations theorists. Perhaps more than anyone else, Melanie Klein is responsible for introducing the study of relationships into a field that had been dominated by notions of pleasure seeking and tension reduction. If Freud is the father of psychoanalysis, Melanie Klein is the mother of object relations.

W. R. D. FAIRBAIRN

Often grouped together with Melanie Klein as part of the "British School" of object relations, William Ronald Dodge Fairbairn published a series of clinical papers in the 1940s which earned him a position in the ranks of object relations thinkers (1954, pp. 1–179). In these papers, he proposed that the ultimate goal of human behavior is not merely satisfaction of bodily pleasure but the establishment of meaningful human relationships. The desire for relatedness was *the* motive force in Fairbairn's point of view. For Fairbairn, libido was not pleasure-seeking, but rather object-seeking.

It was this consideration that led Fairbairn to propose his own relational theory of human development. Rejecting the primacy of Freud's psychosexual stages, he outlined a maturational sequence which focused on relationships rather than on reduction of erogenous tensions. Like Klein, he highlighted the importance of the early mother-child relationship. But unlike Klein, he focused on the operation of dependency in the relationship rather than on destructive fantasies.

Fairbairn's theory of object relations has its beginnings in a description of child development, with particular reference to the role that dependency plays in that relationship. According to Fairbairn, every child progresses through three broad phases of development:

1. early infantile dependency
2. the transitional period
3. mature dependence

Each constitutes a stepping stone on the road to autonomous functioning and describes a particular mode of relating to primary figures in one's life.

At one end of the scale—early infantile dependency—the child is psychologically merged with the primary caretaker. In this stage, there is very little differentiation and a poorly developed sense of self. The child is bound to the mother in a very primitive way, so much so that it is even difficult to speak of an infant ego at this point. Winnicott, for example, suggests that it is more accurate to talk about a "nursing couple" than about two separate human beings. Fairbairn refers to this primitive state of existence as "primary identification."

At the other end of the scale—mature dependence—relationships are marked by mutuality and exchange. In relationships such as these, participants not only are able to acknowledge each other's difference but are also cognizant of the healthy dependence that underlies their interaction. It perhaps is more correct to call this stage the stage of mature *inter*dependence rather than dependence, for it is the recognition of mutual reliance and the ability to tolerate difference that mark maturity for Fairbairn.

The transitional stage is not a discrete stage in its own right but rather a bridge between stages one and three. It entails a lifelong process of breaking away from the one-way dependency of early relationships and a movement toward relationships marked by interdependence. Much of life centers on these transitions (many involving separation), and individuals who cannot negotiate them with some degree of success are prone to psychopathology. In Fairbairn's way of viewing things, neurosis is produced by an inability or reluctance to relinquish infantile dependent bonds.

Though Fairbairn's account of development is painted with very broad strokes, it is clear that he attributes great importance to very early interactions between mother and child. Fairbairn's formulation, consequently, hinges on the way that dependency is experienced and how dependent relations with the mother become structurally incorporated into the child's ego. To understand how this comes about, he relies heavily on the psychological mechanism of splitting.

Fairbairn uses splitting to describe the way the child deals with an inconsistent and unsatisfactory world, that is to say, an inconsistent and ungratifying mother. For the most part, the mother is experienced as good. She fulfills the child's needs and gratifies his wishes. But there are circumstances under which the mother is also experienced as bad. She ignores the child, rejects his advances, and frustrates his desires. This poses a dilemma since the child can neither control her behavior nor leave her. The dependency constrains the child's options and forces the child to search for a solution.

Fairbairn proposes that the child addresses this dilemma by constructing an inner world inhabited by different aspects of the mother. This constitutes the earliest form of splitting. By dividing the mother into good and bad components and psychically splitting off one from the other, the child is able to maintain his dependent ties without constantly feeling threatened. The result is an inner world that is split into "good" and "bad" internal objects, each corresponding to the gratifying and ungratifying aspects of the mother.

The "good" internal object is referred to by Fairbairn as the "ideal object." This inner representation embodies the comforting and rewarding aspects of the mother. It is a part of the mother which, when internalized, is responsible for the child's feeling desirable and loved.

The ungratifying, or bad, object can take either one of two forms. One is the "exciting object." This is spawned by interactions with a mother who tantalizes, teases, and in other ways tempts the child. The result is a child who chronically feels frustrated and empty. The other bad object, "the rejecting object," is created through interactions with a maternal figure who is hostile and withdrawing. The child feels unloved and unwanted and is chronically angry about it. These two versions of a "bad" inner object combined with the "ideal object" comprise a tripartite division of the child's representational world.

Each of these inner objects gives rise to idiosyncratic ego states through what Fairbairn calls parallel ego splitting. The enticing aspects of the mother (the "exciting object"), for example, give rise to an *infantile libidinal ego*. This is a part of the psyche which is always thirsting but never satisfied. The child dominated by this type of ego state is a child who feels perpetually frustrated and deprived.

The rejecting object gives rise to an *anti-libidinal ego*. This is the part of the ego which is hateful and vengeful. It is full of bitterness and rails against the denial it has experienced. It desperately longs for acceptance; it yearns for the union and connectedness it feels it deserves. But it is dominated by the ever present fear that it is unlovable and unwanted. Children controlled by this ego state are filled with rage and feel hateful most of the time.

Finally there is the *central ego*. This is the part of the ego that derives from the ideal object. It is the only part still connected with those parts of the mother which were once gratifying. The central ego results in conforming behavior once the more disturbing aspects of the other two states have been split off.

Of the various states, only the "central ego" is available for relationships with real people in the real world. The other two tend to be repressed because they create pain. But isolation, or splitting off, of these parts leaves the inner world fragmented and leaves large segments of the self cut off from consciousness. This forms the basis for the development of psychopathology.

Abnormal behavior, according to Fairbairn, derives from extremes in splitting. The child's attempts to protect the positive parts of the mother by controlling the negative parts result in the repression of a whole realm of inner experience. Because painful parts of the self are repressed, they are not amenable to conscious control and in the end are experienced as inner feelings of frustration, persecution, and self-denigration.

All this ultimately affects what takes place in the face-to-face world. The same mechanisms that were responsible for splitting in the first place lead to the perseveration of infantile dependence in ongoing relationships. The core fear centers about loss of contact, and the individual does all he or she can to avoid the pain of abandonment. When separation – real or imagined—is threatened, the disturbed individual responds to the interpersonal world with either more intense expressions of neediness or rage.

Fairbairn's vision of the inner world elaborates on Klein's by providing a more detailed picture of various types of object relations as well as the ego states associated with them. In the process, he paints a somewhat different picture regarding the nature of good and bad objects. For Klein, the badness of an object is a product of the child's own innate destructiveness projected onto an external object, typically the mother. For Fairbairn, just the opposite is true. Badness in his view is an internalized aspect of parents who actually are depriving, frustrating, or rejecting.

Fairbairn's view of infant psyche, in sum, is one in which interactions with the mother produce splits in the inner object world. These, in turn, form the basis for splits in the child's emerging ego states. Fairbairn's object relations are more purely relational than Klein's in that real interactions rather than fantasy are afforded primary consideration. Despite his retention of traditional analytic terminology (libido, anti-libidinal, etc.), Fairbairn was one of the first to give meaning to the object relational contention that an ego or true self never develops outside the context of interpersonal relationships.

MARGARET MAHLER

The object relationist who perhaps most decisively placed the mother-child interaction in a developmental context was Margaret Mahler. A Viennese pediatrician, Mahler's interest in the faulty object relations of psychotic children led her to consider discontinuities in the early mother-child relationship. It was her careful study of autistic and other highly disturbed youngsters that led her to appreciate the psychological significance of the child's early attachment to the mother.

Mahler's study of disturbed children eventually evolved into a vision of normal childhood development. By careful observation of the interaction between mother and child in the first few months of life, she was able to chart the nature of early bonding. She saw this bonding and the child's primitive efforts to establish a separate identity as the beginning of a lifelong process called "separation-individuation." Mahler's description of this process and the interactions that fuel it gives her formulation "a simplicity and lyrical power which has made it perhaps the most compelling vision of early childhood since Freud's depiction of the oedipal complex" (Greenberg and Mitchell, 1983, p. 273).

The overall sequence of maturation, as Mahler sees it, is a process in which the child moves from a position of symbiotic attachment to the mother to the realization of a stable autonomous identity (Mahler, 1952). This process is marked by three major developmental phases: the autistic phase, the symbiotic phase, and the separation-individuation phase, the latter made up of a series of subphases. It is within the separation-individuation phase that life's major conflict—the longing for autonomy versus the urge to stay fused with the mother—is played out most intensely. The degree to which children resolve the conflict determines the extent to which they can go through life without pathological consequences.

According to Mahler, the first, or *autistic*, phase, begins with birth and lasts for three or four weeks (Mahler, Pine, and Bergman, 1975). During this period the infant operates as a closed system and typically is unaware of others in the interpersonal sense of the word. It is true that the infant seeks out the breast for sustenance, but much of this is guided by a rooting reflex rather than an awareness that there is another human being "out there" who is responsive to its needs. The infant during this early period of life is concerned primarily with tension reduction and has little awareness that another person is responsible for it.

It is not until somewhere in the beginning of the second month that the connection between tension reduction and the child's primary caretaker (typically the mother) is made. This marks the beginning of the *symbiotic* phase, which lasts from approximately the fifth week till about the fifth month. But even though the mother is in the child's awareness in primitive ways (she dimly is connected with feelings of warmth and fullness), she is not yet experienced as an autonomous presence. The world of the infant is still very much "pre-objectal."

It is during this period of life that the smiling response first occurs in response to the mother's face. Though this seems to connote a certain degree of separateness, Mahler points out that the infant still continues to experience the mother as if she were part of the same interpersonal system. Thus, the infant may react in a distressed manner when the mother is emotionally upset, even though food, warmth, and other physical requirements are present. At this stage of life, differentiation is still a distant goal.

These primitive "pre-objectal" experiences contain the seeds of early splitting. Pleasurable experiences are categorized as "good" while painful ones are classified as "bad." Together they form the basis for memory traces which are the precursors of later interpersonal splits. At this point, though, there is no experience of oneself as a separate human being, no differentiation between the mother and an infant "self," only the experience of symbiotic oneness.

The next and most complex phase, *separation-individuation*, is made up of a series of subphases, each of which signals a unique form of movement on the path towards independence. In order of occurrence, they are the differentiation, practicing, rapprochement, and libidinal object-constancy phases (Mahler et al., 1975, chapters 4–7). Beginning in the fifth or sixth month and extending into third or fourth year, these four subphases essentially dictate the degree of separateness one achieves. One's sense of self and the nature of one's relationships are determined largely by the kinds of things that happen during this phase.

The *differentiation subphase* begins in about the fifth or sixth month and extends into approximately the tenth month. The key mother-child dynamic during this period centers on perceptual discrimination. Distal sensory systems such as vision become more sophisticated; as they do, the infant begins to experience the separateness of the mother (and others) more and more. It is this subphase, for example, that the child first experiences "stranger anxiety." As the child starts to investigate the world and discovers that it extends beyond his lips and fingertips, self and object become increasingly differentiated.

At about 10 to 11 months the child enters the *practicing subphase*. This part of the separation-individuation process lasts until about 15 or 16 months and is marked by quadruped locomotion. The child climbs and crawls, and in so doing is able to bodily separate himself from the mother. This separation from the mother has its primitive beginnings in the differentiation subphase in a phenomenon Mahler calls "hatching." Mahler claims that the child's ability to physically distance himself from the mother marks the true beginning of "psychological birth."

This does not mean that the child is fully able to function on his own emotionally. He still seeks the mother's presence and reassurance at regular intervals for "emotional refueling." One need only to observe the play activities of one-year-olds to verify this. Even though children are actively involved in play with other children, they regularly stop what they are doing to visually check on the mother's whereabouts. Although the end of this period sees the beginnings of upright locomotion and more active exploration of the world, the mother continues to be used as a "home base."

The *rapprochement* subphase of the separation-individuation process begins somewhere between the 15th and 18th month and extends to 30 months, or about the age of two and a half. During this time, rapid gains are made in language ability as the child interacts more and more on a linguistic level with the mother and other significant figures, especially the father. Feelings of self-assertion and separateness come to the fore as the child struts about almost belligerently flouting his newfound independence. But while the child is making increasing strides in separating himself from the mother and establishing himself as an individual, there remains a strong need for help and reassurance. The child tries to deny this, and this culminates in what is known as the "rapprochement crisis."

This so-called crisis is really a series of ongoing struggles between mother and child constituting a conflict between the need for the mother and the need for separation-individuation. The child enters this subphase in an expansive, omnipotent mood due to his budding physical and linguistic abilities. This, however, alternates with clinginess and other expressions of neediness. The "terrible twos" of which so much has been written aptly describes the intense negativism born of this conflict. The mother's ability to successfully provide the child with the right balance of emotional support and firmness, while still allowing the child to engage in a healthy level of independent activity, is an important factor in the resolution of the crisis.

The final subphase of the separation-individuation process is perhaps the most critical because it plays such an important role in the creation and ultimate nature of the self. Referred to as *libidinal object constancy*, this subphase has its onset at about two and a half years and lasts until the child is approximately three years of age. The principal task of this period is the development of a stable inner representation of the mother. Unless this is accomplished, the child continues to depend on the mother's physical presence for security and can never develop an autonomous sense of self.

The successful completion of this task sees the child able to internalize the mother and maintain a stable inner vision of her in her absence. Development of a viable inner maternal presence, i.e., achievement of libidinal object constancy, enables the child to function independently of the primary caretaker and to experience interpersonal separateness. To the extent that this is achieved, or at least a fair start made in this direction, the child incorporates the ability to function on his own and to establish healthy object relationships.

Achievement of libidinal object constancy presumes that positive and negative maternal introjects have been integrated. If integration is incomplete, the child—and later the adult—responds to those in his interpersonal environment either as punitive and rejecting or as unrealistically gratifying. Both positions, to borrow one of Klein's terms, stem from faulty early object relations. Both in their own way lead to the corruption of adult object relationships and to the eventual onset of psychopathology.

One needs to regard the time spans associated with Mahler's various phases and subphases as rough temporal guidelines. Like Piaget's stages of intellectual growth, they fold back onto one another, behaving more like points on an undulating helix than points on a straight line. As anyone who has ever raised children knows, childhood development is more a process of fits and starts, of losses and losses recouped, than a series of predictable events taking place in linear fashion.

Still, one is able to identify concrete behavioral markers in each of Mahler's phases which highlight the important stages of the maturational process. Stranger anxiety in the differentiation subphase, for example, indicates that the infant has learned to perceptually discriminate the mother from other human beings. The ability to move about on one's own, beginning with crawling and ending with the baby's first steps, suggests that the child is in the practicing subphase. And the use of language as an interpersonal tool clearly indicates that the child has entered the rapprochement subphase. Together these markers offer as clear-cut a description of the separation-individuation process as any object relationist has presented to date.

Separation-individuation, in short, comprises two complementary but distinct developmental processes. Separation is the process by which the child emerges from the symbiotic fusion that characterizes the early relationship with the mother. It begins with a process of perceptual discrimination and culminates in an act of cognitive incorporation (libidinal object constancy). Individuation, on the other hand, is marked by concrete achievements, such as locomotion, language usage, and other activities that indicate the ability to function autonomously. Mahler's contribution rests in her ability to document these processes and to show how they are rooted in the child's early object relations.

OTTO KERNBERG

A contemporary object relationist whose work has attracted a great deal of attention, Otto Kernberg has written a number of papers and several books on object relations theory and its use in understanding severe character disorders. A great deal of contemporary thinking on the origin and nature of borderline disorders, for example, is contained in a series of monographs in which he traces the disturbance to pathology in the patient's early object relations (1976, 1982, 1984). According to Kernberg, the origins of severe psychopathology are lodged in deficient or distorted object relations that have become a part of the patient's inner world.

Considering how influential Kernberg is in the object relations arena, it is interesting that he tends not to see object relations theory as a theory in its own right. Instead he views it as an extension of psychoanalysis. This position, challenged by some, will be addressed later. Regardless of the context in which Kernberg's formulations are viewed, they provide a rich and unique perspective on the origins and nature of the relational self and on the types of internalizations that contribute to its development.

Like most object relationists, Kernberg views the mother-child relationship as the key to understanding the nature and direction of psychological growth. He contends that the essence of this relationship is encapsulated in something he calls "bipolar intrapsychic representations." This is Kernberg's term for the inner relational counterparts of the child's interpersonal, i.e., self-other, experiences. Lodged in the infant psyche as relational enclaves of sorts, these bipolar representations not only influence how the child perceives the world but act as a template for what takes place in ongoing relationships.

Every bipolar representation is constructed of three components: an image of the self, an image of the other, and an affective coloring. The latter is dictated by the particular drive state active at the time the child is interacting with a significant other. Thus, if the self-other interaction occurs when the child feels deprived, the bipolar representation will be experienced as frustrating and depriving. If self-other exchanges occur in the context of satisfaction, the resulting internalization will be experienced as positive and fulfilling.

Taken together, the various bipolar representations are "metabolized" by the young child to form the foundations of human personality. The metabolization metaphor is used by Kernberg to describe a process by which experience is transformed from interactions "out there" to interactions that are experienced as an integral part of the self. It is his way of depicting how outer presences become inner presences. To the extent that Kernberg is describing the structural makeup of the human psyche, his bipolar intrapsychic representations are nothing less than the building blocks of the mind.

Each tripartite configuration—the representational self, the representational other, and its affective coloring—contributes to what is known as an "internalization system." Such systems constitute different types of inner experience, reflecting the shifting nature of the mother and child as the two interact. As might be expected, they are intricate and complex. Not only are internalization systems affected by the idiosyncratic characteristics of mother and child, but they also fluctuate over time as a function of changing affective colorings.

The infant, for example, is a very different child at six weeks than at six months. The mother, moreover, may be a very different caretaker at different points in the mothering process. She may be completely at home with herself when the baby is first born but find herself becoming more irritable and impatient as the child becomes more demanding. Just as normal maturational processes (e.g., crawling) transform the child, so mothering transforms the mother. Growth means change and change means that internalization systems constantly are in flux.

Bearing this in mind, Kernberg describes three different types of internalization systems, each reflecting a different type of mother-child experience. Each depicts a shift in the internalized relationship between the child and the primary caretaker. Each dominates the mother-child relationship at different points in the child's life. To the extent that they form a progression over time, the three "systems" are essentially Kernberg's way of portraying stages in childhood development.

Kernberg's first internalization system, which constitutes the most primitive form of development, is labeled *introjection*. In this system, self-images and object-images are incorporated in the context of highly labile, unmodulated feeling states. The child experiences primitive feelings that occur in his relationship with the primary caretaker without being able to make rational sense of who is responsible for them. The child is unable to understand the source of feeling states or fathom their significance. Experiences are swallowed whole, so to speak, and assigned either positive or negative valences.

Introjection is the stage of intrapsychic existence in which splitting is first evident. Initially, the child only incorporates good experiences (e.g., the good breast) and ejects all those that are bad. This act of defensive ejection ("not me") is perhaps the child's first primitive experience of selfhood (a "me") and produces what Kernberg calls a "purified pleasure ego." But as the child matures perceptually and motorically, and the mother becomes increasingly experienced as more than a gratifying part object, positive and negative experiences are introjected as images of a good or bad mother. Splitting then emerges as a defensive attempt on the part of the child to keep the two separate.

This is a normal phenomenon. The infantile ego is not able at this point in development to cognitively process relational nuances. Experience is organized primarily on the basis of affect. The child, for example, is unable to appreciate that the same person who rewards can also be the one who punishes. Only with the advent of more advance internalization systems do good and bad experiences become progressively integrated. Until then it is only natural that the child's world and his internalization system are split.

The second internalization system is termed *identification*. The child operating within this system is conceptually able to transcend the highly labile emotional responses of the system preceding it. As the child cognitively matures, undifferentiated responses are replaced by an appreciation of the dyadic and reciprocal nature of self-object interactions. The child now has the capacity to see himself operating within a specific role and to see the "other" as another human being capable of complementing that role.

At this stage of psychological development, the child is better able to modulate the emotional responses associated with the internalization system. The bipolar images of self and object are not at the mercy of the affective coloring as much as they were in the previous stage. One might say that "identification" ushers in a more cognitive state of being. The child begins to develop a sense of himself more as a player in a complex interpersonal drama than as a helpless leaf swirling about in an emotional maelstrom. But even though "identification" constitutes a developmental advance, the various bipolar representations are still not fully integrated with one another. The child still does not possess an integrated ego.

Integration is achieved in the third and most highly developed system in Kernberg's sequence: *ego identity*. It is within this system that the various bipolar representations are synthesized into an integrated sense of self. The different identifications, each born of multiple self-object transactions, are consolidated into one overriding personality organization. The "self" now truly comes into its own and acts as a central directive force that guides behavior and sustains relationships.

Ego identity is what gives the self a sense of consistency. Instead of simply reflecting the particular identifications that are momentarily in effect, it reflects *all* the bipolar representations that have been incorporated into the inner world. The self is now able to transcend particular situations and particular relationships. According to Kernberg, at this point the self is " . . . the sum total of self representations in intimate connection with the sum total of object representations" (1982, p. 900).

Psychopathology, in Kernberg's system, largely derives from defensive splitting which not only interferes with the integration of self-images and object-images but also blocks their metabolization. In Kernberg's words, "The persistence of 'nonmetabolized' early introjections is the outcome of a pathological fixation of severely disturbed, early object relations, a fixation which is intimately related to the pathological development of splitting" (1976, p. 34). Under these circumstances, relationships with others tend to be guided by highly unstable bipolar representations and consequently are unpredictable, if not chaotic.

Kernberg's descriptions of bipolar intrapsychic representations and the way they evolve into various types of internalizations comprise his version of childhood development. Erogenous zones, fixations, and psychosexual conflicts, while they still exist, recede into the background. The focus instead is on a series of "internalization systems" that depict movement from diffuse and emotionally labile self-other representations to ones that are highly differentiated and capable of organizing experience.

Though elegant and persuasive, Kernberg's developmental theory does not possess the detail and specificity that Mahler's does. This is understandable. Most of Kernberg's work has been with adults and many of his formulations are drawn from therapy with borderline patients. His formulations nevertheless are consistent in large part with the work of other object relationists, and his contributions have been valuable in demonstrating how object relations theory can be used to explain specific pathological states.

HEINZ KOHUT

Another psychoanalyst who has made a significant contribution to object relations theory is Heinz Kohut. Like Kernberg, Kohut's formulations were developed out of work with pathological populations, specifically patients suffering from narcissistic personality disorders. His work led to the construction of a perspective in which the notion of the "self" plays a major role. Of all the object relationists, Kohut perhaps is most noted for his introduction of a self psychology into psychoanalytic work. The titles of his two major works: *The Analysis of the Self* (1971) and *The Restoration of the Self* (1977) reflect the importance of the self concept in his theorizing.

As is the case with other object relationists, Kohut feels that it is important to focus on the mother-child relationship in order to understand the nature of the human psyche. In doing so, he highlights some important dynamics underlying the intense interactions between the mother and infant; he then uses these to explain the development of the self. It is the construction of the self and its role in human affairs that dictates what is normal and abnormal. Psychopathology is viewed as a disturbance of the self, with very severe disorders rooted in very early disturbances of the mother-infant relationship.

For Kohut, the child is born into a social milieu, and relatedness with others forms a basic prerequisite for psychological survival. The child needs adults from the very beginning not only to fulfill physical requirements, but also to fulfill psychological needs. Perhaps the most important of these is support for a vague and undifferentiated sense of self. Whereas in the beginning that sense of self may amount to little more than a set of reflexes and an innate potential, through parental expectations and encouragement it quickly becomes transformed into a central organizing force in the psyche (Kohut, 1977, p. 99).

Kohut refers to the parents, and more generally to any significant objects in the child's life, as "selfobjects." He uses the term to refer to distinct, objectively separate individuals in the child's life who eventually become incorporated into the self. Kohut's "selfobject" should not be confused with Kernberg's "self-object." Kernberg's hyphenated version refers to *inner* bipolar representations. Kohut's "selfobjects" are actual people, not imaginal representations.

The significance of selfobjects lies in the psychological "functions" they contribute to the nascent self. Selfobject responses, such as praise or the induction of shame, for example, are "taken in" by the child and experienced as pride or guilt. Greed, envy, guilt, and pride are not mysterious affairs. They are psychological functions whose origins lie in the concrete, observable communications that make up the mother-child interaction. The communications that make up these selfobject interactions form the building blocks of what ultimately comes to be known as the self.

But the child and his caretaker communicate in more than concrete ways. They communicate in empathic ways as well. Kohut regards these empathic interchanges as highly significant elements in the child's burgeoning sense of self. They constitute a connection with other human beings, and are uniquely and quintessentially human. The ongoing empathic interactions between the child and his selfobjects form the basis for a psychic infrastructure that affects how the child relates to others as well as to himself.

To the extent that the child is naturally concerned with developing a positive and rewarding self-structure, it is correct to say that the developing child is basically narcissistic in nature. Kohut contends that there are two basic narcissistic needs that the child seeks to satisfy through early selfobject relationships. One is the need to show off developing capabilities and to be admired for them: "If others see me as good, then I must be good." The other is to form an idealized image of one of the parents, usually the mother, so as to experience a sense of merger. Both needs are normal. The first constitutes a healthy omnipotence and the second a healthy desire for connectedness.

The significance of these tendencies is that they become incorporated in one's representational world. By means of a process that Kohut terms "transmuting internalization," the two types of external object relations are transformed into two inner relational configurations. The first, comprised of grandiose, exhibitionistic self-images, is the result of interchanges with "mirroring selfobjects." The second, consisting of more muted self-images involving fusion, evolves out of interchanges with "idealized selfobjects." The first self-image is made up of messages that take the form: "I am perfect and you must admire me." The second consists of messages that approximate: "You are perfect and I am a part of you."

Whereas both configurations are healthy parts of the infant's representational world, they need to broaden as the child matures. Relations with selfobjects need to extend beyond mere satisfaction of narcissistic needs. If they do not, the inner structures deriving from them eventually will interfere with adult functioning and lead to abnormal behavior.

In Kohut's system, psychopathology represents an inability to transcend the narcissistic internalizations of infancy. It is not surprising, therefore, to find that these internalizations play a major role in the analytic treatment of disturbed individuals. In the course of treatment, the patient develops either a mirroring or idealized transference—or both. In the mirroring transference, the patient casts the analyst into the role of admiring audience; in the idealizing transference, the patient's view of the therapist is extraordinarily inflated.

The beginning of therapy is marked by the analyst's willingness to allow the patient to dwell in the infantile aspects of the relationship. As the therapy progresses, the patient outgrows the narcissistic, infantile aspects of the transference and moves on to more mature ways of relating. Resolution of the transference, i.e., relating to the analyst as a positive and healthy selfobject, provides for a positive transmuting internalization. Psychoanalysis thus is seen as providing the patient with an opportunity for a developmental second chance.

Of course, it is all a bit more complex than this. But the general outline of what goes on in psychotherapy reflects the object relational features of Kohut's overall approach. There is an emphasis on one's earliest "selfobject" relations, a focus on how these relationships have become part of the self, and a statement of how selfobject failures early in life have led to deficiencies in the self. All this, combined with Kohut's emphasis on the changing nature of the psychotherapeutic relationship, guarantee his place as one of the major contributors to contemporary object relations thought.

There are other theorists who have made significant contributions to object relations theory. Among them are Edith Jacobson, D.W. Winnicott, and Harry Guntrip, to mention just a few. One also could include representatives of the neoanalytic school such as Harry Stack Sullivan (1953) and Karen Horney (1939). Many consider Sullivan's interpersonal psychiatry the American counterpart of British object relations theory.

My purpose, however, is not to present a compendium of object relations thought. It is to provide an appreciation for what is meant by "object relations" by summarizing the ideas of some of the major contributors to this school of thought. As indicated earlier, there is no one approach that can lay unqualified claim to the title "object relations theory." There are many different approaches, many different views of childhood development, and many different ideas about the nature of the self. Similarities nevertheless do exist, and closer examination may uncover the common denominators underlying an object relations perspective.

THE TIES THAT BIND

If there is one dimension along which all the various formulations cluster, it is the primary role accorded human relationships. The need for other human beings does not simply subserve other needs; it is motivational in its own right. As Klein and Tribich put it, " . . . object relations theory is first and foremost a reaction against the Freudian motivational concept of instinctual drives" (1981, p. 30). Greenberg and Mitchell echo this sentiment in their belief that, "The relational model establishes relational configurations as the bedrock of existence; all other human behavior and experiences . . . are relational derivatives" (1983, p. 404). Though some object relationists continue to include tension reduction notions and libidinal conflicts in their formulations, most have shifted either explicitly or implicitly to a relational perspective.

This constitutes a major shift in the way one approaches the study of human beings, for it says not only that human behavior is fueled by relational concerns, but also that the human psyche is fundamentally relational in nature. The "stuff" of which mind is made has less to do with libidinal impulses and psychic energy than with the internalization of relationships. To understand what motivates people and how they view themselves, one needs to understand how relationships are internalized and how they become transformed into a sense of self.

Of the various relationships that make up the human drama, perhaps the most important is the relationship with an early caretaker. "The unique, central, and unitary claim of object relations theorists is that optimal development and individuation is predicated upon an optimal early human relationship" (Klein and Tribich, 1981, p. 30). In most instances, this early caretaking relationship is with the mother. Because this relationship occupies so much of the early life of the child and because it is so tied up with emotional gratification (and deprivation), object relationists believe it forms a template for all subsequent relationships.

The focus on the mother as a major developmental force in the psychic makeup of the child constitutes a major change in emphasis insofar as traditional psychoanalysis is concerned. In psychoanalysis, it is the father who occupies center stage. By creating castration anxiety in the young boy and penis envy in the girl, he powerfully influences whether or not the child successfully negotiates the oedipal period. In object relations theory, it is the relationship with the mother that predominates.

Shifting the emphasis from the father to the mother represents more than just a minor theoretical point. It represents a significant conceptual reorientation. To begin with, it says something about the types of experiences and conflicts that are important in normal development. Issues of intimacy and nurturance, for example, begin to overshadow issues of power and control. At another level, it indicates something quite revolutionary about the significance of the oedipal conflict. For object relations theorists, preoedipal occurrences are more important for personality development than oedipal ones.

This strikes at the very heart of psychoanalytic doctrine. Whereas traditional analytic thinking places the key to optimal psychological development in occurrences that take place in the fifth or sixth year, object relationists place it much earlier. Mahler, Kernberg, Kohut, and others believe that events occurring in the first year of life dictate the course of human development. According to object relations theory, the critical events that shape people's lives occur not at five or six years, but at five or six months!

If this is the case, then one needs to have a systematic way of describing what goes on in the first few months of life. And all the theorists ranging from Klein to Kohut take some pain to depict what happens between mother and child during this early period. Of those surveyed, Mahler perhaps is the most successful. Relying on the notion of separation-individuation, she not only demonstrates how each stage fits into the overall maturational process, but documents the behavioral markers that differentiate one stage from another. However, the fact that all the theorists attempt in one way or another to account for what goes on interpersonally in the preoedipal years attests to the importance they give to relational phenomena in the early life of the child.

The singular importance of these phenomena is that they underlie the construction of the child's representational world. Most of the theorists, except perhaps Melanie Klein, see the infant psyche as a relational tabula rasa. Early interactions with the mother are internalized as relational configurations that are transformed over time into a sense of being. This internalization process—along with its aggregate projections and identifications—forms the basic ingredients of what eventually comes to be experienced as the "self."

Melanie Klein's contribution lay in the fact that she was one of the first to clinically document this process. Drawing on her work with disturbed children, she was able to depict the inner world of the child as a complex web of fantasied relationships evolving out of the child's relationships with others. Her formulations lie at the bottom of Kernberg's "self-object representations," Kohut's "transmuting internalizations," and Mahler's "emotional object constancy." All object relationists owe a debt to Melanie Klein, in that she not only was the first analyst to envision the inner world as representational, but was also able to describe its operation.

Finally, all object relationists seem to take note of a goodness-badness dynamic operating deep within the self. In its most primitive expression, this can be seen in Klein's depiction of a flowing "good breast" and an empty "bad breast." At a more advanced developmental level, the dynamic is expressed in good and bad self-object representations (Kohut) and in Fairbairn's notion of a central, libidinal, and antilibidinal ego. The importance of this dynamic is that it forms the basis for "splitting." The fact that the world of the infant is suffused with bad (frustrating) and good (gratifying) experiences leads to a partitioning of the inner world which has important implications for later functioning.

OBJECT RELATIONS: THEORY AND THERAPY

Considering all the similarities, one might think that it would not be too difficult to come up with an object relations therapy. There seem to be enough parallels among the various perspectives to allow for construction of a set of principles that would fall under the rubric of object relations treatment. However, a review of the different perspectives covered in this chapter indicates that this is not the case. Instead we find each theory generating its own unique approach to treatment. Thus, there are therapies based on the work of Klein, of Kohut, as well as others, and therapists who identify themselves as Kleinians, Kohutians, and the like. Instead of a relatively discrete, identifiable object relations therapy, we have a series of treatment procedures, each with its own object relational emphasis.

If there a common ground among the various theories insofar as therapy is concerned, it is their continued reliance on psychoanalysis as a treatment modality. This does not mean that psychoanalytic treatment is adopted in totality, but merely that it is molded to conform to object relational demands. Thus we find references to modifying the analysis, minimizing interpretation, and dealing with the "real" relationship. But this does not change the fact that the patient still is in psychoanalysis. Much of what passes for "object relations therapy" nowadays is essentially a reworking of traditional psychoanalytic technique.

It is not difficult to surmise why this is the case. For one, much of what is considered object relations theory evolved in the context of traditional psychoanalysis. One could, in fact, argue that object relations developed as a reaction to a perspective that was heavily dominated by biological, i.e., instinctual, concerns. Furthermore, most object relationists are themselves practicing psychoanalysts. A great deal of writing in the field of object relations comes out of work with psychoanalytic patients. We therefore should not be surprised to find object relations and psychoanalysis so intimately intertwined.

This, however, creates epistemological problems. Perhaps the most striking arises from the fact that the two perspectives contain very different assumptions regarding human nature. Greenberg and Mitchell (1983) point out that the basic premises of object relations (the relational model) and psychoanalysis (the drive model) differ in so many ways that the two may be incompatible with one another. They write, "The drive model and the relational model are complete and comprehensive accounts of the human experience. The premises upon which they rest constitute two incompatible visions of life, of the basic nature of human experience" (p. 406).

To the extent that this is true, it creates theoretical discontinuities of serious proportions. An example regards the status of the ego. Should the ego continue to be viewed as part of an id-ego-superego system or should it be replaced by the "self"? This is not merely a semantic consideration; it alludes to whether relational structures (representational schema) are subordinate elements of the psyche or whether they are primary. A growing number of theorists seem to favor the latter position. Guntrip, in fact, proposes that the concept of a "systems ego" be replaced by that of a "person ego" (1971, p. 103–139).

The confounding of psychoanalysis and object relations theory creates more than just conceptual problems; it creates definitional problems as well. Reference was made earlier to how the term "object" takes on a different meaning within an object relations perspective. The same holds true for "libido." There are vast differences in the way the term is employed in traditional analytic circles and the way it is used by object relationists. Most object relations theorists, for example, use "libido" to refer to events which clearly do not possess the energy or biological drivenness that the term typically connotes. Fairbairn's "infantile libidinal ego" and "antilibidinal ego" clearly are interpersonal constructs and have little to do with any sort of energy, libidinal or otherwise. And Mahler's "libidinal object constancy," referring to the child's ability to imaginally preserve the mother, is as far from the traditional meaning of libido as one can possibly get.

This lexical confusion is carried over into the psychotherapeutic arena as well. Object relationists, for example, write a great deal about the use of the countertransference in therapy (Epstein and Feiner, 1979; Searles, 1979; Spotnitz, 1985). For them, the countertransference represents the therapist's experiential response to the patient's pathology and is a valuable part of the treatment procedure. Not only does it perform a diagnostic function but it also guides many of the therapist's interventions.

The term is used very differently in psychoanalysis. In psychoanalytic treatment, the countertransference normally describes pathological responses on the part of the therapist. Countertransferential responses typically are viewed as remnants of the therapist's own unresolved oedipal conflicts. One therefore does not "use" the countertransference in psychoanalysis. One gets rid of it. Using the same term to refer to two very different phenomena tends only to confuse matters.

Is there a solution to all this? The most obvious perhaps is to extricate object relations theory from psychoanalysis. Though the two are related, they constitute two different perspectives on the nature of the psyche and on human functioning. If object relations is to become a powerful conceptual and clinical tool, it has to be afforded status as a theory of human relationships in its own right.

This does not mean that object relations theory has to totally divorce itself from psychoanalytic thinking. The findings and conclusions of psychoanalysis can continue to inform object relations thinking and vice versa. But unless object relations theory acquires its own identity, it never will achieve the explanatory potential of which it is capable.

OBJECT RELATIONS THERAPY

The question remains: Is there such a thing as an object relations therapy? If we look to the theories in this chapter, the answer has to be no. As indicated earlier, each theory generates a set of therapeutic procedures that are more psychoanalytic in nature than they are object relational. Perhaps a better question is whether an object relations therapy is possible. The answer to this question is an unqualified yes! This is especially true if the therapy is bound to those parts of object relational theory that are predominantly relational in nature.

What form might such a therapy take? For one, it would place a great deal of emphasis on relational pathology. The patient suffers not from "symptoms" but from what Kaiser (1965) refers to as a "contact disturbance." Instead of suffering from an inability to reconcile inner impulses, there is an inability to meaningfully engage others in sustained and/or gratifying relationships. The meaning of psychiatric symptoms (anxiety,

depression, somatic complaints) is that the patient's relationships are dete-
riorating or are threatening the patient's sense of self.

The focus in such a therapy would consequently be on the role that
internal object relations play in the creation and maintenance of these
relationships. Of the various relationships that make up the patient's life,
prime consideration would be given to the relationship with the therapist.
Not only does it occur in the phenomenological here-and-now, but it also
contains many of the critical elements operative in the patient's relationships with others. The therapist-client relationship consequently would be
viewed as an in vivo expression of what is pathological in the patient's life.

If this were the case, it would be reasonable to conclude that the
therapist-patient relationship contains the greatest potential for change.
Rather than being viewed as a means of producing insight, self-awareness,
or other changes "in the patient," the therapist-patient relationship *itself*
would become the focus of change. Issues of psychological differentiation,
faulty internalizations and pathological splitting could then be addressed
through this relationship. To the extent that relationships form the foundation for the self, one might say that the therapist-patient relationship would
function as a crucible of the self.

In the pages that follow, an attempt is made to develop an object
relations framework that can act as a basis for this kind of therapy. My aim
is not to build a grand theory, but rather to provide a framework that is
consistent with the relational aspects of the formulations already presented.
The focus will be on "splitting" as a central relational dynamic and the
effect it has on the development of good and bad object relations. From
there, I will show how pathological splits lead to different forms of relational pathology. This ultimately will be applied to what happens in psychotherapy, with particular reference to the meaning it has for the therapist-
patient relationship.

CHAPTER 2

Object Relations: A Developmental View

Roy, a stocky black child with pudgy features, had not quite reached his ninth birthday when he first was admitted to a children's psychiatric hospital. He had a history of truancy and minor fire-setting; in addition, he had been in and out of a series of foster homes and reportedly was difficult to control. The record indicated that he would burst into explosive fits of anger for no apparent reason and was highly abusive to his foster parents. But the main reason for Roy's being hospitalized was that he suffered from a psychiatric eating disorder called pica.

Of the various eating disorders that affect children, pica is one of the most enigmatic (Bicknell, 1975; Cooper, 1957). Like bulimia, pica centers around gorging. But unlike bulimia, which is marked by the ingestion of large quantities of food, pica is marked by the consumption of inedibles. Children who suffer from pica gnaw on furniture, devour garbage, and even scrape wallpaper off the wall to satisfy what seems to be an insatiable appetite.

Roy was no exception. The childworkers assigned to care for him indicated that the boy continually tried to eat chalk, crayons, and other inedible objects. They constantly were prying things out of his mouth, and it was all they could do to keep him under control.

The original circumstances underlying the pica were not difficult to understand in Roy's case. The clinical notes revealed that the boy had received very little nurturance in his early years. The father was a chronic alcoholic who was rarely around. The mother was a part-time prostitute who deserted the family shortly after Roy was born. The child consequently never had a chance to experience a relationship with a consistent caretaking figure. Nurturance, particularly of a maternal sort, was virtually nonexistent.

The only "mothers" Roy knew were the various women the father took up with after Roy's real mother left. Information about these women was sketchy, but it was evident that none provided any maternal care to speak of. One by one they entered Roy's life, only to disappear once the father tired of them or vice versa. One winter day, the father also took off, leaving his three-year-old son locked in a cold-water apartment, crying, hungry, and scared out of his wits.

It was not until three days later that a neighbor heard the child's mournful cries and called the police. When they broke into the apartment, they found Roy sitting in the middle of the kitchen floor eating pieces of plaster. The boy apparently had scraped the plaster off the wall with a spoon. There was a bag of half-eaten garbage by his side and scraps of food and paper strewn all about.

Despite the efforts of the police and social work agencies, neither the father nor the mother was ever found. Roy became a ward of the state and spent the next six years of his life in a succession of foster homes. Despite some caring and devoted foster parents, he proved a very difficult child to manage. The social workers reported that he would strike out at his foster parents at the least provocation and that he constantly was getting into fights at school. His teachers threw their hands up in despair.

It was somewhere in these turbulent early years that the pica developed. One foster parent after another told of Roy's uncontrollable urge to consume inedibles. A diagnosis of pica was established and an attempt made to treat it on an outpatient basis. Nothing worked. The realization that the pica was getting worse, coupled with the fact that it was becoming increasingly difficult to maintain Roy in a foster home, eventually led to his placement in a psychiatric facility.

It was under these circumstances that I first met Roy. I was a psychology intern at the time and Roy was one of the first cases to which I was assigned. As one might suspect, I was not greeted with open arms. Roy was suspicious of everyone, particularly those who tried to get close to him. I was no exception. He met my efforts to engage him with violent curses and attempts to escape the therapy room.

It was only with great effort that any headway was made. As is often the case with young children, this was accomplished not through talking but through play (Schaefer and Millman, 1977; Thompson and Rudolph, 1983). Very early in treatment it became apparent that Roy liked to draw.

One day, upon entering the therapy room, I found him eyeing a blackboard that stood on the far side of the room. Sensing an opening, I offered Roy a piece of chalk and encouraged him to draw whatever he liked.

This momentarily took Roy aback. He was accustomed to having people take chalk out of his hands lest he try to eat it. The fact that someone actually would give him chalk or crayons apparently came as a shock. He nevertheless took the chalk and began to draw. From that day on, Roy spent many hours painting his thoughts and feelings on paper.

The drawings that Roy produced in the early part of therapy were graphic representations of his inner turmoil. One early picture showed a boat sailing across an expanse of water. The drawing, reproduced in Figure 1, depicted several airplanes, each raining bombs on the ship and strafing it with machine gun bullets. Alongside the ship were two submarines firing torpedoes at it. The beleaguered ship was returning fire, so by the time the painting was finished the paper was crisscrossed with bullets, torpedoes, and cannon fire. The result was a chaotic representation of unbridled aggression.

FIGURE 1

As the therapy progressed, Roy's drawings became much less disorganized. They began to include human figures; as Roy and I drew closer, he

began to include me in his paintings. These were not always complimenta-
ry. One of Roy's early drawings pictured him holding me at bay with sharp
talon-like fingers. I was on one side of the paper and Roy was on the other.
As time went by, though, the distance between us decreased. A later
drawing, a winter scene, showed Roy pulling a sled through the snow with
me standing quite close by.

Of all the pictures that Roy produced in therapy, one in particular sticks
in my mind. It was a picture of the moon replete with craters and volcanoes
(see Figure 2). Hovering over the barren surface were different colored
spaceships in the process of taking off. Whereas at first glance it looked like
a happy enough scene, a closer look revealed just the opposite. Hidden
among the craters in one of the crevices was a tiny creature. Apparently it
had been abandoned by the departing spaceships and left to fend for itself.
What Roy could not express in words was poignantly expressed in his
drawings.

FIGURE 2

Roy's artwork provided the communicative scaffolding upon which the
therapy was built. By exploring the emotions associated with each of his
paintings, Roy was able to get in touch with the feelings of abandonment
that lay behind his simmering rage. Accordingly, he was better able to

manage his anger so that it did not constantly interfere with his relationships. Still, the part of therapy that stands out in my mind has less to do with the drawings themselves than with a particular incident surrounding them.

It took place one day as I was about to begin a therapy session with Roy. Upon entering the room where we met, I found Roy standing in a corner facing the wall, his arms hanging loosely at his sides. From my vantage point I could see that he was fingering a piece of chalk in one hand. The blackboard on which he sometimes drew was on the other side of the room, so I naturally was perplexed. For a moment I thought that Roy might have reverted to the pica, which over the course of therapy had essentially ceased. But as Roy turned to face me, I realized that something very different was going on.

The scene that greeted me was heartrending. For a split second, I didn't recognize Roy. Looking forlorn and bewildered, he had ground the chalk into a fine white powder and smeared it all over his face. He looked like a small white ghost. There were tears streaming down his face, and brown streaks showed beneath the white where the tears had washed away the chalk. Standing alone in the corner, he was a pitiful sight.

I went to Roy and held him in my arms until he stopped crying. After a while he told me what had happened. He apparently had been spending a lot of time trying to figure out why his parents had left him. He had given a lot of thought to it and in the process had become confused and depressed. In an effort to make sense of his jumbled thoughts and jumbled feelings, he reasoned that it must have been because he was black.

It then all seemed to make sense to him. Most of the other children at the hospital were white and their parents were still around. In fact, he was one of few children who did not have visitors on visiting day. In attempting to fathom why his parents had left him, he concluded that it must have been because of his color. To be black must mean he was bad. If only he were white, he might be wanted. If only he were white, he might be able to feel good about himself as a human being.

THE ORIGINS OF GOODNESS:
SPLITTING AND HUMAN DEVELOPMENT

What does it mean to be good? What does it mean to be bad? Where do feelings of goodness and badness originate? Do human beings come into the world tainted or do they, like Snow White, emerge from the womb "pure as the driven snow"? These are not easy questions. Philosophers and theologians have been grappling with them for years. It is only recently that clinicians have tried to tie these concerns to complex clinical phenomena, and to consider how they figure into the makeup of the human psyche.

It is fairly evident in Roy's case that concern over being a good or bad human being was intimately tied to feelings of personal desirability. It is also true that fears of desertion in his case were rooted in an actual abandonment. But issues of lovability and acceptability are a pervasive part of all object relations, regardless of whether or not physical abandonment is at issue. Children as well as adults have deep concerns over whether they are acceptable human beings. These concerns have at their basis an inner conflict over "goodness" and "badness."

We saw in the last chapter that the polarization of good and bad self-representations occupies a major position in contemporary object relations thought. The position taken in this chapter is that the dichotomy of goodness-badness not only constitutes a powerful and pervasive dynamic in human functioning but also creates a deep pervasive split in interpersonal consciousness. The way that this split manifests itself in the course of maturation depicts the child's movement from extreme dependence to psychological autonomy.

The focus in this chapter consequently is on splitting as a major development dynamic. Four phases in interpersonal splitting will be described, each comprising a phase in the overall process of human development. The first three phases constitute childhood expressions of splitting while the fourth extends the phenomenon into adulthood and adult relationships. We begin, however, with the mother-child relationship, for it is within this relationship that splitting originates and unfolds.

PHASE ONE: MATERNAL SPLITTING

According to modern object relations theory, splitting begins in the very early days, even hours, of life. The process begins with the infant's primitive division of the world into satisfying and unsatisfying sensations: fullness is good, emptiness bad; warmth is good, cold bad; to be held is good, to be denied contact bad. Long before children are able to assign labels to what is good or bad, much less conceptualize it, a primitive sensory intelligence exists that enables the child to recognize that the world—or whatever it is that is out there—is divided into good and bad (Myers, Clifton, & Clarkson, 1987; Ziajka, 1981). Before children are even aware that people exist, the foundations of their interpersonal worlds are being set down.

At this early stage of development, the infant does not associate specific sensory experiences with being lovable or unlovable, worthwhile or worthless. Only much later do these adult overlays come into being. The neonate does not even associate these experiences with specific people. The notion of a living, thinking, breathing human being "out there" is beyond the child's cognitive capabilities. In the first few weeks of life, the infant does not yet interact with people as we know them but with parts of them—a hand, a cheek, a hank of hair—or what object relationists refer to as "part-objects."

Since much of the infant's waking life centers about eating, it is not surprising that one of the earliest and most potent part-objects is the breast. And it is through interaction with the breast (or bottle) that one's earliest splitting experience takes place. When milk is flowing, the breast is good; when it is not, it is bad. And even if it is good, it may not be good all the time. The nature of life is such that the most well-intentioned mother cannot always respond to the child's beck and call. She cannot drop everything at a moment's notice and run to the infant every time the child is hungry. Even under the best of circumstances, the infant naturally comes to experience the world as split.

This early division of part-objects into good and bad is the precursor of relationships with whole objects, i.e., human beings. As the child develops, there comes a dim but growing awareness that whatever it is that is "out there" is more than just a disembodied hand or breast. It is a human being. As the infant's perceptual and mental capacities mature, unrelated images, sounds, and smells coalesce in the figure of the child's earliest caretaker, usually the mother. She now becomes the flesh and blood embodiment of all that has come earlier—good and bad. It is in this stage of development that relationships with part-objects are replaced by relationships with whole ones.

But not entirely. Part-object relationships often persist into adulthood. When they do, they may take the form of excessive interest in parts of the body, such as hair, breasts, and feet. Most of the time, such "interests" represent harmless residuals of an early stage of life when part-objects were associated with pleasure and gratification. If such interests come to dominate one's interpersonal existence, however, they can turn into fetishes. Foot fetishes, hair fetishes, and obsessive preoccupations with other parts of the body represent instances in which part-object relationships come to be preferred over, and sometimes even replace, whole-object relationships.

The fervent wish of each and every child is that its primary object of gratification, the mother, will meet its every need. Hopefully she will be loving, giving, and unconditionally accepting. By epitomizing all that is good in the world, she will satisfy the needs of the child and turn what often is an inconsistent and frustrating environment into one that is dependable and gratifying.

But this can never amount to anything more than a dream, not because most mothers wouldn't like things to be this way—most probably would—but because they are human. Like everyone else, mothers get tired, impatient, frustrated, and just plain fed up. One of the sobering realizations of childhood is that mother is not perfect. This does not stop the child from clinging to the fantasy of perfection or from idealizing the mother. But deep down the child knows that the dream is flawed. With the dawn of interpersonal consciousness, the child realizes that there is trouble in paradise. The split is there and it is not going to go away.

Splitting, phenomenologically speaking, is not abnormal. In fact, it is quite commonplace. It is a direct consequence of being born into an imperfect world and being subjected to imperfect mothering. Winnicott purposely uses the term "good enough mothering" to refer to the waxing and waning of nurturance that describes normal mother-child interactions (1971, p. 11). He purposely does not speak about perfect or ideal mothering because he knows that the unconditional gratification associated with this kind of mothering is at best illusory.

This does not mean that abnormal splitting in childhood does not occur. As with everything else, abnormal outcomes develop when matters are taken to extremes. Thus, abnormal splitting occurs when "bad mother" experiences are particularly frustrating or when they border on wholesale rejection. The child finds these experiences so painful that they are pushed out of awareness. It is under circumstances such as these that the seeds of interpersonal pathology are sown (Cicchetti, 1987).

It is difficult, however, to accurately describe the nature of these abnormal experiences since they often occur, as it were, in the nooks and crannies of the mother-child interaction. What's more, the pathological impact of these experiences may be felt only years later. Nevertheless, there is a growing body of empirical research that gazes into these nooks and crannies to try to capture what takes place within them (Stern, 1977, 1985; Tronick, 1982). Analysis of high speed motion picture film and video tape, for example, reveals that the seemingly ordinary "social moments" which comprise the mother-child relationship in the first six months are among "the most crucial experiences in the infant's first phase of learning . . . " (Stern, 1977, p. 5). Most of this research, however, deals primarily with ostensibly normal interactions and their immediate impact on the mother-infant relationship.

It obviously would be useful to have video playbacks of childhood experiences which could provide clues as to the types of early interactional patterns that contribute to abnormal development. But these don't exist. Researchers, however, have come up with something that is almost as good:

old home movies. Using slow motion analysis of films gathered from families of disturbed children, they have been able to identify patterns of mother-child interactions which appear to lead to pathological outcomes.

In one set of studies, Massie and his colleagues were able to describe some of the patterns by which infants establish visual contact with their caretakers (Massie, 1975, 1978a, 1978b). One of these focused on "gaze avoidance" and the manner by which it characterized the interaction between an autistic child named Joan and her mother (Massie, 1982). A frame by frame analysis of movies taken early in Joan's life showed that the child's mother turned away from Joan every time the infant tried to look her in the eye. After trying repeatedly to make visual contact with her mother, the child became increasingly confused and responded with a look of unmistakable dejection. This pattern was apparent even in films taken at four months, long before a diagnosis of autism was ever made.

Something similar occurred in the case of a child named Ann. The interactional pattern in this case, however, took place in the realm of body contact, and entailed an inability on the child's part to achieve chest-to-chest contact with the mother. Analysis of normal patterns of mother-child interaction in our culture reveal that it is common for new mothers to lean towards their infants whenever the infant arches his or her chest. Films taken at six months revealed no evidence of this in Ann's case. Whenever the child arched her chest, the mother remained immobile, suggesting an inability on her part to respond to her child's need for physical closeness. Ann was diagnosed as having childhood schizophrenia.

Fortunately, the majority of mother-child interactions do not take on the pathological quality of those just described. Most frustrating experiences in infancy typically take place in the context of an overall positive relationship. The anger the child feels in response to being frustrated can be tolerated if the frustrating experiences are not too severe. Transient experiences of noncontact are counterbalanced by the warmth and comfort the mother typically provides. Or, as Massie puts it, "Frustrating experiences within the context of a positive reciprocal relationship are the nontraumatic frustrations that advance psychological development" (1982, p. 177). Under circumstances such as these, splitting remains within normal bounds and becomes a part of normal development rather than obstructing it.

One consequence of early splitting—even in cases where it is considered in the normal range—is that it produces strong feelings about oneself that may not have any logical foundation. One of my patients, a young man in his early thirties, became somewhat depressed after being denied tenure at a small, prestigious New England college. This was entirely comprehensible since he had taught there for nearly six years and was well regarded by students and colleagues alike. But the school had a ceiling on the number of tenured faculty and that ceiling had been reached. The decision to release my patient was based solely on administrative grounds.

Fortunately, things were not as bleak as they seemed. Not long after he was told he would have to leave, he was able to secure a job at another school in the area which gave him a promotion and a handsome raise in salary. His depression, however, did not lift. It seemed that the experience at the first school struck a chord that touched on early feelings of undesirability. Despite his intellectual acceptance of the reason for his dismissal, he was left with the nagging feeling that there was something wrong with him. He must be a bad teacher, a bad scholar, a bad something or other. For reasons they often do not fully comprehend, people tend to place a goodness-badness template on many of the significant occurrences that shape their lives.

The reason for this is that early splitting is largely "pre-linguistic." That is to say, it occurs long before people learn how to use words. Language is a major way by which human beings order their worlds, the means by which they categorize their thoughts and feelings (Vygotsky, 1986). To the extent that words allow people to place their feelings in perspective, they enable them to make sense of emotional reactions that might otherwise seem irrational. But sometimes these reactions are tied to events that take place so early in interpersonal existence that they literally are "beyond words" (Ziajka, 1981, p. 138).

One of the significant contributions made by Melanie Klein was to call attention to the fact that the child's world is characterized by feelings way before it is ever filled with words. She was the first object relationist to portray the early world of the child in terms of experiences which were felt even before they could be conceptualized or put into verbal form. It is no wonder that people intuitively sense that certain things are good or bad without being able to explain rationally why it is they feel the way they do.

Taking all this into account, how does the child deal with the unsettling proposition that the mother is split? By idealizing her. In an effort to build a more internally satisfying picture of the most significant relationship in his world, the child represses the bad parts of the mother and reifies the good parts. By behaving as if the bad parts of the mother do not exist, or by minimizing them, the child transforms the mother into a perfect, all-good human being.

But this isn't always successful. Mothers are human. They get angry, depressed, and behave inconsistently despite the mental machinations of their young charges. The child nevertheless tries to make the best of things and labors endlessly to reconcile the split. Much of what goes on in the first few months of life centers on the infant's fledgling attempts to cope with the maternal realities of his limited world. These primitive efforts to deal with the polarized nature of early experience ushers in the next phase of the splitting process.

PHASE TWO: PRESERVATION AND IMAGINAL SPLITTING

At the same time the infant struggles with the early effects of splitting, he remains highly dependent on the mother. Part of this is rooted in physical reality. Children are helpless creatures and must rely almost entirely on their primary caretakers for survival. At the same time, the infant is also inextricably bound to the mother in psychological ways. At this point in development, children do not have a separate sense of self. They are still very much a part of the person who is responsible for their care.

Mahler, as well as other object relationists (e.g., Bowlby), contends that early bonding and the child's response to it form the foundation for all future growth. Her depiction of the painstaking moves the child makes towards independence provides us with a meaningful way of looking at a process that begins with fusion and culminates in the birth of the self. But as Mahler aptly points out, the infant behaves very early on as if he and the mother were a single entity. At this point in development, these still is no true individuation, no sense of what it means to be a separate human being. The existential formula in the earliest phases of infancy is: *Mother = Me*.

If that is the case, then *No Mother = No Me*, and constant disappearance of the mother, no matter how brief, can cause considerable distress. At one moment the mother is holding the child; the next moment she is gone. Now the child hears her voice; then there is silence. The ebb and flow of mother-child interaction in the first few months of life are characterized by a series of vanishing acts. The nature of early childhood is that it is marked by countless disappearances.

These mini-abandonments cause quite a bit of consternation. Even when children begin to make their first halting attempts at independence, they still constantly check up on the mother's whereabouts. Mahler uses the expression "hatching" to describe this early phase in the separation-individuation process in which the child stays close to his mother even though he ostensibly is playing "on his own." In this phase, the child plays with toys or with playmates but crawls back to his mother every now and then to make physical contact. Though the child may venture farther away later on, he nevertheless continues to visually check on the mother's whereabouts, using her as an emotional "home base."

Attempts to cope with the distress that abandonment produces can be seen in many of the games children play with their mothers. In peek-a-boo, for example, the mother hides her face from the child, making sure to pop back into sight before too much time has elapsed. The infant squeals with delight, if not relief, when the mother "reappears." Later on, children cover their own eyes with their hands to make the mother vanish. After a moment, the hands are taken away to make her magically reappear. Peek-a-boo obviously is more than just a game. It is one of the earliest means by which children deal with issues of abandonment. By turning maternal disappearance into a game, the child gains control over the fear that the mother might vanish. Peek-a-boo and other activities like it are ways through which children gain mastery over the transitory nature of their social world.

But games are games, and the child still has to deal with ongoing, and typically upsetting, maternal disappearances. How does the child accomplish this? The answer is through the use of imagery (Lichtenberg, 1983). By conjuring up a mental picture of the mother, the child internally "captures her" and in so doing invests her with a psychic permanence of sorts. The inner image acts as a substitute while the mother is gone and mitigates the panicky feelings her absence might otherwise produce. Much of the child's attempt to "preserve" the mother are wrapped up in efforts to create an inner maternal presence.

This process has its parallel in Piaget's classic work on object constancy (Flavell, 1963). In attempting to assess the stage of development at which children imbue inanimate objects with constancy (permanence), Piaget designed a series of experiments in which objects were systematically removed from the child's field of vision and made to "disappear." In one of these experiments, a ball was rolled under a couch to determine the circumstances under which children would try to retrieve it once it vanished from sight. Piaget found that older children tended to search for the ball while younger children tended to quickly lose interest, responding as if it had ceased to exist.

Object relationists contend that something similar takes place in the sphere of early human interaction. A major difference, though, is that the object here is not a lost toy but the absent mother. To lose a ball is one thing; to lose one's mother is quite another. Since the mother is so critical for the child's sense of being, it is understandable that children respond with apprehension rather than indifference when the mother "disappears."

The capacity to preserve lost objects by substituting inner images for them constitutes a developmental milestone in the cognitive life of the child. Current thinking suggests that the capacity to engage in "maternal imaging" begins as early as one or two months, although the first stable mental representation of the mother may not take form until the child is five or six months old. It then takes a year or two until a "primary maternal presence" is firmly established. Mahler and others feel that the ability of the child to maintain a sustained image of an object when the object is missing is not fully consolidated until almost three years of age (Mahler, Pine, and Bergman, 1975).

One or two years, though, is a long time in the life of a child. In the time it takes for an inner maternal presence to become established, the child may have to withstand many worrisome moments. At this point in the child's life, the phrase "out of sight, out of mind" more rightly reads "out of sight, out of existence." The young child naturally searches for ways to compensate for the life-threatening effect of the mother's absence. That search is rewarded by what is known as "transitional objects."

Transitional Objects: Solace and Security

What exactly are transitional objects? Very simply, they are special toys or playthings that act as maternal substitutes. They are, according to Winnicott (1971), the infant's first real possessions. But a transitional object is not just any possession or any toy. To function in this way, it must seem to the infant to "give warmth, or to move, or to have texture, or to do something that seems to show it has vitality or reality of its own" (p. 5).

Some of the more common transitional objects are teddy bears (and other stuffed animals), dolls, pieces of clothing, and the ubiquitous security blanket. These and similar playthings function as maternal surrogates; they substitute for the mother when she is out of earshot or out of sight and provide the child with comfort and security. Transitional objects enable the child to "hold" the mother until the time comes when she can securely be held within. By functioning in this way, they smooth the transition from the mother as outer object to mother as an inner presence.

Transitional objects not only act as surrogate maternal objects but fulfill splitting functions as well. This can be seen in the emotional way children respond to them. At times, children treat transitional objects as if they exuded goodness; at other times, the object is treated quite cruelly. In Winnicott's words, "the object is affectionately cuddled as well as excitedly loved and mutilated" (1971, p. 5). One of the reasons that toys such as this are utilized in play therapy is that they offer the child the opportunity to express in concrete ways the struggles that are taking place within.

Obviously not all toys function in this way. What then qualifies one toy as a transitional object and not another? While the answer to this is not as yet fully understood, it is likely that the choice has less to do with the physical characteristics of a toy than with its availability. Thus, some children may adopt a rag doll as a transitional object, whereas others might choose a teddy bear or a blanket. It may be that certain toys or playthings become transitional objects simply because they are available at a point in the developmental process when the child is dealing with issues of separation.

Since the major function of a transitional object is to provide the child with comfort and a sense of security, it does not necessarily have to be an object in the physical sense of the word. Horton (1981) suggests that tunes, jingles, and magic sayings can fulfill transitional functions as well. In fact, he prefers to use the phrase "transitional relatedness" so as to broaden the concept and to place the focus on the relationship rather than the object per se. It nevertheless is the case that most transitional objects take the form of stuffed animals, dolls, or blankets. It is hard for a jingle to be "warm" or have "texture."

What about the specific characteristics of transitional objects? Is one transitional object any better than the next? Probably not. One could argue that dolls and teddy bears are "better" transitional objects because they represent an anatomical advance over blankets and fuzzy articles of clothing. Since they possess eyes, ears, and limbs, one could say that they constitute more accurate representations of the mother than do shapeless forms. This may be true, but in the end it probably is the emotional significance of the object that counts rather than its size or shape. At this stage of development, feelings far outweigh logic.

One thing we do know about transitional objects is that children have a hard time separating from them. A case in point is that of a three-year-old named Jonathan whose mother related the following incident to me. It centered on a stuffed animal, a small giraffe, that belonged to her son.

The giraffe had been the boy's faithful companion since he was an infant and held a special place in his life. Not only did the giraffe sleep with Jonathan, but it also accompanied him to the bathroom and to the dinner table. Jonathan obviously was very attached to the animal. It would not be exaggerating matters to say that the animal hardly ever left his side.

Over time, the giraffe naturally began to show signs of wear. Not only was it coming apart at the seams, but it had acquired a distinct odor. This was not surprising in light of the fact that Jonathan had been "feeding" the animal for years. The giraffe's "fur" was impregnated with applesauce, mashed bananas, and other delicacies, and one could easily sympathize with the mother's desire to get rid of the toy.

At the same time, the mother was aware of Jonathan's extreme attachment to the giraffe. She therefore sought to replace it with a giraffe just like it. This was not easy. Years had passed since the toy had first been purchased and she doubted that she could find one identical to it. Nevertheless, she decided to give it a try and spent the next few weeks searching through various toy stores. Her search was rewarded one day when she stumbled across exactly what she was looking for. She purchased the new giraffe and brought it home to Jonathan.

Was Jonathan delighted? Did he embrace his new giraffe and shower his mother with thanks? Far from it. Not only did he display little interest in the new toy, but he became very upset when his mother tried to foist it on him. Try as hard as she could, she could not coax Jonathan into trading his old giraffe for the new one. In the end, his mother decided to abandon her efforts and leave well enough alone. She returned the new giraffe to the store and focused her efforts instead on trying to get the old one into the washing machine.

Does there ever come a time when people outgrow their need for transitional objects? Generally speaking, the answer has to be yes. Otherwise transitional objects wouldn't be "transitional." But do people ever reach a point when they forsake these objects altogether? Are they ever able to leave them behind once and for all? Probably not. The fact that there exists a thriving teddy bear revival, complete with festivals and antique shows devoted exclusively to these cuddly "toys," suggests that transitional objects continue to hold special meaning for many far into adulthood. And then, of course, there is *Rosebud*.

But even though many of the transitional objects of childhood are retained by adults as fond reminders of an earlier time, the adult world contains its own objects, many of which also possess transitional significance. Horton (1981) indicates that certain household objects (and even people's homes) may in some cases function in this way. This is especially true when people find themselves alone and away from loved ones. Explorers who wander far from their normal surroundings often carry household mementoes with them as a concrete reminders of the safety and security a home provides.

Something similar could be said about the transitional significance of money. Aside from its more pedestrian uses — buying groceries, paying bills, and buying movie tickets — money often is instrumental in filling deep emotional needs. For some, money is synonymous with power and independence. But for others, money (including stocks, bonds, and other "securities") connotes safety, protection, and lovability. For certain individuals, just handling money can be reassuring; fondling a wad of bills may not be that far removed from stroking a blanket or squeezing a stuffed animal.

Returning to childhood, we find that most children manage to negotiate the transition from "mother-as-outer-object" to "mother-as-inner-presence" somewhere near the end of their third year. By then, most children have developed enough constancy to feel secure when they are separated from their mothers:

By three years, a child will have achieved his initial sense of separateness and identity. . . . The three-year-old has but a small degree of constancy—just enough to allow him to feel safe in the world even though his self is separate from the self of his mother. (Kaplan, 1978, p. 29)

Children may yearn for the mother when she is absent, but they do not turn this into a frightening fantasy that they too will disappear.

This does not mean that children do not occasionally get panic stricken once they pass their third birthday. But it does mean that the mother's absence becomes less traumatic once the child is able to spontaneously evoke an imaginal representation of her. Children nevertheless continue to hold on to their transitional objects throughout their childhood, even into adulthood, as hedges against abandonment.

Attainment of a inner maternal presence is a significant developmental breakthrough. Once children can evoke a maternal image in the absence of the mother, they are well on their way to becoming individuals in their own right. The capacity to function on one's own, to experience what is known as "intrapsychic separateness," is dependent on the ability to evoke and sustain this image. The importance of transitional objects is that they allow this process to take place gradually over time so that the child does not feel totally overwhelmed by the thought of desertion or feelings of abandonment.

There is, however, a hitch in all this. Since the mother is by her very nature split, her inner representation is also split. To the extent that the maternal image is a derivative of the mother, it too is separated into good and bad. Like the mother "out there," it may be idealized, but its basic makeup remains the same. While the second (imaginal) phase of splitting is a significant developmental advance, it leaves the child no closer to solving the question of how to deal with the goodness-badness split within.

PHASE THREE: SELF SPLITTING

Up until now, the inner maternal representation has largely been visual in nature. The child "preserves" the mother by generating a mental image of her which is essentially iconic in nature. This changes rapidly as language begins to be used more and more as an interpersonal tool. As the child increasingly relies on spoken language to engage those about him, he also uses language to engage those within (Bretherton and Beeghly, 1982). The mother now can be called up through the use of words instead of just through imagery. In other words, the child now is able to engage the mother in inner conversation.

One of the most exciting developments in childhood—for both children and parents alike—is the appearance of language in human interaction. A memorable moment in the lives of parents occurs when the child utters his first word. Fathers and mothers often get in heated arguments over whether that word was "momma" or "poppa." Whatever the word may be, it represents the child's initial linguistic contact with those about him.

From this rudimentary beginning, language fans out and expands to where it is used increasingly to interact with others—both inwardly and outwardly. The child engages the mother in face-to-face dialogue when she is present and her maternal representation in inner dialogue when she is not. As a consequence, the inner maternal representation which previously existed only as a visual presence becomes more linguistic in nature. Since the mother leaves the child alone more and more during this phase of development, much of the child's interactions with the mother take the form of "inner dialogues."

Most of this dialogue is silent. Nevertheless, there are occasions when one is able actually to eavesdrop on it. An example is the "conversation" that sometimes takes place during toilet training. It is during this period that a crucial shift occurs from the mother's external management of the child to the child's management of himself. Somewhere towards the tail end of this process, you sometimes can hear children exclaim "naughty, naughty!" While it is obvious that the child has had an accident, what you are hearing is one side of an inner exchange in which the child is acting out the part of the inner maternal representation.

This kind of inner interaction takes place in other contexts as well. When small children do something they shouldn't do—steal a cookie from a cookie jar, overturn a lamp—and then mutter "bad boy" or "bad girl," they momentarily provide us with a glimpse into the private recesses of their inner worlds. The conversation we overhear is one that actually is taking place between the child and the inner mother. At this stage of development, this inner maternal representation is experienced by the child more as an inner voice than a visual presence.

As the interpersonal world of childhood continues to expand, the child's inner dialogues extend beyond the mother to include conversations with a whole host of others. They come over time to include playmates, relatives, TV characters, and even make-believe friends. The childhood phenomenon of "imaginary companions," once thought to be quite rare, even abnormal, is now regarded as a healthy childhood occurrence. Studies indicate that a great many children converse with so-called "invisible friends" whom only they alone can see. What one witnesses when one sees a child speaking to thin air is only the outer linguistic counterpart of an inner world dialogue.

The reason that more of these "conversations" aren't actually heard is that over time they are increasingly driven inward. In most social situations, "talking to oneself" is frowned upon, even regarded as a sign of mental disturbance. The older children get, the more they are instructed to stifle their inner dialogues and to "keep their thoughts to themselves." Parents admonish their children not to move their lips when they aren't actively engaged in conversation. Little children should be seen and not heard, especially if they insist on carrying on conversations with persons their parents cannot see or hear.

As time passes, verbal expressions of the inner world become less and less obvious, until they disappear entirely from view. Ultimately they fade from our inner worlds as well. As social interactions become increasingly complex and involve more than just a few select individuals, it becomes increasingly difficult to monitor and manage one's inner dialogues. Children, and for that matter adults, do not have the cognitive capacity to keep up scores of simultaneous inner conversations. It would be like trying to keep four or five telephone conversations going at the same time.

Aside from the sheer complexity of the inner world, other factors come into play that discourage the continuance of inner dialogues. There is the need, for example, to make quick decisions. The day-to-day demands of social interaction require that people respond in relatively rapid fashion to what is going on about them. If human beings had to engage in lengthy inner conversations every time they had to make a decision, things would never get done. Even crossing the street could assume major proportions. Imagine if someone had to go through the following "conversation" before setting out to reach the other side of the street:

"Is it safe to cross now?"
"Have you looked both ways?"
"I think so."
"Did you make sure the light is green?"
"Uh huh."
"Then go ahead."
"Are you sure it's safe?"
"Hurry up before the light turns red."

Obviously, it is grossly inefficient, even immobilizing, for people to preface everything they do with lengthy inner consultations.

For reasons having to do with the richness and complexity of our interpersonal worlds, the inner presences of childhood consequently undergo one final transformation, this time into something called the "self." By the time the splitting process has progressed through its various phases, the maternal presences of childhood have largely been psychologically metabolized. They no longer are experienced as inner entities but as part of one's own being.

This transformation is similar to the process Kohut describes when he speaks of "transmuting internalization." The incorporation of relationships, beginning with the mother and fanning out to include other significant figures in one's life, forms the foundation for what ultimately becomes a "self." The child does not begin life with a self but incrementally constructs one through socially engaging others. Though the self probably is more rightfully considered a process than an entity, it ultimately comes to be experienced as the essence of one's being.

The emergence of the self is marked by the appearance of the word "I" in the child's vocabulary. The young child no longer refers to himself or herself in the third person: "Jimmy wants a cookie," or "Nancy go beddy-bye." Instead the child announces, "*I* want a cookie," and "*I* want to go to bed." When children replace "Mommy says do this or that" with "I want to do that," they are on the threshold of becoming autonomous human beings. The decision to cross the street ultimately is transformed from "Mommy says it's all right to cross" into "I am heading for the other side."

The self, in its most elemental form, is the linguistic culmination of a rich and ongoing social incorporation process. It is not a conflict-ridden mélange of drives striving to seek expression, nor is it a bundle of habits waiting to be triggered by external stimuli. It is a complex configuration of multiple object relations which make up people's inner sense of who they are. As one relational theorist puts it, "We are our others." To the extent that this is the case, we become our others by incorporating significant others and psychologically transforming them into a self.

It is not surprising therefore that our language and interactions with others are permeated with terms containing self references. It is hard to talk about who we are without speaking of self-esteem, self-worth, and self-regard. It is not uncommon to hear people declare "I love myself" or "I hate myself," and to speak of self-acceptance or self-actualization. As people mature and their "selves" become the center of their existence, a language of the self develops through which they describe how they feel about who they are and how they relate to others.

One can view these self-interactions as a type of dialogic interaction. Instead of "talking" to our inner others, we talk to ourselves (our selves).

This type of interaction is very private and stands in contrast to public interactions with figures in the outer, or face-to-face, world. But it still constitutes a form of interpersonal communication. When a person says, "I don't like myself," he may not realize it, but he is indicating that there are figures in his inner world who put him down and actively disparage him.

Se ef ✶

In the last analysis, the self is the linguistic derivative of internalized relationships that have their beginnings in childhood. It comes to include more and more relationships as time goes by, but the early relationship with the mother is the one that is most influential. Over time, this relationship goes through a number of transformations. Though it initially makes its psychological presence known through proprioceptive channels (vision, touch, smell, etc.), it ultimately undergoes a linguistic transformation to become an integral part of what is eventually experienced as a self.

But just as early splitting of the mother creates a split in the inner maternal presence, so the split in the inner maternal presence creates a split in the self. Early splits give birth to later splits. The result is that people come to regard themselves as relatively "good" or "bad" depending on the quality of experiences that have accompanied splitting in the early years. Whether we refer to this as self-worth, self-esteem, or self-regard, it constitutes an interpersonal legacy that affects our entire existence. The way people deal with this legacy largely determines how they organize their lives and whether they go though life feeling good or bad about themselves as human beings.

PHASE FOUR: IDENTITY SPLITS

The fourth phase of self-development extends from childhood throughout one's entire adulthood and could properly be considered the phase of adult lifespan development. By the beginning of this phase, the infantile self is relatively intact. Object constancy has been achieved and the child has become increasingly facile in the use of language. The self becomes a font of security for the child and leads to increased efforts to engage others.

The ability to feel secure about who one is enables the child to embark increasingly on interpersonal forays. This marks the beginning of a lifelong effort to psychologically engage others. It signals an attempt to expand upon a self which until now has been constructed almost entirely out of interactions with the mother and perhaps a few other significant figures. The rest of life constitutes a process of internalizing meaningful relationships and using these relationships to reconcile the goodness-badness split.

How is this is accomplished? Is the adult self simply a mirror image of the infantile self? Are adults merely larger children playing out infantile themes in different playgrounds? There are some who subscribe to this position, but in doing so they ignore the richness of adult relationships and the unique contributions they make to the self in their own right. Issues surrounding adult sexuality, success in one's work, and the ability to sustain a marriage are uniquely adult and need to be considered on their own merits. While all may contain conflicts that have roots in early infantile splitting, they introduce into human interaction elements that are qualitatively different from those that concern infants.

One perspective that approaches object relations from an adult vantage point is "symbolic interactionism." A branch of sociological thought, this viewpoint was developed by sociologist George Herbert Mead and focuses on the way that the adult self is linguistically codified (Blumer, 1969; Mead, 1934; Strauss, 1956). At the core of the perspective is a vision of the adult self based on interpersonal relationships. As such, it expands upon object relations theory, which tends to focus almost exclusively on the mother-child relationship and the prelinguistic period of child development.

According to Mead, the individual self is the mechanism by which society becomes incorporated into the human psyche. Because the self is constructed out of relationships with others and therefore involves the internalization of societal codes and conventions, it can be considered a miniature society within the individual. Just as the broader society guides the operation of its institutions, so the inner miniature society guides the behavior of the individual. As mother and child are inextricably bound in object relations theory, so self and society are bound up in symbolic interaction.

If the self is a society in miniature, one needs a way of describing the elements that comprise it. Mead does this by sorting the interpersonal elements contained within the self into two intrapsychic components: the "I" and the "Me." He uses the term "I" to refer to the active, initiating component within the self. It is the part of the self that reacts to changes in the outer world in a spontaneous and immediate, i.e., nonreflective, fashion. Although the "I" is eventually expressed through specific behaviors, it initially is experienced as a feeling or as a fleeting impulse.

Ultimately, whether the potential behavior contained in the "I" will be consummated depends on a set of inner considerations that Mead subsumed under the term "Me." This is Mead's term for the representational society that is symbolically embedded in each and every individual. Embracing the imagined response of the world at large, the "Me" symbolically interacts with the "I" and determines whether initial impulses are expressed or inhibited.

Adopting a dramaturgical metaphor, Mead sees the interactive relationship between the "I" and the "Me" as a series of inner rehearsals. Before action contemplated by the "I" ever surfaces, it is subjected to an imaginary audience (the "Me") and modified accordingly. "Minded" behavior, i.e., behavior that is socially responsive, is behavior that has been molded by a pattern of inner action and inner responses. To the extent that the "Me" allows people to monitor their ongoing behavior, it is the seat of reflection and forms the basis for what ultimately comes to be known as "self-control."

The "I" and the "Me" act in concert to make up the self. Together they roughly correspond to the "self-other" distinction in object relations theory. Just as the child interacts internally with representational others to create a sense of self in object relations, so the "I" symbolically interacts with the "Me" to create a sense of self in symbolic interactionism. The two perspectives are essentially opposite sides of the same relational coin, with object relations focusing on childhood internalizations and symbolic interactionism on adult ones.

But *how*, precisely, do the "I" and the "Me" interact? The answer, very simply, is through conversation. Much of what is considered "mental activity" by symbolic interactionists entails the linguistic codification of interactions with others. Cognitive activities that normally fall into the category of "thinking" are regarded as transformations of conversations people hold or have held with significant figures in their lives. For Mead, the "I" and the "Me" essentially comprise an "inner forum" which he regarded as the essence of the self.

The question still arises as to the concrete makeup of the inner forum, particularly the "Me." Mead tends to be somewhat vague about this. He speaks about the forces in the "Me" as constituting a "generalized other," representing, as it were, a composite of the various forces in society that affect people. One gathers that Mead is using the notion of a "generalized other" to refer to various societal institutions such as marriage, school, and the family.

People, however, do not interact with composites or with "institutions" but with human beings. Some of these human beings are spouses, and interactions with them dictate how people see themselves as husbands and wives; others are coworkers or clients and dealings with them affect how people feel about themselves as teachers, nurses, or therapists. And yet others are children; interactions with offspring strongly influence how people see themselves as parents. All this suggests that the self may not be a single "I-Me" configuration, but rather a series of "I-Me's."

There is growing recognition among social theorists that the self, rather than being monolithic, is composed of a series of subselves. Cottrell (1969) refers to these as "self-other systems" and contends that the self is a congregate of different self-other systems. Each of these systems, moreover, is activated by social circumstances relevant to that system. Cavorting with one's children triggers the *parental* self-other system, flirting with someone the *sexual* self-other system, and doing one's job the *work* self-other system.

The phrase "self-other system" tends to be a bit cumbersome and somewhat removed from daily experience. It perhaps is more phenomenologically accurate to refer to these various systems as "identities" and to simply talk about family identity, sexual identity, career identity, and so on. Sexual identity thus would be seen as more than just a term depicting gender or erotic preference. It would be regarded as a set of feelings one has about oneself generated by complex interchanges with internal and external figures around issues of sexuality. This might range from early interactions with one's parents to symbolic interactions with a figure in an X-rated movie. Combined with ongoing sexual transactions with figures in one's contemporary life, they define the totality of sexual selfhood.

Identities, in the last analysis, are essentially subselves. They are constructed out of relationships and rely on relationships to remain viable. This is why relationships are so critical for psychological survival. They fuel and sustain the different identities that make up the self. In the words of Harry Guntrip, "the identity problem is the biggest single issue that can be raised about human existence. It has always been the secret critical issue; only in our time have we become explicitly conscious of it" (1971, p. 119).

[margin note: Identity problem = biggest single px]

Bearing all of this in mind, we find that the fourth and final phase of self-development describes a lifelong phase of self-differentiation. It is in this phase of development that different types of interactions are sorted, so to speak, into various identities. Most of the major identities can be counted on the fingers of one hand. To the ones already mentioned (parental, sexual, marital, and career identities), one probably can add ethnic or religious identity. Much of people's adult lives involves establishing relationships which will enhance these identities. To the extent that each is a part of the self, the process contributes to one's overall sense of "self-worth."

As is the case in each preceding stage of development, the fourth stage also contains its own variant of the splitting process. Every identity in its own idiosyncratic way is deeply affected by issues of goodness and badness. What originated in good and bad experiences in the mother-child relationship and evolved into good and bad feelings about the self comes to be expressed in feelings about being a good (or bad) husband, a good (or bad) wife, a good (or bad) parent, and a good (or bad) lawyer or teacher. What began as a central issue in the infant-mother relationship has become an issue in all relationships.

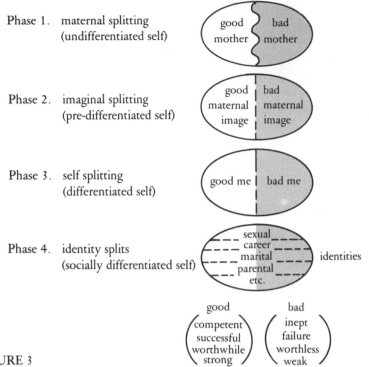

Phase 1. maternal splitting
          (undifferentiated self)

Phase 2. imaginal splitting
          (pre-differentiated self)

Phase 3. self splitting
          (differentiated self)

Phase 4. identity splits
          (socially differentiated self)

FIGURE 3

Figure 3 depicts the four phases of developmental splitting in schematic form. The first three phases portray the goodness-badness split as it is transformed from an experience of the mother "out there" to an experience of self. The fourth phase indicates how splitting is embedded within the various identities that make up the adult self.

It is evident that concerns over goodness and badness never disappear. Quite simply, the salient issues of early childhood—desirability, acceptance, and the emergence of a viable self—are replayed and reworked in richer and more diverse contexts. The extent to which resolution of these issues leads to a more integrated and satisfactory vision of the self is a fairly reliable measure of the extent to which individuals successfully can lay claim to psychological health.

Much of what is considered psychopathology in object relations theory centers about maladaptive efforts to redress the goodness-badness balance of the inner world. This typically is accomplished by means of psychological mechanisms called projective identifications. Aimed at dealing with unsatisfactory object relations that are largely historical in nature, projective identifications distort and undermine the patient's current relationships. The next chapter addresses the different forms that these projective identifications take and the way individuals use them to deal with some of the deficiencies in their inner worlds.

CHAPTER 3

Object Relations Pathology

The question of what constitutes psychopathology is a key consideration in any systematic approach to human behavior. In psychoanalytic circles, psychopathology is defined in terms of psychosexual fixations and the inability to adequately discharge libidinal tensions. In perspectives with a cognitive emphasis, e.g., cognitive behavior modification, psychopathology develops because the patient interprets events falsely or harbors unrealistic expectations. And in phenomenological approaches, psychopathology tends to emerge out of incongruities in the patient's experience of his existence. The particular stance taken towards psychopathology is a direct derivative of the theoretical perspective to which one subscribes.

In object relations theory, psychopathology is viewed as a disturbance in the makeup of the self. Symptoms, mood alterations, distorted perceptions of the world—all are construed in terms of one's object relationships and the ways in which they have been internalized. The nature of the patient's difficulties can be traced to arrests in the development of the self and anomalies in splitting. The critical considerations have to do with how early the arrest occurs, the precise character of the splitting, and the degree to which both permeate the patient's various identities.

Since the self is interpersonally constructed, so-called "mental disturbances" are tantamount to disturbances in interpersonal relationships. If one's early object relations have been particularly debilitating, i.e., if the maternal relationship is characterized by gross abuse, chronic separation, or straight out abandonment, the chances are that difficulties will arise in practically every sphere of self-functioning. This was the case with Roy, whose story is told at the beginning of Chapter 2. His relationships with foster parents, peers, and teachers all demonstrated the impact that his early abandonment had on his sense of self.

But early relationships are not the only ones that affect one's sense of self-worth. Intervening internalizations take place throughout life, making the self more than simply a mirror of what happened in the early years. Because of the makeup of the self, individuals subject to a critical and harsh upbringing may, for example, develop positive feelings about themselves as professionals if interactions with coworkers are positive and rewarding.

The compensatory quality of adult object relations can be seen in a patient named Cynthia who entered treatment for mild but recurrent depression. A 26-year-old graduate student in economics, Cynthia had a history of poor sexual relationships with men, especially those with whom she was romantically involved. She would meet a man, spend a great deal of effort trying to establish a relationship, and then find that the man would lose interest in her. This happened with some regularity and seemed to fall into some type of pattern.

At the same time, Cynthia was doing quite well in her studies. She stood at the top of her class and was highly regarded by both her instructors and fellow students. She was close to finishing her dissertation, and at the time she entered treatment had already been offered several attractive positions once she received her degree.

Early in therapy, Cynthia reported that she had been raised in the South and that her family had more or less planned her life for her. They fully expected her to attend a small local college (which was more like a finishing school), marry one of a number of eligible businessmen in town, and settle into the life of a genteel Southern belle. Cynthia decided instead to enroll in the state university. There she met a mathematics professor who felt she had unusual potential. He took her under his wing and encouraged her to pursue a graduate career.

Once the therapy got under way, it became evident that Cynthia's depressions were associated with overdetermined efforts on her part to please her partners—sexually and otherwise. It also became evident that this was related to subtle messages she had received from her mother regarding what it meant to be a desirable woman. These largely had to do with the need to take a subservient position in relationships with men. Not surprisingly, this was the stance her mother had adopted in her own life.

It was revealing that Cynthia's difficulties did not extend to her performance in school. She had to deal with many male figures in the mostly male economics department and might easily have assumed a meek and submissive posture there as well. But she did not. Her confidence in herself in the academic arena clearly was influenced by the man who acted as her mentor while she was an undergraduate. At one point in treatment, she told me that this man "lived inside of her" and that his presence had sustained her throughout the years.

Within object relations theory, interactions with significant others act to sustain people's various identities. Maintaining marital identity, for example, involves a whole host of subtle relational responses through which husband and wife legitimize one another. Through the various and seemingly innocuous tasks that make up marriage, the wife sustains the spouse's identity as "husband," while he sustains her identity as "wife." The two identities are so mutually interdependent that one cannot be considered separately from the other. In transforming each other into husband and wife, marital partners socially "create each other" and in so doing create their own marital identities (Berger and Kellner, 1964).

What this means is that the relationships people establish with one another are instrumental in maintaining a viable sense of self. Human beings constantly engage in self-other internalizations that complement and enhance each other's respective identities. Relationships are not simply welcome additions to human existence. They are what existence is all about. If human beings hope to retain an ongoing sense of who they are and where they fit in the world, they need to form meaningful relationships with significant others. What's more, they need to ensure that these relationships endure.

But what if people have grave reservations about their self-worth? What if they not only question their ability to form meaningful relationships but to sustain them? For such individuals, human relationships are at best tenuous affairs. They cannot assume that others will stay involved with them of their own volition. They consequently search for means by which to ensure that significant figures in their lives remain bound to them. The results are seen in patterns of adult object relations that fall under the rubric of "projective identifications."

PROJECTIVE IDENTIFICATION

In object relations theory, projective identifications are patterns of interpersonal behavior in which a person induces others to behave or respond in a circumscribed fashion. This differs from ordinary projection, which is essentially a mental act and need not involve overt responses of any sort. In the projection of hostility, for example, the person who projects assumes that people are angry or ill-tempered regardless of how they actually may feel or behave. What is more, there need not be any face-to-face interaction for the projection to occur. Projective identification, on the other hand, actually involves the behavioral and emotional manipulation of others.

Projective identification lifts projection out of the inner world and deposits it in the realm of interpersonal relationships (Grotstein, 1981; Racker, 1968; Sandler, 1987). Persons who are targets of another person's projections may never know of it—but not those targeted with projective identifications. In projective identification, the recipient is forced to respond to the projective fantasies of the projector. Without realizing it, the target unwittingly becomes a repository for the feelings and inner representations of the person doing the projecting. The result is a relationship in which "the recipient is pressured to think, feel, and behave in a manner congruent with the ejected feelings and the self- and object-representations embodied in the projective fantasy" (Ogden, 1982, p. 2).

Thus in the projective identification of hostility, a husband who is unaware of his own inner hostile urges may constantly provoke his wife and incite her towards anger. He may stay out late, leave a mess throughout the house, and fail to keep promises. After having been pushed to the limit, the wife responds by lashing out at him, to which the husband reacts with surprised indignation. The two make up and things are smoothed over—until next time. The husband's projective identification acts as a way both of discharging a projective fantasy and of manipulating his wife to respond in a circumscribed way.

A key dynamic in projective identification is the *induction* that underlies it. Individuals who rely on projective identification engage in subtle but nonetheless powerful manipulations to induce those about them to behave in prescribed ways. It is as if one individual forces another to play a role in the enactment of that person's internal drama—one involving early object relationships. The target of the manipulation is induced to engage in an *identification* with a disowned aspect of the person doing the *projection*—hence the term "projective identification."

The elements that makes up a projective identification and the sequence in which they occur can perhaps best be described in terms of a three stage process (Ogden, 1982). The first stage in the process centers on the wish to get rid of a part of the self because that part either is experienced as bad or threatens to destroy the self from within. This wish takes the form of a *projective fantasy* in which an individual "places" a part of himself in another human being and tries to control that person from within. This fantasy is very primitive and is a vestigial remnant of pre-objectal thinking processes.

In the next stage of the process, the person engaging in the projective identification pressures the recipient to behave in a way that conforms to the projective fantasy. The goal is to get the recipient to actually experience the feelings associated with the fantasy—to become submissive, dominating, sexually aroused or whatever—and behave accordingly. The pressure put upon the recipient is not fantasy pressure; it is real pressure derived from real interaction. Projective identification by definition exists only where there are behavioral and emotional interchanges. It does not exist when there is no interaction between projector and recipient.

In the final stage of the process, the recipient responds to the feelings and responses that have been induced by the projective manipulations. The recipient may in some cases tolerate these feelings and even be able to integrate them into his or her own personality structure. Or they may be able to use the feelings to form a basis for relating to the person doing the projecting in a new way (Ogden, pp. 17–20). This, at least, is what the projector hopes will happen. The secret desire of the person engaged in the projective identification is that the feelings "deposited" in the recipient will enhance the relationship.

This wish clearly is a part of the projective fantasy and rarely comes true. More often than not, the target of the projective identification feels used and manipulated. Once a person is aware of what is going on, a typical response is anger or withdrawal. This confirms the original belief of the projector (that part of him is bad and undesirable) and perpetuates the pathology. This is not to say that a positive outcome cannot occur, only that it is unlikely under normal circumstances.

Projective identifications can be seen as powerful relational artifices that straddle the intrapersonal and the interpersonal. An individual unconsciously projects a part of the self into another human being as a means of converting an inner struggle over badness and unacceptability into an external one. The hope is that the forces of goodness will prevail and the individual will feel better about himself as a human being.

That projective identifications almost always lead to relational fiascos should not obscure the fact that they possess a positive side. Projective identifications represent serious efforts to undo a pathological conflict in the self. The problem is that they do so at the expense of ongoing relationships. In the end, projective identifications only prolong and intensify the patient's pathology.

Why do people allow themselves to become targets of projective identifications? Why do recipients subject themselves to manipulations that only end in anger and frustration? Why don't they simply bail out before matters get totally out of hand? Sometimes they do, and many broken relationships are the results of projective identifications that have been pushed to the limit. But just as often they do not. Many individuals stay in relationships marked by projective identification, despite the fact that they get anxious, depressed, and chronically frustrated. The reason they stay usually can be traced to guilt, obligation, or fear of loneliness.

There is, however, another reason that people remain in relationships marked by projective identifications. And this has to do with the fact that every projective identification contains a powerful injunction—a promise or a threat—that keeps the recipient bound in the relationship. For every projective identification, there is a Damoclean sword with an "or else" etched on its blade. It is this hidden threat that keeps people in relationships even though they are taken advantage of and manipulated.

Projective inductions can be found to some extent even in normal relationships. Under ordinary circumstances, people induce those closest to them to behave in ways that will enhance their idiosyncratic selves. But in the process they allow themselves to be "used" as well. Healthy interactions are built on implicit quid pro quos in which relational enhancement is seen as a two-way street. In pathological interactions, there is usually only one person who reaps the benefits so that ultimately the other party feels used.

Ogden (1982) suggests that the secret messages and covert threats contained in projective identifications have their counterparts in the mother's attempts to pressure the infant to comply with *her* pathology. The ultimate threat is that the infant will cease to exist for the mother if the child doesn't comply with her demands. Through her actions and emotional responses she communicates: "If you are not what I need you to be, you don't exist for me."

Just as children who are abused by their parents end up as abusers themselves later in life, so children who are the recipients of childhood threats end up using threats when they become adults. The interaction patterns of such individuals tend to contain nonverbal messages designed to coerce key individuals to stay in relationships with them. These coercive threats often are contained in hidden messages known as "metacommunications."

Modern communication theory suggests that much of what takes place between human beings can be described in terms of "communications" and "metacommunications." At the communicative level one finds the behavioral messages, or face-to-face communications, that make up the bulk of human interaction. Most of this is verbal in nature and embraces the actual demands and requests that people make of one another, e.g., "Please take out the garbage." The metacommunicative level, on the other hand, operates nonverbally and consists of messages that are more difficult to pin down. At this level one typically finds such messages as "or I'll make your life miserable." More often than not, the metacommunicative level registers most accurately the emotional quality of a relationship.

Metacommunications are particularly revealing in pathological relationships since they supply the muscle behind the various projective identifications. The projective identification of dependency, for example, contains messages at the communicative level that take the form of "take care of me" or "tell me what to do." The "metacommunication" that lurks beneath these messages conveys the more ominous "or I will perish." A person thus may respond to the overt communications in the relationship without realizing what he is being drawn into. To the extent that one person in a relationship unwittingly is manipulated into responding to the hidden message, the relationship takes on unhealthy, i.e. pathological, overtones.

Projective identifications are the pathologic sequelae of disturbed object relations, most of which have occurred early in life. Because these relationships are largely pre-verbal in nature and unavailable to consciousness, it is often difficult to pinpoint their precise character. Still, one can identify the various projective identifications by means of the different communication patterns associated with each.

In the pages that follow, four major patterns of projective identification are described, along with their characteristic communications and metacommunications. They are the projective identification of dependency, power, sexuality, and ingratiation. Each is a derivative of early pathological object relations. Each describes a clinically identifiable means by which individuals structure their relationships in pathological ways.

Projective Identification: Dependency

The projective identification of dependency in adult object relationships is characterized by statements which signal chronic helplessness. The interactions of persons who relate to others in this fashion are punctuated by expressions such as:

- "What do you think?"
- "What should I do?"
- "Can you help me . . . ?"
- "I can't seem to manage this on my own."

Persons who use this form of projective identification look to others whenever there is a decision to be made or some independent action to be taken. One often is taken aback by their requests since they seem capable of doing what has to be done on their own. This perception usually is not far from the truth. Persons who employ dependency projective identifications are, for the most part, quite intelligent and resourceful. Their use of this form of interpersonal manipulation has little to do with pragmatic or real needs. Instead it represents a style of interpersonal relating that is instigated by inner considerations.

A case in point is a woman named Bettina who was seen in individual therapy. The mother of two, Bettina was married to an electrical engineer named Tom and was active in town politics. At the time she entered treatment, she was a member of the town council and held a board position in the League of Woman Voters. She entered therapy to seek help in dealing with growing fears that her husband was going to leave her. Although he denied it, she was convinced his departure was imminent.

From the first session, it was evident that Bettina was a bright and capable person. She had graduated with honors from a prestigious university and had a master's degree in arts administration. She seemed to be able to deal with most problems that arose—except those that occurred at home. The problem was that Bettina could not make a decision, even the most trivial one, without seeking the advice of her husband.

Things that Bettina should have been able to handle on her own tended to immobilize her. If a faucet failed she had to call Tom before venturing to call a plumber. If a decision had to be made about the children's schooling—something as minor as giving permission for a hastily scheduled trip— she would put it off until she consulted Tom. Often she would call him at the office and interrupt an important meeting to seek advice about a trivial matter. On some days Bettina was on the phone with Tom two or three times.

Tom was relatively easygoing and initially did not make much of his wife's behavior. In the early years of their marriage, when he was not that busy, he tended to regard it as a minor bother. Over the years, however, he became more and more annoyed at her intrusions. Bettina told me that he had spoken to her about it more than once, but she dismissed his concern, insisting that he was blowing things out of proportion.

Eventually Tom's patience wore thin and he responded with angry outbursts. At one point Bettina said he accused her of acting like a two-year-old. She promised to change, usually after a tearful confrontation, but eventually she fell into the same pattern. The problem was taking its toll on the marriage and Bettina, perhaps realistically, decided that it was time to seek help.

Bettina's behavior highlights an important characteristic of people who projectively identify through dependency. They honestly do not believe that they can make it on their own. A feeling of helplessness is constantly with them, even though they seem on the surface to be quite competent. Such individuals are convinced that the success of their relationships, particularly close ones, hinges on their ability to convince people that they cannot exist on their own. They consequently adopt the emotional demeanor of a young child and coerce (induce) those about them into taking care of them.

The concrete messages or communications that make up a projective identification of dependency involve seeking advice, asking for directions, and other seemingly innocuous expressions of help-seeking. The patient usually targets someone—a spouse or parent, a friend, a guru, or sometimes a therapist—and relies on that person for assistance and support. On the surface it all seems harmless and benign. But beneath all this is a metacommunication which signals something more malignant. The embedded message typically takes the form of "I can't survive on my own." Persons who use projective identifications of dependency are intent on convincing those about them that dire consequences will ensue if the help they feel they need isn't forthcoming.

What are these consequences? What is the nature of the "or else" that is built into the metacommunication? One is loss of control. Persons who employ a projective identification of dependency have temper tantrums, hysterical crying fits, and other outbursts that suggest their world is coming apart at the seams. Another common response is depression. The projector feels left on his own, withdraws from the relationship, and becomes despondent. Finally, there are statements of suicidal intent or even actual suicide attempts. What better way to play out the inner threat contained in the metacommunication but to offer conclusive proof that one cannot, in fact, "make it on his own."

The projective identification of dependency clearly figures in a number of psychiatric syndromes. Perhaps the clearest example can be seen in severe cases of major depression, where patients are unable to perform such basic tasks of self-maintenance as dressing or feeding themselves. When this happens, friends, relatives, and nurses are forced to take over caretaking functions that the patient ordinarily manages. What we are seeing in such cases is the formation of a relationship between the patient and others in which the early infant-caretaker relationship has been reconstituted.

Another more subtle but nonetheless clear expression of a projective identification of dependency can be seen in the following description of a woman who showed up at a psychiatric clinic suffering from a severe anxiety reaction:

The 26-year-old wife of a successful lawyer came to a psychiatric clinic with the complaint that she had "the jitters." She said she felt that she was going to pieces. She had fears of being alone, of screaming, of running away, and of committing suicide. . . . One of these attacks occurred in the middle of the night when her husband was out of town. She awoke crying and shaking violently, and remembering thinking in terror, "I'm sick here alone and my husband is away and nobody knows who I am." (Cameron and Magaret, 1951, p. 307).

The anxiety was so disabling that eventually she had to be hospitalized.

It was during the hospitalization that the patient's extreme dependency on her husband became evident. This was reflected in her feeling that she could not exist independently of him. If her husband were not there to look after her, her entire sense of being would become shaky ("nobody knows who I am"). It is also telling that during her hospitalization she often thought of running away, and when she was asked where she would go, she said "probably to [my] husband's office" (p. 309).

Another syndrome in which the projective identification of dependency seems to play a significant role is agoraphobia. An interesting demographic feature of this disturbance is that most individuals who suffer from it are housewives. But these are not ordinary housewives. They are women whose overall sense of self is concentrated almost entirely in their marriage and marital identities. They are intensely bound to their husbands. Their relationships seem heavily rooted in dependency, and they spend a great deal of energy making sure there is always someone around to take care of them. Whenever they feel threatened, they respond by placing the husband (or a surrogate figure) in a caretaking role. In extreme cases this expresses itself as agoraphobia, and they literally cannot go out of the house by themselves.

Whether a person is depressed, suffers from an anxiety reaction, or is agoraphobic, using a dependency projective identification constitutes a way of structuring and sustaining a relationship. Patients who employ projective identification of dependency in therapy frequently solicit advice ranging from financial matters (buying a new car, investing their money) to what kinds of books to read or movies to see. One of my patients was drawn to psychological self-help books and insisted that I counsel her as to which were the best. When I declined, she became angry and abusive. What sometimes seem like minor requests for advice often mask attempts to enmesh the therapist in a dependency interaction.

To the extent that targets of a dependency projective identification—be it a therapist or other persons in the patient's life—offer help or advice, they fuel the projective identification. This perpetuates the projective fantasy, so that targets of the identification find themselves in the unenviable position of caring for someone who really doesn't need to be cared for. This ultimately takes its toll. It is very difficult to sustain a relationship where all the giving is one way. Persons who become the targets of dependency projective identifications eventually feel drained and exploited. Wittingly or unwittingly, they have become drawn into a relationship in which they are asked to provide things that only a mother could reasonably be asked to provide.

The origins of a dependency projective identification, as well as of most other projective identifications, can be traced to the individual's early object relations. As one might expect, advice and guidance are prominent features of the mother-child interaction in these relationships. Bettina, for example, had only vague recollections of her very early years, although she recalled that her mother and she were very close. She was able, however, to remember some significant facts about her preteen years. Specifically, she recalled that her mother constantly told her what to do and advised her regarding even the smallest choices she had to make in her life. These ranged from choosing the "correct" clothes to advising about the proper makeup to wear.

The striking part of Bettina's description was that as Bettina matured, her mother's "hovering," as she called it, increased instead of diminishing. As Bettina got older, she found herself consulting with her mother as to her choice of girlfriends as well as boyfriends. With some embarrassment, Bettina admitted that the decision to marry Tom was as much her mother's as hers. Throughout her growing years, Bettina was subtly and sometimes not so subtly taught that she could not rely on her own judgment or make it on her own.

Of the various projective identifications one comes across, those rooted in unresolved dependency seem to be the most prevalent. This is not surprising since dependency is the bedrock of early childhood. If something is going to go wrong in the early years of life, it most likely will take place in the context of the child's early dependency on the mother.

Winnicott's "good-enough mother" is the inverse of the mother who inculcates projective identifications of dependency in her child. The good-enough mother is not merely an object who gratifies but a person who selectively frustrates the child's needs. Winnicott writes:

The good-enough mother . . . starts off with an almost complete adaptation to her infant's needs, and as time proceeds she adapts less and less completely, gradually, according to the infant's growing ability to deal with her failure. (1971, p. 10)

In "failing" to respond to the child at critical transitions, the "good-enough mother" succeeds in encouraging the child's emerging autonomy. "Failure to fail" on the part of the mother creates a child whose projective fantasies are filled with images of helplessness.

The major paradox of early childhood is that autonomous growth occurs in the context of a highly dependent relationship. In healthy mother-child transactions, autonomous behavior on the part of the child is welcome and met with praise. In unhealthy transactions, the same behavior is met with emotional withdrawal, punishment, and sometimes even abandonment. It is as if the mother cannot tolerate her child unless the child is weak and needy. And to the extent that the child responds in a weak and needy fashion, the mother dispenses whatever love and affection there is to dispense. What the child comes to learn through this type of experience is that to be good (loved, accepted, retained) is to be weak and helpless. This becomes a distinguishing feature of inner self-object representations and an integral part of the self. Once it is a part of one's inner world, it forms the basis for external interactions. Such individuals then seek out relationships in which "helplessness" is the dominant theme.

Individuals who use projective identifications of dependency occasionally find someone whose life goal is taking care of others. If they do, all is well and good. If, on the other hand, interactions with others fail to take on caretaker-child characteristics, they set out to recreate this kind of relationship on their own. This is what the projective identification of dependency is meant to accomplish. Individuals who relate in this way spend a large part of their lives inducing those closest to them into becoming caretakers, believing that interactions of this sort form the foundation for lasting relationships.

Projective Identification: Power

The projective identification of power has its basis in an internal struggle having to do with dominance and control. The struggle is rooted in early object relations in which power was associated with issues of acceptability and goodness. It is played out in the interpersonal arena by inducing feelings of weakness and incompetency in others.

Examining the behavior of persons who employ this type of projective identification, one finds statements that take the form of:

- "Do exactly what I say."
- "Follow my lead."
- "Do it this way."
- "Obey my directions."

The overall purpose of these kinds of communications is to create a relationship where the recipient is forced to take a subservient role. Whatever else goes on in the relationship, issues of power and control predominate.

An example of a projective identification of power can be seen in an exchange that took place between a couple initially referred because of problems having to do with their 11-year-old daughter Melanie. It seems that Melanie had been skipping school on certain days and covering this up by forging letters excusing her absence. She also had been caught shoplifting. A merchant who knew the parents told them that Melanie had been taking small items from his store. He caught her taking colored shoelaces on one occasion and plastic barrettes on another. Because he was a friend of the family, he decided to alert the parents before taking more drastic action, such as notifying the police.

Initially Melanie and her parents were seen together to sort out what was going on. The girl at first denied that she had shoplifted but broke down after her parents threatened to confront her with the shopkeeper. Over the course of a few sessions, it became evident that Melanie was not a delinquent child. Her behavior was a way of calling attention to the fact that she was troubled by the state of her parents' marriage. Because of the heightened marital tension in the family, a decision was made to see the parents alone. The father was less than happy about this arrangement, but agreed to be seen with his wife "if it would help Melanie."

The way Melanie's parents interacted with one another in the therapy session indicated that her father dominated the relationship. He was somewhat older than his wife, had been married once before, and was intent on making this marriage work. His determination to ensure a marital success led to his virtually controlling his wife's life. He was sure, for example, to oversee practically every aspect of how his wife ran the household. He commented on her housecleaning, corrected her bookkeeping, and even checked over her shopping list before she went to the supermarket. It was clear that he didn't trust her to do things on her own.

Over the course of couple therapy, the marital relationship was explored and the nature of the spouses' interactions probed, particularly those that occurred in the room. During the sessions, I often had to stop the husband from answering questions for his wife. Since she would habitually defer to him, it took a great deal of effort to get her to speak for herself. As the therapy progressed and the wife slowly became more assertive, she began to challenge her husband's statements. She also reported that she was beginning to relate to her daughter more as a person in her own right rather than as a mouthpiece for her husband.

The father did not take kindly to all this. He began finding excuses not to attend the sessions. Since I had stipulated early in treatment that I wanted to see them together or not at all, this meant we had to skip several meetings. In one session, he claimed that I was disturbing his marriage and threatened to stop coming to therapy altogether if I did not back off. His wife responded by telling him she would leave him if he did. He scoffed at her, obviously taken aback by the fact that she had the gumption to make such a threat. When she made it patently clear that she meant business, he responded by saying, "Go ahead, see what happens if you leave. You won't be able to make it on your own." He paused, adding, "You'll be crawling back on your hands and knees in a week begging me to take you back."

Whatever else one might say about this marriage, it was a showcase for the projective identification of power. In relationships founded on this type of projective identification, the face-to-face messages typically involve giving orders, making criticisms, and challenging the competency of the person who is the target of the projective fantasy. The metacommunication behind the surface message is "You can't survive without me."

This is the hidden threat that lies at the bottom of all projective identifications of power. In this couple, it surfaced at the point where the existence of the relationship itself was menaced. But it was there all along, perhaps from the beginning of the marriage, and was used to persuade the wife that she could not function on her own.

It perhaps is evident that a projective identification of power is the inverse of a projective identification of dependency. In the latter, the projective identification invests the target of the projection with caretaking powers, whereas in the former efforts are made to convince the target that he or she needs to be cared for and looked after. Both projective identifications are similar in that they entail manipulation of an external relationship so as to deal with unresolved conflicts in one's internal object relations. But while the communications in the case of dependency signal "Take care of me," those in the case of power signal "You need to be taken care of."

Marriage is not the only place where one finds projective identifications of power. It is just that marriage, because of the emotional and physical proximity of husband and wife, tends to magnify whatever disturbances existed in the participants' early object relations. But there are numerous other examples of how projective identifications of power tend to subvert the nature of male-female relationships.

A flagrant and all too common example is described by Susan Forward (1986) in her research on misogynistic men. Her study of "men who hate women" indicates that a great many men structure their relationships so as to regularly abuse the women with whom they get involved. This abuse can range from implied threats to physical assault and often includes unrelenting criticism and vicious verbal attacks. Paradoxically, the behavior of these men often is excused by the women who "love them."

Forward's examination of the interaction between these partners reveals that their relationship is fueled by an intense power dynamic in which the man needs to dominate and overpower the woman. The key element is one of control: "The misogynist must control how his partner thinks, feels, behaves, and with whom and what she involves herself" (p. 42). Forward contends that these men feel that women can destroy them by abandoning them. To counter these fears, they must make the women less powerful. If a woman is weak and helpless, she cannot help but be bound to him. Forward's description essentially portrays the slave-master relationship that is at the basis of projective identifications of power.

Similar projective identifications can be seen in relationships where gender is not a primary factor. Corporate life, for instance, contains abundant examples of how power disparities contribute to relational fiascos—and also affect productive capacity. Every organization has its share of middle managers and executive officers who cannot seem to delegate responsibility. Such individuals constantly indicate to their subordinates that they "can't seem to do things right," treating them as if they were just barely competent. A great deal of organizational consulting is directed at resolving institutional relationships in which projective identifications of power seem to have gained an upper hand.

The origins of projective identifications of power, like those of projective identifications of dependency, can be traced to early object relations. The particular interactions that contribute to their development are those in which caretaking figures communicate that they are unable to care for the child. Instead they communicate that they need to be cared for themselves. This inversion reverses the normal caretaking relationship between parent and child and paradoxically places the child in the position of a surrogate parent.

In the field of family therapy this kind of pattern produces what is known as a "parentified child" (Boszormenyi-Nagy and Spark, 1984; Karpel & Strauss, 1983; Minuchin, 1974). Parentified children are children who are thrust into the role of caretakers for parents who are emotionally (and sometimes physically) unable to care for themselves. This requires major psychic dislocations for as Boszormenyi-Nagy and Spark put it, "the person of the child first must be transformed into that of an imaginary adult" (p. 152).

Patterns of this sort very often are seen in alcoholic families. In such families one or both parents typically are incapable of managing for themselves much of the time. In the course of growing up, the child learns that the people closest to him are weak, if not inept, and unreliable. The result is that the child has to care not only for himself but for the parents as well.

It is not surprising that feelings of goodness and positive self-regard are at a premium in families with parentified children. The parentified child discovers that feelings of competence and self-worth can be achieved only if he controls what takes place about him. To ensure success, the child is transformed into a "little parent" and charged with the responsibility of making sure everything takes place as it should. This can range from making sure the parents eat two or three solid meals a day to getting them into bed at night. It is almost as if the child has been prematurely thrust into the future and is taking care of elderly parents. Only these parents are not old; they simply are unable to care for themselves.

Parentification, whether it occurs in alcoholic families or non-alcoholic families, constitutes a developmentally advanced expression of a projective identification of power. Since it requires the child to act as caretaker, the child has to have reached a relatively mature level of development. A seven-year-old may be able to instruct the parent to take off his clothes before getting into bed; an infant cannot. Nevertheless, one can safely assume that the types of expectations and feelings associated with concrete acts of parentification reflect feelings that were experienced much earlier. An alcoholic parent does not become an alcoholic parent overnight.

Another pattern of early infant-mother interaction that can lead to the development of a power projective identification involves mothers who are withdrawn or unavailable rather than helpless. Forward suggests that an early object relational pattern in misogynistic men is one in which the mother withholds love and affection and makes the child feel as if he were unwanted. The threat of abandonment hangs over the head of the child and produces feelings of impending catastrophe. To forestall these feelings, the child tries to control the mother's behavior through fantasy. In adulthood, such individuals play out their control fantasies in relationships with women. By making the women around them feel inadequate and fearful of functioning on their own, they assure that they will not be abandoned.

An example of how a projective identification of power operates in therapy can be seen in a patient named Celia. A therapist by profession, Celia was prone to intellectualize and would constantly reflect on what was happening in the therapy. She would respond to my comments with "That's an excellent interpretation. You really hit the nail on the head." At other times she would say something along the lines of, "That's not quite right. I don't think you've given enough thought to what I've been saying." I sometimes had the feeling that I was back in graduate school and the patient had mysteriously been transformed into one of my supervisors.

A clue to the presence of a projective identification of power in therapy is the criticism that pervades the sessions. Like Celia, some patients comment critically on the correctness or incorrectness of the therapist's interventions. It is almost as if they feel that they would know how to do the job more effectively if they were in charge. Other patients comment on the surroundings or even on the therapist's clothing. One of my patients said to me in the course of a therapy session, "You could use someone to help pick out your clothes." I probably could, but I think the Pygmalion-like quality of the patient's remarks indicated that she was doing more than just giving me a helpful bit of advice.

To the extent that the metacommunication in the projective identification of power signals "You can't survive (or at least manage) on your own," it places individuals who are targets of these projections in uncomfortable positions. Competency, control, and power seem always to be at issue. This does not bode well for a relationship, and it is not long before rebellious confrontations and angry outbursts begin to appear. If there is one thing that people dislike—and dislike intensely—it is being told they are inept. However incompetent they may be, human beings resent hearing that they cannot make it on their own.

Not unexpectedly, projective identifications of power tend to be more prevalent among men than women. Just the opposite holds true for projective identifications of dependency. Jessica Benjamin (1986) proposes that differences of this sort stem from the way gender identity is constructed in patriarchal western society. Commenting on the way men and women achieve "object status" in our culture, Benjamin proposes that the quest for selfhood and desirability leads to submissive behavior in women and dominant behavior in men.

If this the case, one would expect women to be more prone to use projective identifications of dependency. Such patterns derive from developmental experiences in which women are forced to become objects rather than subjects of desire (Benjamin, 1986, pp. 87–88). In contrast, the male sense of self, rooted in experiences in which control and dominance are valued, is more likely to be expressed through projective identifications of power. Clearly there are exceptions. But it is not surprising to find broader cultural patterns mirrored in clinical work.

Projective Identification: Sexuality

The projective identification of sexuality is an interpersonal dynamic meant to establish and sustain relationships through sexual means. It is specifically designed to induce an erotic response in the person toward whom it is directed and to keep the relationship operating on this basis. Sexual arousal thus becomes the mainstay of the relationship and ensures that the relationship will prove attractive to the person who is the recipient of the projective identification.

The kinds of behaviors that make up sexual projective identifications are not that different from the sexual behavior one sees in any relationship where sexual intimacy is a factor. These range from flirtatiousness and suggestive dress to blatantly seductive come-ons. The difference between normal relationships and relationships marked by sexual projective identifications has mainly to do with the driven nature of the sexual activity and its exclusive character. In relationships where sexual projective identifications operate, sex overshadows all else. Instead of being a part of the relationship, it *is* the relationship.

The unspoken assumption in relationships of this sort is that sex is the glue that keeps everything in working order. The unspoken fear is that the relationship would deteriorate and eventually crumble if sex weren't the major component. This can be seen in two separate cases in which a projective identification of sexuality was the basis for relationship formation. The first involved a woman named Ingrid who sought therapy because of chronic insomnia and unhappiness over being unable to establish long term relationships. The second involved a patient who was having difficulty dealing with women after his divorce.

A 36-year-old elementary school teacher, Ingrid left Norway at the age of 12 to come live with an aunt and uncle in America after her father passed away. She was attractive and dated men regularly but over the years had been unable to form lasting relationships. Since she described her dealings with men in vague ways, it was difficult to get a precise picture of what her interactions with them were like. Much of the early portion of therapy was spent recounting her involvement with various men she had dated over the past few years.

There was a strained quality to Ingrid's dating pattern. She would meet a man, go out with him, and orchestrate matters so that the two ended up in bed on the first or second date. This was not strange in and by itself except for the almost compulsive regularity with which it occurred. Even stranger was the way she behaved the morning after.

If the two had spent the night in the man's apartment, she would be very reluctant to leave. If they had spent the night in her apartment, she would insist that her date stay with her the entire day, or at least part of the morning. Often she would plead with him to stay, usually to no avail. She had no appreciation of the effect her behavior had on the men she dated, and no inkling of why most never called again.

In the course of treatment, Ingrid revealed more about her chronic insomnia. It turned out that her inability to sleep was tied to a specific recurrent nightmare. At first she would only say that it was sexual in nature and involved vivid scenes of two people having intercourse. She later revealed that she was the woman in the dream and that the man was her father. Although the dream didn't occur that frequently, it occurred frequently enough to make her anxious about going to bed at night lest the dream return. She told me she was afraid that she would eventually "go crazy" if something weren't done about it.

The connection between Ingrid's dream and her interactions with men began to make sense as she talked about her early childhood. She was a late and only child of parents who were quite wealthy and played a prominent part in the Oslo social scene. Her father headed an industrial conglomerate and spent most of his time at the office or traveling to other countries on business. Ingrid had few memories of her mother, who died before Ingrid reached her second birthday. The father never remarried and Ingrid was essentially raised by a nanny.

The thing that Ingrid remembered most vividly about her childhood was the succession of beautiful women who paraded through her house. They would come in the evening, sometimes dining with her father and her, and then not reappear until the next morning. She told of admiring these women from afar and at the same time envying them for their ability to apparently obtain what she so desperately wanted: the love and attention of her father.

Only when Ingrid was a bit older did she come to realize that the women were her father's mistresses. He was an attractive and wealthy man and it was easy for him to attract young and beautiful women. It also was apparent to her that the basis of these relationships was primarily sexual. The dream was an object relational expression of a small child's wish to be loved by her father fused with a grown woman's ideas about what made a woman attractive to men. It contained the same dynamic that lay behind her use of a projective identification of sexuality.

Jackson's case was not as dramatic as Ingrid's although in some ways it was not that different. Jackson had been involved with other women on and off for a good part of his 14-year marriage, although his wife had not learned about it until ten years or so into the marriage. When she first found out about his extramarital ventures, she threatened to leave him; however, she decided not to after Jackson promised to stop seeing other women. He failed to keep his promise and his wife finally filed for a divorce after two years of bitter accusations and constant quarreling.

Jackson's decision to enter therapy was prompted by a string of failures in maintaining lasting relationships with women, and episodic depressions which had resulted in heavy bouts of drinking. After he divorced, he thought that he would enjoy leading a bachelor existence. He did at first, but after almost three years of aimless dating and playing the field he decided he really wanted something more substantial. He found, however, that what he was searching for was not that easy to find. The women in whom he was most interested tended to shy away from him, particularly when he brought up the subject of commitment. Some of the same women he had dated when he was married seemed to be less enamored of him now that he was single and available. As time passed, Jackson became increasingly perplexed and, as he put it, "out of it."

A major concern for Jackson was why his relationships with women left him feeling so empty. Though his involvements were sexually stimulating, they seemed to have a barren quality about them. The reason for this became evident as he described his relationships with women, particularly their nonsexual aspects.

The simple truth of the matter was that for Jackson a relationship meant sex. This was true not only for casual involvements but for serious ones as well. It was not so much that he viewed women as sexual objects as that he saw himself as one. Jackson just could not see himself as attractive or desirable outside a sexual context. This, more than anything else, formed the basis for his projective identification of sexuality.

The key to understanding projective identifications of sexuality can be found in the patterns of communications and metacommunications that comprise them. On the communicative level are double entendres, sexual posturing, and other forms of erotic maneuvering designed to attract the recipient and create sexual arousal. The projector is the proprietor of a sexual candy store in which fun, excitement, and escape from boredom are offered for little more than a couple of nights' involvement.

The metacommunication, on the other hand, offers more than sensual delights. Contained within it is a message of sexual fulfillment that goes far beyond orgasmic satisfaction. It signals more than "I will turn you on." It promises "I will make you feel sexually competent." The metacommunication, in short, promises to make the recipient sexually whole. Conversely, it also contains the implicit threat that recipients will feel less whole, less sexually competent, if they do not respond to the message contained within.

The overall intent of patients who use projective identifications of sexuality is to ensure interpersonal desirability by making sure they are sexually valued. As is the case with other projective identifications, this form of relational pathology derives from disturbed object relations in which the child is exclusively valued for one rather restricted form of behavior. The earlier "loaded" messages about one's sexual desirability are conveyed and the more pathological early object relations are, the more damaging the results will be.

An instance of this can be seen in the case of a highly disturbed seven-year-old child whose life was a mass of sexual pathology. The boy had a tendency to exhibit himself from the time he was very young and would masturbate in public as he got older. This became such a frequent occurrence that he was barred from attending school. The child was totally preoccupied with sex and eventually had to be hospitalized in a children's psychiatric hospital, where he received a diagnosis of childhood schizophrenia.

Though I did not treat the child, I did have the opportunity to see the mother as part of a comprehensive treatment program. In the course of an initial interview, I learned that the father had deserted the family some years back and that she was the only available parent. But it was evident from the first time we met that she wasn't much of a parent. The woman was near-psychotic herself. Her thinking was very disorganized and she spoke about the child as if he were an object. She really didn't comprehend why he was in the hospital and agreed to place him there only because of pressure put on her by school authorities.

During the therapy, I learned that the mother had been treating the child as a sexual object from the time he was born. She told of playing with the boy's genitals while bathing and diapering him, and of instances in which she would rub him against her body. She seemed unaware of what she was saying and giggled much of the time while describing these episodes. But perhaps the most pathological example of the way she sexualized the relationship involved certain incidents that revolved about play.

The mother told of times in which she would take the boy to an outdoor playground not far from where they lived. The boy was one or two at the time, and she particularly enjoyed playing with him on the see-saw. She did this by first sitting herself on the end of the see-saw and placing the boy between her legs while she rocked up and down. From her description of what went on and the licentious looks and giggles that accompanied it, I had little doubt that she was using the boy to masturbate herself. She as much admitted this later on. Though one might argue that an infant really doesn't know what is going on at this young age, something has to be conveyed along sexual lines.

Individuals who utilize projective identifications of sexuality learn early on that they are wanted as long as they provide some form of sexual arousal for the adults in their lives. However it is communicated, the message the child receives is "You are desirable as long as you excite me." This is the basic message that is incorporated into the infant's representational world and which ultimately forms the basis for interacting with others later on.

Structuring one's relationships entirely on sexual lines is one way of assuring that one is valued. The fact that this places serious constraints on the range and quality of one's exchanges with other human beings becomes a secondary consideration. Once inner object relations of this sort are incorporated into the self, an individual has little choice but to follow their dictates.

Projective Identification: Ingratiation

The fourth major form of projective identification entails structuring relationships so that the major emotional component is that of self-sacrifice. In the projective identification of ingratiation, relationships are orchestrated so that others are constantly aware that the person doing the projecting is giving up something or putting the recipient's interests before his own. There is a concerted attempt to induce others to be grateful for the things that one does and the sacrifices one makes.

The kinds of statements one hears when interacting with individuals who use projective identifications of ingratiation are:

- "I try so hard to make things easy for you."
- "I work my fingers to the bone."
- "You don't appreciate how much I do for you."
- "You always take me for granted."

Whether a statement depicts something about oneself ("I work so hard") or a failing in the respondent ("You never do enough"), it is meant to elicit appreciation in the person toward whom it is directed.

Persons who are the targets of a projective identification of ingratiation constantly find themselves in situations in which they are expected to be thankful and appreciative. They are required to comment on how much easier their lives have become in light of the constant attention paid them. In a multitude of explicit and implicit ways, they are forced to provide assurance to the person doing the projecting that whatever he does or says helps make life easier. Above all, individuals who employ a projective identification of ingratiation need to know they are *helpful*.

Henrietta, a middle-aged single mother, was seen in family therapy with her two teenage sons. This was prompted by the fact that the boys were causing problems in school. Their teachers reported that one of the boys had become very belligerent and was getting into fights at school over trivial matters, while the other was becoming more and withdrawn. Whereas initially the problem was regarded as wholly school related, there were indications that it might be reflective of difficulties at home—hence the recommendation of family therapy.

Exploration of the family dynamics revealed a great deal of anger in the family, much of it rooted in Henrietta's way of relating to the boys. Some of the difficulties were prompted by the simple fact that the boys were growing up. But a larger part seemed to be related to their unwillingness to respond to Henrietta's need to have them appreciate how much she did for them. Their angry refusal to respond to Henrietta's "sacrifices" left her feeling dejected and unwanted.

A family scenario that pointed up these dynamics centered on rides in the family car. Neither of the boys had his license and each had to depend on Henrietta to chauffeur him about. Whenever they got into the car, Henrietta would remind them to put on their seatbelts and to lock the doors. Before they had a chance to move, however, she reached over and pressed down all the door buttons herself. This was done in a ritualistic fashion. The boys reported that they felt put upon and annoyed by what they interpreted as unnecessary intrusions. On one occasion they stormed out of the car and refused to ride with her.

During one of the therapy sessions, a lengthy discussion took place about what went on in the car. One by one, each family member told his or her side of the story. At first it didn't seem like a big deal. After all, what did it matter who pushed down the door buttons? But as the family members recapped what happened, the interchanges became more and more heated. There was a fair amount of bickering regarding the door buttons, with the boys arguing that they could take care of it themselves and Henrietta insisting that she was just trying to be helpful.

At this juncture, I asked Henrietta what she thought might happen if she refrained from reminding the children about the door buttons. A doleful look appeared on her face and she lapsed into a long silence. At one point, I even thought that she was holding back tears. Some minutes passed and I asked her what she was thinking. She responded in a very dejected tone of voice, "Then what would I be good for?"

It is sad that a woman who has spent the greater part of her life raising a family derives her entire sense of self-worth from "doing things" and being appreciated for them. It is even sadder that this mode of interaction undermines what she desperately yearns for most: the feeling that she is loved for what she *is* rather than for what she *does*. Instead of fostering interactions which are based on caring, she spends a lot of her energy making sure that she is appreciated. And it is this way of relating to others that is the essential feature of projective identifications of ingratiation.

Persons who employ projective identifications of ingratiation need to be appreciated for the many acts of self-sacrifice they perform. They need to know that the respondent is aware of what they are doing for them. But beneath all this is a deeper, more potent communication, one that says something about the underlying bargain that is being struck. It is contained in the metacommunication "You owe me." Persons who use projective identifications of ingratiation expect something in return. And that "something" is a pledge that other people will stay in a relationship with them no matter what.

This, of course, is what all of us would like to believe about our closest, most intimate relationships. We all want to believe we are worthwhile human beings and to know that those closest to us feel we are worth being with. Persons who relate through a projective identification of ingratiation have little faith that this is the way the world works. They do not really believe that other human beings, even their own family members, really love them for what they are. They are convinced that they need to ingratiate themselves to ensure that they will be wanted. And to make sure this happens, they establish relationships in such a way that others feel indebted to them.

The early maternal messages instilled in children who later employ projective identification of ingratiation are that they need to do things for those who care for them or they will not be loved. Such children are taught that their intrinsic worth lies in their ability to be useful. Only by performing various utilitarian deeds are they able to convince themselves that they are "good." As a consequence, they spend a good part of their lives ingratiating themselves to others as a way of being in a relationship.

PROJECTIVE IDENTIFICATIONS
AND INTERPERSONAL PATHOLOGY

Projective identifications, in sum, are the behavioral offshoots of projective fantasies whose origins lie in pathological object relations. They function to constrain relationships in which they occur and dictate the tenor of what takes place within them. In the projective identification of dependency, the major relational themes have to with helplessness. In the projective identifications of power, sex, and ingratiation, they center, respectively, on control, eroticism, and self-sacrifice. All of these in turn are driven by potent metacommunications designed to make sure that the projective identifications succeed.

Recalling what was said at the beginning of the chapter about the various components of a projective identification, we now can perhaps appreciate how each contributes to the perpetuation of interpersonal pathology. The *projective fantasy*, for example, is contained within the metacommunication. It is the metacommunication that secretly signals what the relationship is really all about. The object relational wish that drives the projective fantasy is transformed into hidden messages designed to control and constrain the behavior of the recipient.

The *behavioral inductions* are contained within the various communications that make up the projective identification. They constitute the concrete interactive manipulations that define the nature of the ongoing relationship. The actual messages that make up the moment-to-moment interactions of projector and recipient give behavioral form to what heretofore existed only in the realm of imagination. Whether sexual, dependent, sacrificial, or controlling in nature, they give the projective identification its peculiar stamp.

Finally, the fate of the projective identification is embedded in the *response of the recipient*. If an individual who employs projective identifications targets an individual whose idiosyncratic needs conform to the projective identification, no problems need necessarily arise. A person who engages in a projective identification of dependency may be fortunate enough to stumble across someone whose life desire is to take care of people. If, on the other hand, the target offers resistance, the projector may experience anxiety, depression, rage, and other "symptoms" attesting to what amounts to projective failure. These are the people who most often end up seeking help.

Bearing these distinctions in mind, the four projective identifications discussed in this chapter are listed in Table 1. Each is identified by the relational stance taken by the person using the projective identification,

TABLE 1 MAJOR PROJECTIVE IDENTIFICATIONS

Proj. Ident.	Relat. Stance	Metacommunication	Induction
Dependency	Helplessness	I can't survive	Caretaking
Power	Control	You can't survive	Incompetence
Sex	Eroticism	I'll make you sexually whole	Arousal
Ingratiation	Self-sacrifice	You owe me	Appreciation

along with its respective metacommunication and the inductive response it is meant to produce in the recipient. Thus, in the case of the projective identification of dependency, the relational stance is that of helplessness, the metacommunication a statement to the effect that one cannot survive without help, and the inductive response caretaking.

In addition to the patterns listed in the Table 1, there are patterns in which the various projective identifications merge, e.g., dependency-sexuality. Some of these will be discussed in a later chapter. In most instances, though, the four configurations that have been described tend to exist as independent patterns in their own right. They are readily identifiable in clinical work and form the focus for object relations therapy.

SECTION II

The Therapy

CHAPTER 4

Stage One: Engagement

THE THERAPY RELATIONSHIP: FOUNDATIONS OF CHANGE

Projective identifications are the residuals of early object relations that are expressed as disturbances in interpersonal relationships. Persons who use projective identifications have learned early in life that staying in a relationship requires that they be dependent, controlling, sexual, or ingratiating. The decision to behave in these ways may not be entirely rational, but many of the things that people learn when very young are not based on reason or logic. Patterns of object relations formed early in one's life are usually influenced more by emotional factors than intellectual ones.

But there is another motive behind the use of projective identifications, one that is more optimistic insofar as psychotherapy is concerned. Though undeniably pathological, projective identifications also represent an effort to rectify relational deficiencies. Replaying pathological object relations scenarios of one's early years constitutes an attempt to reverse the bad endings of early childhood. People who resort to projective identification as a means of structuring their relationships desperately yearn for a "good" ending. They want to know that those closest to them love them for what they are, not because they fulfill specific needs.

It is this secret hope that brings people into therapy and keeps them in treatment in spite of setbacks and disappointments. At one level, people enter therapy to deal with panic attacks, broken marriages, depression, and other forms of emotional malaise. If you ask them why they are in treatment, they reply, "to feel better." But at another level, a much deeper one, they want to be able to be psychologically "held" by others, to be connected without feeling compromised. Unfortunately, the only way they know to achieve some semblance of connectedness is through the use of projective identifications. As one patient put it, "I know in my heart there is a better way, but I don't trust it."

Object relations therapy constitutes a way of countering these projective patterns and changing these feelings. Using the therapy relationship as a staging ground for the emergence of the patient's relational pathology, the therapist confronts the metacommunications that are lodged within the patient's projective identifications and responds to them in a contradictory, i.e. therapeutic, manner. In the course of treatment, the patient may gain better understanding of current object relations or even gain insight into past object relations. But understanding of this sort is epiphenomenal. It has little to do with the essence of change as it is conceived within an object relations framework. Instead, it is the concrete alterations in the therapist-patient relationship that are responsible for whatever lasting changes occur.

Within object relations therapy, the therapist-patient relationship is seen as a special and unique object relation. What makes the relationship particularly unique is that one of the participants voluntarily allows himself to be drawn into a relationship in which he knows he will become the target of a projective identification (Ogden, 1982, p. 54). The therapist enters the relationship with the knowledge that the interaction with the patient will sooner or later take on manipulative qualities. By creating an interpersonal milieu in which projective identifications are likely to occur, the therapist creates an in vivo opportunity to deal with them in the here-and-now.

Malin and Grotstein (1966) contend that the fundamental goal of therapy is modification of the patient's inner object world through altering projective identifications. This belief is echoed in Ogden's statement that:

. . . the essence of what is therapeutic for the patient lies in the therapist's ability to receive the patient's projections, utilize facets of his own more mature personality system to process the projection, and then make the digested projection available for reinternalization through the therapeutic interaction. (1982, p. 20)

In order for this to happen, the therapist must ensure that the projective identification surfaces and becomes part of the therapeutic relationship.

Once the projective identification becomes part of the relationship, the therapist can respond in a manner very different than that to which the patient is accustomed. This is what makes the therapy relationship different from most other relationships. Most people who interact with the patient, particularly in intense long-term relations, ultimately become angry, depressed, and upset. Some even abandon hope in the relationship and leave. The object relations therapist does not. It is the therapist's atypical response to the patient's projective identification and his commitment to the treatment process that gives object relations therapy its unique character.

On a pragmatic level, this means that therapists who do object relations therapy have to rely on their own responses to the patient's projective identifications to advance the treatment process. These responses are used both as a source of information regarding the precise nature of the patient's pathology and as a basis for therapeutic interventions. Thus, in object relations therapy an "interpretation" is more likely to involve an analysis of one of the patient's manipulations than an analysis of something that happened in the past. By actively confronting the patient and refusing to conform to the projective identification, the therapist uses the relationship to alter the patient's habitual and self-defeating ways of relating to others.

The foregoing is a brief synopsis of what obviously is a sensitive and complex procedure. The actual interventions that make up the therapy are contained in a four-stage process which involves eliciting the projective identification, confronting it, and reconstituting the relationship in which it occurs. The first stage of this process is labeled "engagement" and involves active efforts to emotionally engage the patient in the psychotherapeutic process.

ENGAGING THE PATIENT

Most individuals who enter therapy have only a scant appreciation of what they are getting into. They know precious little about psychotherapy as a discipline or the various interventions used to bring about change. Most are simply looking for a way to alleviate their suffering. They want to feel less anxious, less depressed, and less overwhelmed by the vicissitudes of life. In return, they are willing to give up some of their time, a part of their earnings, and perhaps even some of their ways.

It is rare for patients to enter treatment with the idea of making radical changes in their personality. Only infrequently do patients indicate that they are interested in changing longstanding patterns of behavior. Even patients who sincerely want to change rarely are aware of how much pain and discomfort such change actually may incur. Most patients approach therapy in much the same way as they approach their family physician: They know something is wrong and they want a pill to make them feel better. The smaller the pill, the happier they are.

But psychotherapy is not a medical procedure. There are no pills, no "magic bullets" that can dissolve the kinds of problems that bring people into treatment. While there are drugs to suppress anxiety and medications that alleviate depression, there are no drugs that can change frustrating and nongratifying relationships into gratifying and productive ones. The fact of the matter is that therapy, particularly one that deals with disturbances in object relations, is likely to be a difficult experience.

One can explain all this to the patient at the outset. This usually does more good for the therapist than for the patient. Even patients who acknowledge that therapy will involve tough choices and difficult times cannot really appreciate what this means experientially. It is one thing to *know* what therapy is all about; it is quite something else to actually *experience* it.

Many patients consequently have misgivings over what they have gotten themselves into soon after treatment begins. They are uncomfortable about what is taking place and wonder whether their decision to enter treatment was the right one. Very often they find themselves more anxious than when they began. The engagement phase of object relations therapy is meant to deal with the incongruity felt by the patient and ensure that the patient remains in treatment.

The therapist does this by transforming what is a distant professional relationship into one that contains elements of caring, commitment, and involvement. One cannot assume that patients will stay in treatment simply because they are hurting or because the therapist has impressive credentials. Patients need to feel that the therapist can satisfy some of their object relational needs even if the precise nature of those needs is still vague and ill-defined. "Without sufficient trust in the therapist's ability, they will leave therapy or remain nonparticipants in the therapeutic interaction" (Beitman, 1979, p. 306).

Not infrequently, patients decide to terminate treatment before it even has a chance to get off the ground. The therapist receives a telephone call or some other message indicating that the patient has decided to try something else. Sometimes the message indicates that the patient is feeling so much better that he has decided he does not need help after all. Such messages rarely mean what they say. Although life circumstances something change radically, they don't change *that* radically.

The reason that patients flee from treatment in the early stages is that the therapist has failed to successfully engage them in a therapeutic relationship. Things are said and issues raised under the assumption that a relationship already exists. Since it does not, patients begin to wonder whether they have gotten in over their heads. Often patients will take off before the therapy goes beyond the first or second session.

THERAPEUTIC BONDING
AND PREMATURE TERMINATION

Premature termination is a pertinent issue throughout therapy, but especially in the early stages (Hoffman, 1985). One of the chronic complaints of beginning therapists is that their patients fail to show up regularly or that they terminate treatment before the therapy has even begun. A close look at what happens in the early sessions tends to reveal that the therapist has tried to do too much too soon. Instead of concentrating on engaging the patient, a suggestion is made or an interpretation offered for which the patient is ill prepared.

An example of this can be seen in the work of a clinical supervisee of mine named Lorraine who had just begun seeing a patient for problems having to do with his "love life." Though a good number of patients enter therapy because their romantic involvements have become destitute and depleted, this particular patient suffered not from a paucity of romantic involvements but from an overabundance. He told the therapist that he was seeing three woman at the same time, was seriously involved with two of them, and wanted the therapist to help him sort out his commitments.

The therapist was somewhat taken aback by the business-like quality of the patient's approach to his predicament. The way he described his problem indicated that he really wasn't very distressed about it. He envisioned himself as a Don Juan of sorts and liked the idea of having so many women in his life. His problem was not emotional as much as it was logistical.

Lorraine spent the first two sessions soliciting information about the patient and exploring the quality of his interactions with the women in his life. From his description of the way he dealt with his girlfriends, she concluded that he was a self-absorbed, somewhat narcissistic individual whose relationships were rather shallow. His narrative was punctuated with remarks to the effect, "I need to feel this" and "I need to have that." A common remark began with, "It is very important for me that I . . . " and finished off with something that he felt he should say, do, or, have. Rarely did he show concern over the effect his needs had on others. There was a facade of confidence and assurance about him that was difficult to penetrate.

The patient's confidence and self-assuredness started to unravel somewhere around the third session. He arrived at the therapy session looking out of sorts and rather dejected. After a bit of prompting, he confessed that something very terrible had happened. One of the women with whom he had been involved had left him for someone else. As he told the story, he burst into tears and began sobbing. He went on to say that what had happened had shook him up so much that he had contemplated suicide. He still was worried about hurting himself and was not sure what he might do.

It was all very dramatic and Lorraine clearly was shaken. But from where I was sitting, it looked like a sham. I was watching the proceedings from behind a one-way mirror, and the tears just weren't convincing. As he "sobbed," the patient repeatedly sneaked glances at Lorraine to see how she was reacting. The pictures of the patient as someone cool and self-assured about his relationships in one session and completely torn to pieces in the next didn't mesh. Something just didn't seem right.

As the session progressed, Lorraine became more and more uncomfortable and somewhat at a loss as what to say or do. She responded by making an interpretation, suggesting to the patient that his girlfriend's rejection had been experienced as a failure and that the episode quite likely threatened his masculinity. The patient straightened up in his chair, pulled himself together, and spent the rest of the session calmly discussing some of the things that happened to him at work that week.

That for all intents and purposes signaled the end of the therapy. Much to Lorraine's consternation, the patient did not show up for the next session. After waiting a week, she tried to contact him by phone but her call was never returned. She did receive a note some weeks later thanking her and telling her how well things were going. Though Lorraine and I hoped this was true, we had strong doubts as to whether in fact it was.

Later in the course of supervision, the two of us discussed what had taken place during the last session. Lorraine admitted that she had become very frightened at the mention of suicide. She naturally worried that she might lose her patient and desperately searched within herself for something to say that was "therapeutic." She felt she needed to *do* something and what she did was interpret. It was not that her interpretation was incorrect; it probably was not far off the mark. But it came at a point in treatment before Lorraine had fully engaged the patient, before there was some semblance of therapeutic bonding.

The need to engage the patient early on is something of which experienced therapists are well aware. The simple fact of the matter is that without a patient you cannot do therapy. The therapist may have the best intentions and be highly skilled, but unless the patient sees something in the relationship besides an expert with an advanced degree, his initial motives for entering treatment quickly wane. When this happens, the patient typically is not interested in exploring why his interest has flagged. Very often, the therapist also is not that eager to investigate the reasons for the termination. The patient either was "not ready for therapy" or "not psychologically minded." The chances are, though, that the issue of premature termination probably has less to do with patient variables such as psychological mindedness or low motivation than with the therapist's failure to establish a "therapeutic bond" early in the treatment process.

Another reason that therapeutic bonding is so important in the early stage of treatment has to do with what goes on in subsequent parts of the therapy process. Even if patients are able to get beyond early fears and apprehensions, they may not be able to withstand the kinds of pressures that are encountered in later stages of treatment. If object relations therapy is to succeed, the patient is going to have to deal with challenges to his projective identifications. Since this can be quite threatening, there may be times when the patient feels like quitting treatment. The nature of psychopathology and psychotherapy is such that the pain of getting better frequently seems worse than the pain of staying sick. It is for this reason that what happens in the engagement stage of treatment is so important.

How specifically does one engage the patient? How does the therapist foster therapeutic bonding? The object relations therapist does this by going beyond the presenting problem, by letting go of any immediate inclination to "do something," and by demonstrating interest in the minute details that make up his patients' lives. What do they do for a living? Who are their closest friends? What disappointments have they faced lately? But "getting the facts" is not as important as the attitude one maintains in obtaining them. Therapy isn't Dragnet and the therapist isn't Jack Webb. Information gathering has to be done with care and an eye to the engagement function it performs. One way of accomplishing this is through "emotional linking"

EMOTIONAL LINKING

The term emotional linking refers to a variety of techniques designed to convey empathic understanding (Beitman, 1987, pp. 48–52). With roots in the client-centered approach, these techniques enable the therapist to communicate to the patient that the patient's feelings are shared and appreciated. The major way the therapist does this is by responding to the emotional, usually nonverbal, messages embedded in the patient's remarks.

There are a number of ways to accomplish this. If the patient says, for example, that he shuns TV shows and movies that contain violent themes, the therapist might respond along the lines of "It seems that physical violence makes you feel very *anxious*." Or if the patient indicates that he has to be careful about what he says at work or to whom he says it, the therapist might say, "It often is *depressing* not to be able to trust the very people you work with." By taking factual reports ("I don't like certain movies", "I have to be careful at work", etc.) and highlighting the emotional message contained in them, the therapist establishes an empathic base for emotional linking (Cashdan, 1973).

Employing emotional linking leads to interventions such as:

- "It makes you *happy* when you talk about _____"
- "You seem *upset* whenever the subject of _____ comes up."
- "You're really *annoyed* at _____"
- "_____ makes you *embarrassed*." (Cashdan, 1973, p. 66)

Comments such as these foster therapeutic bonding by transforming the conversation from a dialogue that is largely factual to one that is emotional in character.

Another way of advancing the goals of this stage is to let the patient know that you are on his side. Individuals with deficient object relations often arrive at treatment with stories of how they have failed in romance, in their jobs, in school and in other important areas of their lives. It is easy for a relatively astute therapist to pick up patterns of self-defeat and maladaptive ways of doing things in the patient's accounts. It is even easier to comment on these. But it is more judicious in this stage of treatment to keep this to oneself and not come down too strongly on the side of interpretation and self-enlightenment.

This is especially important in therapy with couples where each member of the marriage often enters treatment intent on proving that the other one is at fault. Work with couples suggests that while each member of the couple comes to therapy to ostensibly "save the marriage," each is more interested in proving that he or she is the injured party. Both husband and wife believe that they have been abused and that an unbiased "true" account of what has been going on would substantiate their side of the story. The therapist, of course, is expected by each to be the arbiter of this truth. But marriages contain different truths, each with its own legitimacy. And it is these two truths—one the husband's and the other the wife's—with which the therapist needs to align himself.

Thus, in the early stages of marital treatment, I ask both the husband and wife to present their accounts of what they give to the marriage and what they see as having gone wrong with it. As they present their stories, I engage each in an attempt to create an empathic bond. I encourage the husband to tell "his story," and after he does, I often say something along the lines of, "It must be tough at the office dealing with all the pressures you face during the day. It would be nice to come home and not have to deal with your wife and the kids on top of all that."

I take a similar approach with regard to the wife. I might say to her, "It must be hell having to manage a job and a household, and to have to deal with housework and a bunch of squabbling kids at the end of a day. I bet some days you wish you could turn everything over to your husband and jump into a hot bath." By sequentially engaging both husband and wife, I try to empathically bond both participants to me so as to be in a better position to deal with what lies ahead.

In addition to empathic reflection (emotional linking), there are other effective ways to engage patients. One can accomplish one's ends through humor or even by behaving "irrationally" if need be. An example of this can be seen in the case of a patient who was referred for treatment because of severe depression and a strong likelihood of suicide.

The patient, Isabel, had been seeing another therapist, and in the course of treatment became depressed and suicidal. The therapist, who was relatively inexperienced, naturally became very worried and referred her to a psychiatrist in the area who agreed to see her on an emergency basis. He diagnosed her as suffering from "Major (Unipolar) Depression" and started her on a course of antidepressant medication. After waiting two and a half weeks and seeing no appreciable improvement, he decided to hospitalize her.

The only hospital in the vicinity with psychiatric facilities had no psychiatric beds available at the moment and Isabel was advised that she would have to wait at least three weeks before she could be admitted. The chief psychiatrist suggested she try another setting, but Isabel had three small children and didn't want to be too far from them. She consequently refused to leave the area and decided to wait. The psychiatrist who was caring for her felt somewhat uneasy about this arrangement. He called and asked if I would agree to "look after" Isabel until she could get into the hospital. I agreed and under these circumstances began to see Isabel on a twice-a-week basis.

When I first met Isabel I was somewhat taken aback. Not only was she very pale, but she looked emaciated. Her clothes, hanging on her frame like a shroud, looked as if they were two or three sizes too large. It was evident that she wasn't eating and that over the course of the past few months she had lost a substantial amount of weight. She was so depressed that it was hard for her to speak above a whisper. What's more, her head hung to the side as if she didn't have the energy to keep it erect. It didn't take much to see why the psychiatrist was fearful of leaving her unattended.

In the course of the session, Isabel related some of the circumstances that led to her current condition. The major precipitating event seemed to be that her husband had left her without so much as a goodbye or a forwarding address. Isabel reported that she had wakened one morning to find a note on the kitchen table saying that he had had enough and was leaving. Although the marriage had been going downhill for years, she was completely taken aback by his sudden departure.

Isabel thought she could set things straight once she talked to her husband. The note said that he would be back shortly to pick up his belongings and to explain his departure to the children. But he never returned, and in addition to having to personally cope with his disappearance, she was forced to deal with the children's questions and confusion.

During the course of the first interview, it was evident that Isabel was a serious suicidal risk. Not only was she self-depreciatory (she blamed herself for her husband's leaving and insisted that she wasn't a very good wife), she kept making suicidal-like statements. "I don't know whether it's worth carrying on," she remarked over and over again during the session. She said that she was a burden to everyone, and that everyone including her family would be better off if she weren't around.

Toward the end of the session, I asked her point blank whether she was thinking of killing herself. She sat silent for a long while and then nodded. I called her attention to what might happen to her children if she killed herself. My appeal to her maternal sense was not very successful. "It probably would be better for them if I wasn't around," she replied. "I'm not a good mother. They would be better off with someone who could care for them better than I can." It was clear that I wasn't going to get far with rational arguments.

I decided to try a different tack. Toward the end of the session, I said to her, "I've been thinking things over, and if you're going to knock yourself off, I don't want to see you anymore."

Isabel looked at me in disbelief. "What?" she murmured.

I went on, "It's like this. You're depressed and you look like a mess, but in spite of that I kind of like you." I waited for her to take this in and continued, "The problem is, if I keep working with you, I might get to like you even more. Then, if you go and kick the bucket, *I* will be the one who is going to be depressed."

I went on to tell Isabel that I had enough problems and really didn't need to get depressed on top of everything else. If she really intended to kill herself, we might just as well call it quits right now.

Isabel stared at me for a while, a perplexed expression on her face. After a while she said, "You know, you're a little crazy," and for the first time a faint smile crossed her lips. We spent the rest of the session talking about my commitment to her and hers to me. She ended the hour by asking when we would be meeting again. As she left the office, she remarked, "Don't worry. I won't kill myself."

She didn't. But neither was she able to stay out of the hospital. Her depression was just too severe and the conditions which precipitated it hadn't changed appreciably. But keeping her out of the hospital wasn't the reason I had contracted to see her. My purpose was to engage her enough to keep her from killing herself and to prepare her for what lay ahead—dealing with her children and with her upcoming separation from them. One of the things Isabel said to me during our last session was, "You're the only person who makes me laugh." In the beginning, sometimes that is enough.

Engagement, based as it is on bonding between relative strangers, is seldom simple. This is especially true in work with children. Most children who end up in therapy are there not because they want to but because they are forced to be. They have run afoul of the law, are failing in school, or have tried their parents' patience. Unlike adults who enter therapy of their own accord and see therapy as a reasonable place to seek answers, children are there because they have no choice. It therefore is not surprising that many children offer a great deal of resistance to the therapist's efforts at engagement.

One child I treated for obsessive-compulsive behavior refused even to speak to me. An attractive, well-dressed 12-year-old, Marc was referred for treatment because he seemed apprehensive at school and was falling behind in his schoolwork. The school records revealed that he was fairly bright (his IQ was 116) but not very sociable. The teachers indicated that he was highly anxious about his class work and spent an inordinate amount of time preparing in-class assignments, e.g., writing a short essay.

His parents reported a similar pattern at home; they said he would spend hours going over even simple homework assignments. They portrayed him as highly conscientious and referred to him as a "very good boy." Their accounts of his behavior, however, revealed that Marc's "goodness" derived from overly compliant behavior; it might have been more accurate to describe him as a highly conforming child.

Without a doubt, one of the major frustrations for a therapist is a patient who refuses to speak. It is one thing to work with a schizophrenic who is mute or with an autistic child. You don't expect meaningful conversation. One may even question whether speech exists, at least in the case of autism. But it is particularly annoying to know that a patient who can speak, and even has a facility with words, uses speech—or the absence of it—as a means of avoiding engagement.

Though I tried my best, efforts to engage Marc in conversation proved fruitless. I tried to convince him that dealing with me would help him improve his relationships with the people about him. I told him that everything we spoke about would be held in strictest confidence. I told him that the sooner we got down to business, the sooner he would be able to stop coming. I even tried telling jokes, all to no avail. Every attempt to engage Marc met with failure.

Somewhere along the line, I decided to try some board games. Marc looked at me with disdain as I took out a checker board and carefully laid out the pieces. I didn't get much further with Monopoly. But I did notice a change in his expression when I retrieved a chess set from the closet. That was about the extent of it. For the remainder of that session and the entire next session, Marc refused to do more than sit across from me and stare at the pieces. In the following session, though, he moved a pawn.

Chess became the medium though which Marc and I interacted with one another. It is hard to recall precisely how many sessions we spent playing chess in silence or near silence, but it must have been at least four or five. The only words Marc uttered during this time were "check" and "checkmate," the latter coming in the fifth session when he finally won a game. He was clearly delighted at having beaten me but looked somewhat apprehensive.

I encouraged Marc to share his thoughts about beating me and the feelings he was experiencing. With some prodding, he began to talk about "winning" and his feelings about doing better than adults. In the course of treatment, issues having to do with doing well, acceptance by others, and self-protection formed the focus of our discussions. Interestingly, we continued to play chess throughout most of the times we met so that the bulk of therapy took place over a chessboard.

In thinking about the early sessions with Marc, I recall being somewhat impatient at the time. I wanted Marc to start "talking about his problems," and tended to view the sessions in which we played chess as marking time. In retrospect, I see the time spent playing chess as time well spent. Playing chess was the only way I knew to engage Marc and thus was a critical part of the treatment process.

Students with whom I work often are eager to get through the early part of therapy and get down to the "real clinical work." It takes some experience—and some lost patients—before one is convinced that engaging the patient *is* clinical work. Engagement is a significant part of object relations therapy and needs to be successfully negotiated if later interventions are to be effective.

SUGGESTIONS AND ADVICE

In addition to emotional linking, offering suggestions and advice also may be used to foster engagement (Beitman, 1987). More often than not, patients see the therapist as a source of valuable information regarding how to solve dilemmas. This may or may not be a realistic perception. The therapist is not always that much wiser than the patient when it comes to solving concrete problems. Still, the fact that the therapist is not emotionally embroiled in the patient's difficulties enables the therapist to view things from a different perspective and sometimes allows for a word or two of wisdom. This is illustrated in the following case study.

Eduardo, a successful electrical contractor, was seen in therapy because of residual issues stemming from a bitter divorce. He was successfully remarried but concerned that some of the angry feelings he still bore towards his first wife were spilling over into his current marriage. There also were difficulties surrounding his interactions with his teenage son, Victor. These centered on visits by the boy and the problems these were creating in the context of his new family.

Eduardo's ex-wife had moved to another city approximately 250 miles from where Eduardo now resided. She had been awarded custody of Victor with the proviso that he be allowed to visit his father in the summer months and during school vacations. Though this necessitated long bus trips, the boy was eager to visit his father and the arrangement initially seemed to work out well.

The problem was that the relationship between Victor and his stepmother was less than cordial. Victor would make offhand, usually critical, remarks about the way his stepmother took care of his father, comparing it to the way his father had been treated by Victor's mother. His remarks took the form of "When Dad lived at home . . . " and typically painted his stepmother in a negative light. Eduardo did not confront Victor about these remarks, which he suspected mirrored some of the things Victor had heard his mother say at home.

As time progressed, Eduardo became more and more conflicted about Victor's visits. His new wife, though tolerant, also was getting upset with the boy's behavior. Eduardo spoke to Victor with little headway, and each succeeding visit was looked upon with more apprehension. Eduardo did not want to bar his son from visiting but was feeling the strain that the boy's visits were putting on the marriage.

Somewhere during an early session, I suggested an alternative to the visits which might help defuse what was threatening to become an explosive situation. I wondered whether Eduardo and Victor might meet somewhere in between the boy's home town and where Eduardo and his new wife lived. This would cut down on travel time for Victor, although it would require a two-to-three hour car trip on Eduardo's part.

I proposed to Eduardo that he rent a hotel room for a weekend, have meals out with Victor, and take in a basketball game or a movie in the evenings. The days could be spent sightseeing or doing other things the two liked to do. While this arrangement would not solve the problem of the longer summer visits, it would at least take some of the pressure off the marriage and meet both his and Victor's desire to keep in touch.

Eduardo followed my advice. He and Victor enjoyed their weekend together and spent the latter part of it eagerly planning their next meeting. Eduardo, delighted with the way things turned out, was effusive in his praise for me. I demurred, contending that even though I suggested the arrangement, he was responsible for making it succeed. Still, I was gratified that things worked out, especially since it enhanced the engagement process.

Though giving advice and making suggestions usually seem innocuous, they can backfire unless one observes some caution. Langs (1973) provides an example in which perfectly reasonable advice inadvertently touched on sensitive issues and led to a breakdown in the therapy relationship. The advice involved suggesting changes in sleeping arrangements in a household where there were hidden issues involving incest fantasies. Unless the therapist is reasonably sure that the advice he gives is "safe," it is probably better to avoid offering it.

A general guideline to follow in the first stage of therapy is to offer advice only if it is relatively innocuous and only when it has a good chance of succeeding. While it was conceivable that my advice to Eduardo might have backfired, the chances that it would were slight. The goal in stage one is not to solve problems as much as it is to engage the patient in the relationship.

Patients, in short, need to feel that someone is sympathetic to their plight and is on their side. They need to feel that they can have a sustaining relationship with someone who can help them deal with the vicissitudes of life. At the same time, they are frightened of being in a relationship. They believe that relationships are inherently dangerous and ultimately can lead to rejection and even abandonment. It is not surprising therefore that most patients approach the therapeutic relationship with some ambivalence.

The engagement phase of object relations therapy is designed to overcome this ambivalence. Its goal is to ensure that the patient stays in treatment early on and that a relational foundation is set for what takes place later. Engagement can be accomplished in many ways, limited only by the ingenuity of the therapist. As long as it therapeutically bonds the patient to the therapist, it can involve the use of support, humor, empathic linking and other "techniques."

In the case of Roy (see Chapter 2), the child who suffered from pica, engagement involved something as simple as giving the boy the means by which to express himself. It may be recalled that drawings were used in therapy with Roy to highlight relational issues that were important at different phases in the therapy. His painting of spaceships departing the moon, for example, was drawn in the last stages of therapy, when issues of ending and separation were salient. It touched on object relational issues having to do with abandonment, which the two of us had to confront before the therapy could be concluded. The opportunity to interact on this level might not have come about without the drawings.

The fact that Roy was able to produce these drawings depended on whether or not he had access to crayons and paints. The simple act of giving him crayons early on in treatment constituted a part of the engagement process. It signified that I had faith in him. The therapeutic bonding which ensued enabled me to engage him on an object relational level, and led to changes which I suspect would not have occurred otherwise.

One of the indications that the engagement phase of treatment is nearing completion are patients' remarks that they look forward to the therapy sessions. This is in marked contrast to the first few sessions of therapy, in which patients often express doubts, even misgivings, about what they have gotten themselves into. They don't particularly want to be in treatment, and if they weren't so miserable, they wouldn't be. Therapy at best is like cod liver oil; one swallows it but not without some reluctance.

But if the engagement phase of therapy is successful, the patients' spirits are lightened and therapy begins to be seen in a new light. Patients remark that they feel better, that their interactions have improved, and that life seems a little less bleak. No matter that this is illusory and short-lived. What matters is that therapeutic bonding has occurred and that the therapist has begun to be drawn into the patient's inner object world. Once this happens, the therapist can be fairly confident that the engagement phase has been successfully negotiated and that the therapy is ready to progress into the next stage.

CHAPTER 5

Stage Two: Projective Identification

The character of the therapeutic relationship changes markedly in the second stage of treatment as the patient's relational pathology starts to emerge. This begins with the patient's recognition that the therapist is more than just another professional. Something about the present relationship seems different from relationships the patient has had with lawyers, physicians, and accountants. This perception is fueled by a desire to find someone who "really" cares, to be in a relationship with someone who wants to be involved rather than needs to be. The more this feeling grows, the more likely it is that manifestations of the patient's projective identifications will begin to surface.

By the time this point in treatment is reached, the therapist already has a fair idea of the various behaviors that make up the patient's projective identifications. By carefully attending to the patient's complaints and piecing together what goes wrong in the patient's relationships, the therapist is able to construct a fairly accurate picture of the basis for the patient's difficulties. But listening to someone tell about their projective identifications is not the same as being the target of one. What distinguishes object relations therapy from other therapies is its focus on the way the therapist becomes personally drawn into the patient's pathology.

The first indications that the therapist has been earmarked as a target of a projective identification are vague feelings that things aren't quite right. The therapist finds himself getting very angry and irritated. He begins to doubt whether he is doing a good job. There are instances in which he may begin to be sexually aroused. Thoughts and feelings of this sort, though disconcerting, are a natural part of the object relations treatment process. They constitute a response to the patient's interpersonal pathology and fall under the rubric of "countertransference."

In object relations work, countertransference refers to emotional reactions of the therapist which occur *in response to* the patient's projective identifications. This is in sharp contrast to the way the term is used in traditional psychoanalysis. In traditional analysis, countertransference refers to undesirable responses on the part of the analyst which interfere with the analysis. Their origins lie in the analyst's own unresolved psychosexual conflicts and typically are oedipal in nature. Such responses need to be satisfactorily resolved, and usually this is done through consultation with one's training analyst. If the analytic work is to be successfully concluded, the countertransference needs to be eliminated or at least reduced to manageable proportions (Ernsberger, 1979; Langs, 1982)

Countertransference in object relations work is regarded quite differently. Rather than being viewed as a response to the therapist's unresolved oedipal conflicts, the countertransference is seen as a natural response to the patient's projective identifications. It therefore is viewed as a valuable, even necessary, part of the treatment process (Bollas, 1983; Meyers, 1986; Ogden, 1982). In object relations work, the therapist's emotional response is carefully monitored and used to experientially identify the precise nature of the patient's projective identification and the metacommunication that lies behind it.

It may be, for example, that the therapist consistently feels overprotective towards the end of therapy sessions with a particular patient. He may wonder whether the patient will be able to manage on his own, or even whether the patient will decompensate before the next session. Such feelings, especially when they occur repeatedly, may signal that a projective identification of dependency is operating. Using the countertransference enables the therapist to use his own feelings for diagnostic purposes as well as to make sense of emotional responses which otherwise might prove distracting or disturbing.

The question naturally arises as to how the therapist "knows" his or her feelings are in response to the patient's projective identifications. How does the therapist determine whether a personal reaction is prompted by what is taking place in therapy or by some extraneous life circumstance that has nothing at all to do with the patient? Does sexual arousal mean that the patient is using a sexual projective identification, or does it mean that the therapist's personal life is fraught with sexual difficulties and that the therapy is being used to work these out?

It is obvious that any therapist, particularly one who does object relations therapy, needs to address these questions. To do effective therapy, one needs to be able to separate responses generated by what happens within the therapy from responses generated by what goes on outside of it. A discussion of the way one distinguishes between the two is reserved for a later chapter. For the moment, we need to examine how the various projective identifications are manifested in the therapy itself, for the emergence of the various projective identifications is the salient characteristic of the second stage of treatment.

DEPENDENCY

Patients who rely on the projective identification of dependency in their dealings with others exhibit this in treatment by placing the therapist in the role of caretaker. In cases where this occurs, the therapist is seen as exceedingly sensitive, all-knowing, and omnipotent. Accordingly, therapies in which projective identifications of dependency operate are therapies punctuated with requests for *advice*, *direction*, and *support*. A glimpse of this can be seen in the behavior of a patient who recently divorced his second wife and sought treatment to ensure that his next marriage wouldn't fail.

Somewhere in the course of therapy, the patient, Dom, learned that I was married and had never been divorced. At one point early in treatment, he announced, "Someone told me you've been married to the same woman for over 15 years. You obviously know what makes marriage work. Maybe you could give me a couple of pointers."

My first impulse was to give Dom what he wanted. What harm would it do? At the very least, I could say that staying married requires a great deal of patience and a sense of humor. But I realized that it was presumptive to think that I *really* knew the secret of marital success and foolish to let the patient think I did. As it turned out, this wasn't what the patient wanted. What Dom really wanted to do was to establish a relationship with someone who would tell him how to deal with women.

Patients who rely on the projective identification of dependency relate to the therapist as if the therapist has "the answers." The therapist knows something the patient does not. Or if he doesn't know it now, he will find it out in due course and divulge it later. The therapist, of course, doesn't have the answers. What the therapist has is himself and, though the patient may not be realize it, this is what the therapist has to give.

If patients were in touch with what they really feel, if they were able to verbalize what they truly yearn for, they would confess that what they want most desperately is a relationship in which they feel worthwhile.

They want to be assured that they are valued. The problem is that the only way they know to achieve this is by behaving as if they were helpless. Only by professing neediness, only by acting as if they were incapable of managing their lives on their own, do they feel that other human beings, in this case the therapist, will stand by them.

This was quite evident in the case of Catherine, a legal secretary for a large law firm who sought treatment for deep feelings of insecurity and occasional bouts of anxiety. Catherine reported that she always had a nervous disposition, but that in recent months her nervousness seemed to be affecting her work. She even thought it might get her fired. There was no realistic foundation for these feelings since the lawyers for whom she worked thought very highly of her. Never once did they question her competence or her ability to do her work. Still, she felt that she was getting more and more nervous and that she eventually would "mess up."

In the course of treatment, it turned out that Catherine's feelings of being ineffective and "messing up" were most intense in her dealings with men. She also told me that the happiest time of her life occurred in the early part of her 12-year marriage, which had ended two years earlier in a divorce. Catherine claimed she really didn't know why she and her husband had broken up, aside from the fact that the two had seemed to drift apart over the years.

Over the course of the next few months, we discussed her relationship with her ex-husband and what had gone wrong in the marriage. As she told her story, it became evident that Catherine's relationship with her husband had contained strong dependency components. She relied on him to pay the bills, do the shopping, and take care of household chores. She even relied on him to tell her how to dress. Whenever the two went out, she would ask him to tell her what dress to wear, what shoes would match, and what kind of jewelry to put on. She seemed somewhat embarrassed at telling me all this but explained it away by saying, "I'm a very insecure person."

The kinds of behavior that characterized Catherine's interactions with her ex-husband were a bit unusual. It is not out of the ordinary for a wife to ask her husband to comment on how she looks when she dresses up and vice-versa, but Catherine insisted that her husband actually select her outfits for her. In addition, Catherine's behavior had a ritualistic, almost driven quality about it. She seemed to behave more like a frightened little girl than a 34-year-old woman.

As the therapy progressed, the same kinds of behavior that characterized Catherine's relationship with her husband began to surface in the therapy. Catherine, for example, would "consult" with me about dealings with her employer. How might she go about asking her superiors for a raise? What did she need to do to get a promotion? She felt she had taken on added responsibilities at the office, e.g., training new secretaries, and was not being adequately rewarded for it. Catherine was insecure about her position at work and wanted me to help set things straight by telling her what to do.

Catherine also insisted I instruct her in how to deal with men. She had started dating again, but after being married for 12 years dating was a whole new ballgame for her. She wanted to know, for example, how one goes about meeting eligible men? How far does one go on a first date? Do men expect sex earlier in a relationship than when she first started dating? She directed all these questions to me, expecting that I would come up with the answers. They were all legitimate questions, but one wonders whether the therapist is in a position to answer them.

Seeking advice in and by itself obviously is not pathological. The therapist sometimes may be able to provide a different perspective on the patient's problems simply because he or she has some distance from the emotional turmoil the patient is experiencing. But when therapy sessions are taken up almost exclusively with information-seeking, attempts to secure directions, and pleas, even demands, for support, one wonders whether something else is going on. It quite likely is and more often than not that something is a projective identification of dependency.

A common occurrence in work with patients who structure their worlds by means of projective identifications of dependency is emergency calls and recurrent crises. The patient calls and notifies the therapist that his world is falling apart or that he doesn't think he can make it till the next session. Very often the "crisis" turns out to be magnified way beyond proportion and could easily have been handled in the next therapy session. Though it is difficult for therapists to deny patients who seem to be falling apart, it also is impossible for a therapist to run an emergency room out of the office. Most crises in the case of patients who use a projective identification of dependency are not crises at all but rather attempts to force the therapist into a position of savior.

Behind the manifest requests for guidance and cries for help lies the metacommunication. The clue that tips off the presence of the metacommunication is the therapist's countertransferential response: an urge to "help" the patient in ways that seem to go beyond what one might consider appropriate. The therapist may first experience this as feelings of overprotectiveness. He may worry that the patient may become overly depressed or that the patient may not be able to handle matters without additional support (longer sessions, more sessions per week, the therapist's home phone number). The response induced in the therapist is helpfulness, or more correctly, caretaking.

In trying to be helpful, the therapist may unwittingly provide the advice the patient asks for. More often than not, the advice fails to accomplish what it is meant to do and the patient ends up blaming the therapist. This happened in the case of a somewhat withdrawn and passive woman who complained that her husband always browbeat her. She described him as a pompous, self-righteous individual who always put himself first and regularly put her down.

I encouraged the patient to stand up to her husband, and suggested she try expressing herself more forcefully next time he pushed her around. She returned the next session saying that she had taken my words to heart and decided to put her foot down. When I asked what happened, she replied in a plaintive tone, "He stepped on it." She went on to blame me for giving her faulty advice.

It is better for the most part to resist the urge to be helpful. Holding back and examining one's initial response often reveal it to be countertransferential and highlight the manipulative aspects of the patient's request. Thus, one of my patients complained that he had problems in relating to women, by which he meant sexual problems. He felt awkward in bed and felt that women always tended to take the lead where sex was concerned. In one of our meetings, he produced a copy of *Reader's Digest* and showed me an article he had been reading entitled "Ten Tips to Improve Your Sex Life." He had picked up a copy on the newsstand hoping that the article might help solve his sexual difficulties.

But there was more to it than that. The patient wanted me to go over each item and advise him as to which of the ten I thought might work best for him. While I was tempted to help him (the countertransferential response), I decided to hold back. I clearly was not Dr. Ruth, nor was I more knowledgeable about sex than the authors of the article he was reading. As I reflected on what was happening, I realized that I was being "asked" to participate in a projective identification of dependency. The patient was asking me to make a decision for him which he probably could make on his own. At a deeper level, he was saying that he couldn't make *any* decisions on his own.

"Using the countertransference" means *reacting to one's reaction*. This means (1) allowing oneself to emotionally respond to the metacommunication embedded in the projective identification and (2) using this information as a means of identifying the patient's pathology. It means that the therapist has to be willing to turn himself into an emotional barometer of sorts. The therapist needs to be *emotionally responsive* to what is taking place within himself as well as *intellectually reflective* regarding what is taking place in the relationship. By allowing oneself to be "used" by the patient in this way, the therapist uses the countertransference to experientially assess the nature of the patient's metacommunication.

Once the therapist has a firm sense of what is going on in the relationship, i.e., once the therapist has an appreciation for the precise nature of the metacommunication, it is time to consider the proper response. The therapist could, of course, be "helpful." Where a projective identification of dependency is in evidence, this might mean providing advice, giving directions and offering guidance. But this only reinforces the patient's pathology and is not particularly therapeutic. The proper response requires the therapist to force the metacommunication behind the projective identification into the open so that it can be dealt with therapeutically.

In practical terms, this means the therapist has somehow to get the patient to translate private and hidden communications into communications that are public and interpersonally accessible. In the case of a projective identification of dependency, it means getting the patient to openly declare "I cannot survive without you" or a close approximation thereof. Unless the therapist can get the patient to openly indicate that he cannot make it on his own, the therapy is going to bog down under the weight of ambiguous and inconclusive communications.

How does the therapist accomplish this? How is the metacommunication forced into the open? To begin with, the therapist needs to highlight the interactional nature of what is taking place. He needs to bring the relationship "into the room." The therapist has to concretize and legitimize the ongoing therapist-patient relationship by shifting the focus of what is taking place into the here-and-now.

This is not easy. Patients, and sometimes therapists, find it easier to talk about other relationships than the relationship of which they are a part. It is possible to spend hours upon hours talking about patients' relationships with their parents, partners, and other object relations without ever touching on the object relation which is most immediate and ultimately most accessible. Very often therapists collude with patients in talking about events in the past or other outside-the-room occurrences as a defense against dealing with what is going on in their own relationship.

One of my patients, a schoolteacher with severe obsessive-compulsive symptoms, spent a great deal of time talking about how inadequate she felt at work. During one of our sessions, she began to describe how she needed to control herself in the presence of others for fear that she would "behave like a crazy person." She was vague regarding what she meant by this. I asked her whether she would behave in a crazy way with me. She laughed but whenever she brought up the subject of craziness, I turned it into our relationship until eventually she was able to convey what she meant by it. For her, it meant losing control, sobbing uncontrollably and becoming helpless. The issue then became what it meant to lose control and become helpless with me.

Once the therapy is brought "into the room," the therapist needs to make sure that the communications that make up the projective identification are made as direct as possible. Very often, patients will cloak their requests and demands for help within "What if . . . ?" questions. The patient may ask "What if I asked you to help me with . . . ?" or "What if I asked you to teach me how to . . . ?" Conditional and tentative statements of this sort need to be transformed into concrete interpersonal demands by saying to the patient, "You'll have to ask me to find out," or by responding, "There's only one way to know." Only by forcing the metacommunication behind the patient's vague requests into the open can the therapist hope to make it a palpable part of the therapist-patient relationship.

Finally, the therapist must refuse to offer the sympathy, guidance, and support the patient asks for. This is difficult for most therapists since it seems contrary to an important part of their self-image—that of helping professional. It is very hard to say no to a patient who seems to be in the throes of a crisis and who holds out a hand for help. But sometimes one has to do precisely this if the therapy is to succeed. Complying with the patient's request for help feeds into the patient's pathology. Refusing to comply with it forces the patient to fall back on the threat or injunction embedded in the metacommunication.

The goal of the second stage of object relations therapy is to bring the metacommunication into the open. In the case of projective identifications of dependency, this means getting the patient to actually acknowledge that he cannot survive without the therapist. Once the metacommunication has surfaced, it no longer resides solely within the patient's projective fantasy. It now is a tangible feature of the manifest therapist-patient relationship. The therapist now is in a position to deal with it in a therapeutic fashion.

POWER

Object relation therapies in which the projective identification of power plays a central role are those in which issues of *control* take center stage. In these therapies, the pressing question seems to be who is in charge. The patient operates on the assumption that he has to be in control of whatever happens in the relationship if things are to work out. Thus, we have a situation in which the therapist is supposed to be the expert but the patient strives to direct what goes on. Like Frank Sinatra, the patient seems intent on doing it his way.

The behavior of the patient vis-à-vis the therapist is nothing more than an extension of the patient's relationships with other significant figures in his life. Patients who interact by means of power projective identifications are described by those who know them as domineering, controlling, and overly critical. All their relationships, particularly close ones, are structured hierarchically. The major issues in their dealings with others seem to be who is on top and who on the bottom. Whether we are talking of work relationships or love relationships, the burning question is who is in control.

Examining projective identifications of power and the way they are manifested in interpersonal relationships reveals that in many ways they are the inverse of projective identifications of dependency. In a projective identification of dependency, the assumption is that one is deficient and cannot function without the support of significant others. In a projective identification of power, the assumption is that others are deficient and are unable to function without the powerful one to lead the way. The way this gets expressed in psychotherapy is through attempts by the patient to dictate what happens in treatment.

Projective identifications of power, like most other projective identifications, become most explicit in the second phase of treatment. Occasionally, however, one can pick up indications of their operation early in therapy. This was apparent in the course of my first phone conversation with Nancy, a district coordinator for a national fund raising organization, who called to set up an appointment to discuss ongoing conflicts with her grown children.

After speaking to her for a few moments about the nature of the problem, I suggested that we set up an initial meeting. She asked me to hold on while she went off to retrieve her appointment book. "I suspect you're rather busy," she remarked when she returned to the phone. She asked me what times I had available and said she would check them against her schedule.

It turned out that every opening I offered her just wasn't convenient. Mondays and Wednesdays were her days for meetings. Most other times were spent traveling. We must have spent five or ten minutes trying to find a time that would be mutually suitable. Finally we were able to arrive at one, but it necessitated doing some fancy footwork with my schedule.

The first session turned out to be a replay of our telephone conversation. The time we had set up was not that convenient after all. Nancy wanted to reschedule our meeting. I tried to accommodate her. We spent 15 minutes once again trying to arrange a mutually suitable time. Needless to say, every opening I proposed seemed not to work out. In the end, I again shifted my schedule to accommodate her needs. Though it wasn't evident to me at the time, Nancy's behavior was a coming attraction of later power plays. Her attempt to control the scheduling scenario was a manifestation of a power projective identification and an early indication of her need to dictate who was going to control the relationship.

In retrospect, it was clear that I played into Nancy's hands. At the same time, I probably would have responded in a similar manner had I appreciated what was happening. The time to highlight the operation of a projective identification is in the second stage of therapy, not the first. As was previously pointed out, the therapist needs to tolerate, even encourage, expressions of the projective identification early in treatment if one hopes to bring the metacommunications to the fore. Unless one sets the groundwork for the emergence of the projective identification in the beginning stages of therapy, nothing much is going to happen in later stages.

The full-blown expression of Nancy's projective identification was realized sometime later in treatment. As the therapy progressed, it became increasingly evident that she needed to get her way. If I tried to focus on her relationship with her older son, she would insist that we would be better off discussing the younger one. If I tried to draw a connection between her relations with coworkers and relations with her children, she would insist that there was no connection between the two, and that she didn't come into therapy to discuss her job. And if I tried to shift the focus from what was happening "outside the room" to what was going on inside it, she became very indignant.

At one point, Nancy declared that she would terminate treatment if I persisted in focusing on our relationship. She felt that I was getting "too personal" and that what was going on in the room had absolutely nothing to do with her reasons for entering treatment. But it was an empty threat. I persisted and eventually we were able to deal with her need to dictate the course of therapy. I recall that at one point during this period, she said to me in a half-joking, half-exasperated way, "You don't stop, do you? You just keep coming and coming, like a bull in a china shop."

The need to bring the therapy "into the room" was commented upon in the previous section in the context of dependency projective identifications. The same applies to the projective identification of power. Whereas it is appropriate, even reassuring, for the patients to talk about past relationships in the engagement phase of treatment, this needs to change once the projective identification stage has been reached. To the extent that object relations therapy deals with the patient's projective identifications as they occur in vivo, it is necessary to shift the focus of the therapy from discussion of interactions with others to discussion of interactions with the therapist.

One way of doing this is to inquire whether patients' feelings about other figures in their lives are similar to feelings experienced towards the therapist. One could simply ask whether feelings of anger directed at one's employer, for example, are sometimes also experienced in the therapy room. A more direct way is to make the connection on one's own. Thus when Nancy told of wanting her children to follow her advice in regard to money matters, I responded, "I sometimes get the feeling that you'd like me to follow your advice regarding the kinds of things we should be doing in therapy."

Comments such as these sometimes are rejected outright or are regarded as "foolish" or "off base" by the patient. This should not dissuade the therapist from pursuing them. It is not always necessary to be correct. The correctness or incorrectness of these "interpretations" is not as important as the shift in discourse it promotes. It gets therapist and patient talking about what is going on within the therapy rather than getting into endless discussions about what is going on outside therapy or what has happened in the past. The latter are bound to occur but they must not be allowed to monopolize the treatment process.

The more the therapy is rooted in the here-and-now of the therapist-patient interaction, the more likely it is that the therapist will be able to force the metacommunication into the open. As in the case of other projective identifications, this requires the therapist to change "What if . . . ?" questions into direct declarations and force the patient to make explicit what is being expressed implicitly. Thus, when Nancy made a remark along the lines of "I wonder what would happen if I asked the questions?" I responded, "I think what you are saying is that you would like to take charge of what is going on."

Nancy, of course, denied this, saying that I had a habit of distorting everything she said. She claimed that I misinterpreted her intentions and that she just wanted to make sure "things went well." At the same time, she subtly questioned my competency as a therapist, making off-hand remarks about my training as well as commenting on the appropriateness of my interventions.

The most common countertransferential responses to a projective identification of power are "feelings of inadequacy and emasculation" (Ogden, 1982, p. 49). I recall leaving sessions with Nancy wondering whether I was, in fact, missing the point and mismanaging the therapy. Once I analyzed the countertransference and recognized it as a reaction to the projective identification, I decided to search for an opening which would allow me to highlight the metacommunication associated with it.

The opportunity arose during one session in which Nancy was behaving in a particularly controlling fashion and going on about how, given half a chance, she could probably do a better job at therapy than I could. I stopped her in the middle of her diatribe and, rising from my seat, motioned for her to switch seats with me. She was a bit perplexed but did as I asked her. Having changed places, I said to her "It's all yours. You're in charge. Go ahead and be the therapist."

Nancy looked flustered and spent the next few moments commenting on how silly all this was. This was followed by an extended silence after which she asked to return to her seat. I told her that I wanted her to stay where she was for a little while longer and let me know what was going through her mind. She seemed a little embarrassed, but then began to go on in an "If you really want to know" vein, letting me know that she felt that the success of the therapy depended on her taking the lead. She acknowledged that I was "a pretty good therapist" but insisted that it took cooperative patients such as herself to really make things work.

The metacommunicative message embedded in cases of projective identifications of power is: You can't succeed (or survive) without me. The countertransference induced by this communication produces feelings of incompetence and impending failure. The therapist is criticized for not handling matters correctly and for failing to produce major changes. The patient comes up with "crises" and "emergencies" that the therapist never seems to handle correctly. There is an air of impatience on the patient's part accompanied by the feeling that things would really be moving right along if the patient, rather than the therapist, were in charge.

Therapists faced with projective identifications of power are forced to question whether they are doing things the right way. They begin to wonder whether they really understand what is taking place. The patient views therapy as a job to be done and is dissatisfied with the way it is being handled. To the extent that therapy is less than an exact science and there is much uncertainty in the very nature of the work, therapists prove vulnerable targets for patients who employ projective identifications of power.

It is not usual, therefore, for therapists who treat such patients to become annoyed and develop secret fantasies about getting rid of them. If only the patient would move to another city. If only the patient would find another therapist, or better yet, suddenly become better. Then life could proceed as comfortably and predictably as it did before. Such feelings—and the anger that fans them—are a natural response to the patient's inductive maneuvers. They constitute the countertransference to a projective identification of power.

As is the case with the projective identification of dependency, the therapist uses the countertransference as a relational window into the nature of the patient's interpersonal pathology. The countertransference, in other words, provides the diagnosis. With this "knowledge" in hand, the therapist is able to respond to the patient therapeutically rather than with rejection or anger. To get angry at a patient who provokes countertransference feelings is tantamount to getting angry at the patient because he or she is ill.

Two groups of individuals in which projective identifications of power are quite prevalent are business executives and psychotherapists. For whatever reason, executives and therapists—at least those who enter therapy—tend to establish relationships in which control tends to be a dominant factor. Whereas one would think that therapists would make ideal patients, those in treatment often try to improve upon the therapy. They make reference to their therapeutic accomplishments, to the way they conceptualize treatment, and to "names" in the field upon whom their own work is based. Intellectualization is prominent and therapist-patient interactions are marked by a kind of professional one-upmanship.

But whether the patient is a therapist, a CEO, or a housewife, the task in this phase of treatment remains the same: highlight the operation of the projective identification (in this case, power) and expose the metacommunication. Somehow or other, the therapist must elicit a message to the effect that the therapist cannot survive without the patient, or at least that the therapist is going to fail in what he sets out to do without the patient's help. Once this is accomplished, the main objective of the second phase of treatment has been realized.

SEXUALITY

Of the major projective identifications that are encountered in the course of doing object relations therapy, those that are sexual in nature are the most sensitive. The reason for this is that sexuality in object relations therapy is more than just a topic for discussion. Instead of simply being a part of the patient's life that therapist and patient explore and try to analyze, it is a salient and ongoing part of the therapist-client relationship. To the extent that sexual issues affect how therapists feel about themselves as desirable human beings, interpersonal exchanges which bear on these feelings—therapeutic or otherwise—can be personally threatening.

For these reasons, it is not hard to understand why therapists often choose to avoid dealing with sex as a relational phenomena and to reframe the patient's sexual feelings in less immediate terms, e.g., "Do you recall similar feelings towards anyone else in your life?" or "Does this remind you of something that you felt in the past?" Questions such as these take what is going on between the therapist and the client out of the present and redeposit it in relationships from the distant past or relationships that make up the patient's contemporary existence.

While taking sex "out of the room" makes it less threatening, it tends to skirt object relational issues that are contained in the projective identification. If the point of object relations therapy is to create an in vivo relational enactment of the patient's projective fantasies, the therapist must be willing to become the target of the patient's manipulations. If sexuality is the only reliable way the patient knows to keep people in relationships, the therapist must be careful not to suppress expressions of it.

Patients play out projective identifications of sexuality in therapy by introducing erotic elements into the relationship. Some patients, for example, offer detailed accounts of their sexual problems and proclivities. Women will talk about deep vs. surface orgasms and men will supply details of their sexual conquests. Other patients tend to regularly include double entendres in the conversations, as if they were playing some sort of sexual game with the therapist. Others yet insist on turning the therapy into a classroom where they and the therapist can hold conversations about outdated sexual mores and societal sexual codes.

One patient, a lawyer named Sean, not only described his compulsive need to seduce young female attorneys whenever he attended legal conventions, but also insisted on providing me with blow-by-blow accounts of his conquests. The therapy sessions often involved descriptions of how Sean would spy an attractive woman at a meeting, entice her up to his room, and then get her to spend the night with him. The unusual thing about his accounts was that they included excessively detailed descriptions of his sexual activity. It was almost as if Sean were trying, through words, to involve me in his sexual escapades.

Words are not the only means by which the therapy can be sexualized. Very often, clothing and suggestive posturing fulfill this function. Female patients may hike their dress high up on their thighs and sit in such a way as to strike a seductive pose. Or they may make it a practice to lean forward so as to reveal a bit more cleavage than one would deem appropriate under the circumstances. Male patients sometimes sit facing the therapist with legs akimbo, using body language to signify what they feel to be the most significant part of who they are. Through nonverbal devices, both male and female patients manage to "present" the therapist with those parts of themselves they believe others value most.

Thus, a patient of mine who worked as a parts assembler in a toy factory came to the first few sessions of therapy in work clothes consisting of blue jeans and a baggy flannel shirt. She excused her appearance, saying that she had to come to the session directly from work and did not have time to change into "decent clothes." I didn't give it much thought and said something about it being fine. It was curious, therefore, that soon after the therapy got under way she began arriving in a sheer, low-cut cocktail dress. Whether she made the switch at work or in a telephone booth, it was an indication of how she viewed our relationship as well as a portent of the direction the therapy would later take.

While male patients generally are less likely to use suggestive dress as part of their sexual projective identifications, instances occasionally arise in which they do. A case in point is that of a patient seen in therapy by a clinical graduate student named Judy whom I was supervising. The patient, an attractive male in his early thirties, had entered therapy to deal with feelings of detachment in his relationships with women. Though he was not currently involved with anyone, he had a history of short promiscuous involvements, none of which provided him with any lasting gratification.

An interesting occurrence in therapy was the change in his clothing habits as the weeks went by. In the beginning of treatment, he arrived for his sessions in slacks and a sport shirt. As the therapy progressed and the weather got warmer, he began to shed more and more apparel. Soon he was showing up in tightly fitted short shorts and a white Madras cotton shirt open to the navel. While admittedly it was summertime, the nature of his outfits and the effect his dress had on my supervisee indicated that factors other than weather and fashion were at work.

The overall intent of a sexual projective identification is sexual gratification. Patients who employ these projective devices are convinced that other people stay in relationships with them because they can satisfy them sexually or make them feel more masculine or feminine. From the patient's vantage point, the therapist is no different. Though therapists may profess that they stay with the patient because of professional commitment, humanistic concerns, or even because of the money they earn, the patient at heart believes that the only reason therapists *really* stay involved with them is because of sex. For the patient who employs a projective identification of sexuality, the bottom line in all relationships is providing erotic fulfillment.

The sad fact of the matter is that people who use sexual projective identifications are individuals whose self-esteem is almost entirely enveloped in sexuality. As one patient put it, "The only place I am good is in bed." It is a disheartening commentary on human existence to think that a person's self-worth can be reduced to this. But the fact of the matter is that a great many individuals go through life convinced that their primary value to others lies in the sexual satisfaction they are able to provide.

How does the therapist identify sexual projective identifications? As is the case with other projective identifications, the answer is through the countertransference. The classic response in working with patients who use projective identification of sexuality is, simply stated, sexual arousal. The therapist feels titillated, pruriently attracted, and sexually stimulated. This is what the inductive part of the projective identification is meant to produce. If the projective identification is successful, the natural countertransferential response of the therapist is sexual excitement.

It was not surprising, therefore, that I found myself increasingly captivated by what Sean had to say. At first, I rationalized this by thinking to myself that it was important to know the details of how he dealt with women in order to understand him better. But as I spent session after session allowing him to describe his various escapades, it struck me that I perhaps was *too* interested in his tales. His stories of sexual conquest, peppered as they were with intimate details of how he went about bedding women, were exciting and provided me with what amounted to my own private peep show. Once I was able to appreciate that my interest was not as intellectually motivated as I believed it to be, I was able to use my response for diagnostic rather than for sexual purposes.

Another example of a sexual projective identification is seen in my work with Beata, a 40-year-old artist who sought therapy to deal with chronic gastric pain and episodic depressions. Before considering psychotherapy, Beata had been seen by a number of physicians, including a well-known internist and a highly regarded gastroenterologist. Although at first ulcers were suspected, tests turned out negative and the doctors concluded that there was nothing organically the matter with her. Suggesting that her symptoms might be stress related, they referred her back to her family physician. He suggested she seek therapy.

The daughter of a talented couple, one of whom was an actress and the other a TV producer, Beata led a very unhappy childhood. Her parents spent very little time with her and she was essentially raised by an older sister. Her teenage years were spent in isolation and marked by periods of occasional promiscuity and heavy drinking. It was not until she began to paint that she pulled herself together and began to develop a sense of who she was. At the same time, she still had trouble relating to people.

In the course of therapy, Beata told me of a nude self-portrait she had painted some years earlier. The portrait hung in her living room and came up during a discussion regarding dating. She often invited men up to her apartment and wondered whether it gave them "the wrong impression." At the same time she verbalized her concerns about the portrait, she insisted on describing it—in detail. She told how she had managed to capture the fullness of her breasts and the lithe lines of her body by the delicate use of diffused cross lighting.

I was intrigued by Beata's description. It was like listening to a lecture on Vermeer and the way artists use natural light in their work. But it was more than that. As she went into more and more detail, her description became more and more erotic. By the time she was finished, little was left to the imagination and she might as well have been sitting across from me in the buff. Only after the session was over was I able to recognize that I had been the target of a projective identification of sexuality and that my "interest" in her portrait was more countertransferential than artistic in nature.

Despite the fact that instances of sexual projective identification often are blatantly evident, it sometimes is difficult to recognize the countertransferential nature of what is taking place. This is especially true if the therapist's response is seen as a sign of weakness or as unprofessional. Judy, the student whose patient came to therapy in short shorts, wondered in one of our supervisory sessions whether it was worthwhile to continue seeing him. She felt that the patient wasn't "psychologically minded" and that the therapy wasn't getting anywhere.

This came as somewhat of a surprise and I decided to explore the issue with her. In doing so, I learned that Judy had become very uncomfortable working with the patient. She revealed that she approached each succeeding session with apprehension and during one session had felt like running out of the room. This disturbed her, for it suggested that something might be wrong with her and that she might not be cut out to be a therapist. A competent therapist didn't let her feelings get the better of her.

It turned out that the feelings she was talking about were sexual feelings. Over the course of therapy, the student found herself becoming increasingly attracted to the patient. This was very upsetting for a number of reasons. For one, she was involved with another man whom she planned to marry in the near future. Although her interest in the patient wasn't a real threat, it bothered her. What's more, she felt awkward admitting her sexual feelings to me. She saw her interest in the patient as an indication that she wasn't behaving professionally. Rather than viewing her response as a natural reaction to the patient's sexual projective identification, she saw it as a mark of failure.

It was not of course. If there was any failure, it was a failure to recognize that one can harbor sexual feelings towards one's patients and still be a good therapist. What really constitutes failure is acting upon the countertransference. Ethical issues aside, this is tantamount to failing the patient in the worst possible way. Giving in to the patient's sexual projective identifications only confirms the patient's deepest fears: that he basically is undesirable and tolerated only for the sexual pleasure he can provide.

As is the case with dependency and power projective identifications, the major task with sexual projective identifications is to bring the metacommunication to the fore. The end of stage two is not reached until the seduction is brought into the open. This is not easy since sexual come-ons and erotic maneuvering can easily be excused away. A patient can say that she just happened to wear a low-cut dress that day or that a sexual encounter was described in great detail only because "that's what therapy is supposed to be about." The therapist, in addition, may be accused of everything from being a voyeur to having "sex on the brain."

Accusations of this sort naturally are disconcerting and can lead the therapist to back off and revert to safer areas. This is usually a mistake. A guiding principle in object relations work is that one sinks or swims with the countertransference. The therapist needs to feel confident that whatever feelings are aroused have been precipitated by the interaction with the patient. Though such feelings are awkward and often embarrassing, it is necessary to persevere. Only by pressing forward can the underlying message behind the projective identification become an explicit part of the ongoing relationship.

Keeping this in mind, I responded to Beata by telling her that I thought that her story of the portrait, particularly the way she told it, was her way of undressing herself in front of me. She at first scoffed at my interpretation, but then tried to make light of it by saying, "Well, it's better than actually doing it." I pressed her as to what "it" was and what she really had in mind. She remained noncommittal but after I pressed her she responded by asking whether I would actually like to come up to her apartment and view the portrait first hand. It was evident by now that we had progressed beyond Art Appreciation 101 and that the sexual metacommunication was for all intents and purposes in the open.

There are instances in which the seductive nature of the metacommunication is not that far from the surface and emerges without a great deal of instigation. One patient came straight out and asked me to go to bed with her after I called her erotic posturing into question.

"Where would we go from there?" I asked her, referring to the fate of the therapy.

She shrugged her shoulders. When I asked her whether she thought it would be possible to go on with the therapy if we starting sleeping with one another, she replied, "The hell with therapy. It's not getting me anyplace, anyway." The patient went on to expound on the artificial boundaries in society between psychological and physical expressions of caring. She punctuated her discourse by asking, "If you really care about me, what's wrong with showing it physically?"

In the case of Sean, the attorney, efforts to point up what he was doing in eroticizing the therapy led to his admission that he felt he needed to keep me sexually enticed so that I wouldn't drop him as a patient. He confessed that he wasn't a very interesting person and that he couldn't see why I would want to keep him in treatment otherwise. When I told him that I did care about him as a person and that his stories weren't the reason I kept him as a patient, he reacted as if he hadn't heard me and proceeded to describe another of his sexual escapades.

The session was nearing the end and I again reiterated that I didn't think I could listen to his stories hour after hour. He seemed a bit dejected and the hour ended without much more being said.

Sean opened the next session with "I could bring other stuff."

"Other stuff?" I responded, not sure what he was talking about.

"Pictures, videotapes, anything you like."

I told him in a gentle way that I wasn't interested in turning the therapy room into a sex parlor or the hour into a sex session.

At this point, Sean said, "I'll do anything you want if you let me stay in therapy." I was somewhat taken aback since there never was any question of my dropping Sean as a patient. But rather than pursuing this part of his utterance, I asked him what he meant by "anything."

Sean was quiet for a long time. When he spoke, he said he would perform fellatio on me. He told me that he would do anything I wanted if only I would keep him on. Sean's response had a desperate quality to it, but he was a desperate person where it came to relationships. He assumed that if I wasn't interested in what he had to offer sexually, then I just didn't have any use for him as a human being.

As indicated earlier, forcing full-blown expressions of a projective identification into the open often seems cruel and unfeeling. This seems especially so in the case of sexual projective identifications. But it is no more cruel than leaving the patient to suffer the frustration and emptiness that comes from living a life based on projective identifications.

The therapist does not make up projective identifications. They are not an iatrogenic part of the treatment process. They are a palpable part of the patient's object relations and a part of the psychotherapeutic relationship. If the therapist is to get beyond the second stage of treatment, it is necessary to ensure that the metacommunication behind the projective identification comes to the fore.

INGRATIATION

As pointed out in Chapter 3, the projective identification of ingratiation is made up of interpersonal patterns which contain strong elements of *self-sacrifice*. Individuals who employ projective identifications of ingratiation consistently send out messages regarding how much they put themselves out for others. They notify those about them how much they give of themselves and how unappreciated they feel.

This all is rather innocuous on the surface. All that patients seem to want is a simple "Thank you," a mere acknowledgment that they are appreciated. But closer examination reveals that they expect something more substantial in return. There is a hidden message that lies just beneath the surface. It is the metacommunication "You owe me" and it is responsible for a whole host of pathological interactions.

The particular way that projective identifications of ingratiation are expressed in object relations therapy is through attempts on the patient's part to be helpful and accommodating. Some patients may comment on the office decor as if their advice will prompt changes that might make the office more attractive. Therapeutic designers in more than one way, they try to be of use to the therapist by acting as interior decorators. Others offer to let their friends know how capable the therapist is. It is difficult in such circumstances not to be appreciative. Not only does the patient trumpet your capabilities, but he also provides sources of additional income by drumming up business.

An example of a projective identification of ingratiation can be seen in the behavior of Norman, a patient in a therapy group I led some years back. Norman was different from the other members of the group in that he made a habit of coming early to the meetings, often being the first to arrive. Before the rest of the group showed up, Norman took it upon himself to arrange the seats in the room, see that all the ashtrays were clean, and fill the water pitcher. These were things I typically took care of myself, but since it saved me a little work, I didn't make too much of it. I even welcomed his "thoughtfulness."

Norman's helpfulness did not end there. He would make comments during the sessions themselves which seemed designed to smooth the operation of the group. He would say things like, "I think what Dr. Cashdan is trying to do is get us to be more honest with one another," and "Dr. Cashdan is always punctual; why don't we all make it a point to get here on time?" To round things out, Norman stayed after the others left, ostensibly to help clean up.

I did not question Norman's behavior, at least not in the beginning. After all, someone had to be the last to leave, and what if he lingered five minutes longer than the others? Besides which, it was convenient having someone around to help clean up. But as time went by, it became increasingly evident that Norman's intent was to try to establish an exclusive relationship by ingratiating himself. While he straightened up, he would offer his private opinion of what was happening in the group and make suggestions as to how I might get certain members to participate more fully. By behaving in this way, Norman made it abundantly clear that he was expecting special consideration.

My initial response to Norman was essentially countertransferential in nature. I appreciated his setting up the therapy room and arranging things afterwards. One could, of course, contend that I shouldn't have let myself be "conned" in this way. But squashing the projective identification before it really gets underway prevents a therapist from fully experiencing what it means to be a recipient of the patient's projective fantasy and to accurately identify its precise character (Ogden, 1982, p. 50).

Aside from this, at first it is not always easy to know what is going on. If a patient is skilled in the projective identification of ingratiation (or any projective identification for that matter), the therapist may be drawn into the pathology of the relationship without realizing it. This of course is why projective identifications persist. At some level they succeed, even though the patient ultimately pays a price for their "success."

I therefore found myself responding to Henrietta in much the same way I responded to Norman. She was the woman, it will be recalled, who infuriated her teenage sons by pushing down the door locks whenever they entered the car. One of the problems that arose in the therapy was arrangement of a suitable meeting time for the family. This changed from week to week because the two boys were involved in sports after school. I realized this would be the case when I undertook the therapy and agreed to shift times whenever necessary and whenever possible.

Henrietta took it upon herself to make all the necessary arrangements. She was the one who assembled the family schedules and made sure the family could get together for the therapy. She also called me fairly regularly to let me know of any changes that took place. The nature of our contacts were such that she always let me know how hard she was working to juggle everyone's schedule and how solicitous she was of my time. How could I help but not be appreciative?

Another way that patients act out projective identifications of ingratiation in treatment is by offering to be therapeutic guinea pigs. Some patients will, for instance, offer to act as subjects for new procedures or techniques they think the therapist might want to try. A patient named Danielle spent session after session trying to convince me how hard she worked to ensure that the therapy would be successful. Not only did Danielle keep detailed notes of what occurred in every session, but she used them to prepare for subsequent meetings. In addition to this, she spent a substantial portion of the hour trying in subtle ways to get me to acknowledge that I was her most interesting patient.

As we moved into the second stage of treatment, I directed much of my energy to bringing the therapy into the room. I pointed out to Danielle that her note taking, particularly her efforts to review them with me during the hour, was her way of avoiding dealing with me directly. I told her that I would rather she tell me directly what she saw taking place as it occurred rather than conducting a literary analysis. She nevertheless persisted. I finally refused to go over the notes with her.

Danielle began to pout and to withdraw. She claimed that I didn't appreciate how hard she worked at getting better. None of my other patients were as devoted to me as she was. I agreed that this might by the case, but I still didn't feel that we should be interacting over pieces of paper. At this point she fell quiet. When she broke the silence, she did so by offering to be a guinea pig for me.

"Use any technique," she declared. "If you have any new procedure you want to try on me, you can."

Her offer took me by surprise and I wasn't sure how to respond. I asked her what she had in mind. She merely repeated her proposal. She went on to say that she imagined that therapists were interested in trying out new techniques, and she willingly would volunteer to be a subject if I wanted her to. The offer was made in such an ingenuous way that I was touched by it.

There was, of course, no trial or experiment through which I wanted to put Danielle, but the mere fact that she would offer herself in this manner was somewhat moving. I recall at the time feeling beholden to her and a bit sorry that I had given her such a hard time over the notes. After all, she was just trying to be helpful. It was not until somewhat later that I realized that my response was precisely the countertransferential response to a projective identification of ingratiation.

Once the nature of the projective identification became evident, it became necessary to force the metacommunication behind it into the open. This meant pressing Danielle to acknowledge what she hoped to get in return for her willingness to place my interests before hers. I asked her directly what she hoped to receive in return were I to take her up on her offer. At first she responded by saying, "Nothing." But when I prodded her, she confessed that she hoped I would want to keep her around—even after the therapy was ever—if she could continue to be "useful."

CONCLUDING REMARKS

Whether one is speaking about a projective identification of dependency, power, sexuality, or ingratiation, the task of the therapist is to bring the metacommunication associated with it into the open. The particular way the therapist accomplishes this depends on the therapist's ingenuity and the pace at which he or she prefers to work. One thing, however, is clear. The therapist needs to obtain a clear expression of the metacommunication associated with the patient's projective identification before the therapy can move ahead.

If this is not accomplished, the therapy will tend to bog down and fold back onto itself. If the metacommunication remains vague, ambiguous, and shielded from view, the therapist will find it nearly impossible to achieve what has to be achieved in the stage that follows. If, on the other hand, the metacommunication is forced to surface in the form of a statement that the patient will not be able to survive, or is willing to sexually gratify you, or whatever, there is a good chance that the issues of the next stage can be successfully addressed.

Before moving on to the next stage of treatment, it should be emphasized that although the descriptions of the interactions that make up stage two have an adversarial quality about them, they take place in the context of sincere concern for the patient and the patient's well-being. It is very difficult through the printed word to portray the precise character of the emotional interchanges that take place in any therapy. This is especially true in object relations work where many of the interactions involve subtle but nonetheless intense projective identifications. Sometimes it seem as if patients are being subjected to one more ordeal in addition to the many other ordeals they face in life.

There is truth to this. But at some level, patients know that their way of dealing with others is unproductive, if not destructive. Patients sense that their projective identifications are self-defeating and emotionally draining. For all they are meant to accomplish, projective identifications only disrupt patients' lives and produce unneeded pain. For these reasons, and others to be discussed in the next chapter, patients endure the therapist's challenges and probes. But there also is a sense of relief at the end of stage two. A relational clarity has, for better or worse, been established and the cards, so to speak, are on the table.

CHAPTER 6

Stage Three: Confrontation

Once the metacommunication that is contained within the patient's projective identification has surfaced, it becomes a viable part of the therapist-patient interaction. The subtle and shadowy messages that previously were hidden within the projective identification now are an explicit part of the relationship. The erotic innuendos have turned into direct attempts at seduction; the seemingly innocuous requests for help have been transformed into a demand for wholesale caretaking. Now that all the cards are on the table, the therapist finally can confront the patient's pathology in a direct and forceful manner.

THE THERAPIST RESPONSE

How precisely does the therapist accomplish this? How does the therapist respond to the message contained in the metacommunication? By refusing to concede or conform to the metacommunicative demand. The correct therapeutic response, simply stated, is "no." By confronting the patient's habitual way of structuring relationships, the therapist challenges the very nature of the projective identification.

As one might imagine, this is easier said than done. It is very difficult to turn down someone who is vulnerable. It is not that easy, for example, to say no to patients who appear needy and desperate. The depth of the patient's metacommunicative request seems so psychologically profound that it is almost painful to respond to it in what obviously seems like a negative and degrading manner. How does one tell a patient who threatens suicide that you will not be responsible for what he does if he takes his own life?

By the same token, how do you go about saying no to someone whose sexual metacommunication is out in the open? On the one hand, there are enough available reasons for gracefully declining to become sexually enmeshed. One can fall back on ethical, personal, and therapeutic rationales that argue forcefully and eloquently against sexual involvement with one's patients. Still it is very awkward to communicate this to someone who has lain himself sexually bare. Refusing to capitulate—even for the best of reasons—has to feel to the patient like a rejection of the highest order.

To avoid this, some therapists retreat to interpretation. Patients are asked to explore what their statement "means" or perhaps invited to consider to whom their message is "really" directed. Therapist and patient huddle and together agree that it is high time to explore the patient's early object relations. By engaging in interpretive activities, therapist and patient nimbly sidestep the relational implications contained in the metacommunication.

One might ask what is wrong with making an interpretation at this point. The answer is that interpretation acts to defuse the emotional impact of what is taking place in the present. Whatever good comes of understanding the reasons for one's behavior pales in comparison to the emotional learning that needs to occur in this stage. If any interpretation or analysis takes place, it must take the form of "silent interpretation" (Spotnitz, 1985, p. 167). Making outright interpretations at this stage of treatment acts only to shift the tenor of the therapy from emotional confrontation to intellectual analysis.

A more telling argument against making interpretations at this stage in object relations therapy is that it relies on cognitive, verbal devices to address matters which are essentially preverbal in nature:

One of the problems with [verbal interpretation] is that a patient's reliance upon projective identification as a predominant mode of communication, defense, and object relatedness is frequently a reflection of the fact that he is currently unable to make use of verbal symbols either intrapsychically (as part of an inner dialogue) or interpersonally. As a result, he can neither comprehend nor utilize interpretations offered in a verbalized form. (Ogden, 1982, pp. 76–77)

In object relations therapy, the bulk of the patient's pathology exists in the form of feeling states and needs to be confronted on a feeling level. The things the patient has learned about relationships has come from *being* in them, not analyzing them. This is not to say that interpretation does not have its place, only that it does not belong in this stage of therapy.

If the true benefits of object relations treatment are to be realized, the therapist needs to send an unmistakable, unambiguous signal regarding an unwillingness to participate in the patient's pathology. The therapist must question neither the propriety of the patient's demand nor the patient's right to make it. The therapist should not request an explanation of what the patient's request "means," nor should the therapist attempt to get at its underlying basis. All the therapist should do — must do — is refuse to bow to the patient's demand.

The precise way in which the therapist says "no" depends upon the specific projective identification and the unique demands associated with it. Though the precise words may differ, the therapist needs to say to the patient: I am not going to sleep with you (sexuality), I am not going to lead your life (dependency), I do not need your help to succeed (power), and I do not owe you anything (ingratiation). By directly challenging the inherent demand that lies within the projective identification, the therapist challenges its legitimacy as a basis for the relationship.

At the same time, the therapist needs to affirm the relationship. The therapist needs to let the patient know that the commitment that existed at the beginning of therapy is as strong as ever and that the therapist still cares. As Mann puts it, "Gentle, caring concern of the therapist for the patient may well be the most important element in a proper, effective confrontation" (1973, p. 44). The therapist needs to communicate that it is the projective identification that is being rejected and not the patient. The only way to accomplish this is to restate one's commitment as directly and concretely as possible.

What the therapist should *not* do is deflect the threat, calm the patient, or get into long explanations of what is happening. The patient has to confront that which he or she fears most: loss of human contact. The patient needs to learn that the split-off "bad" parts of the self are not grounds for abandonment. The issue is not reexperiencing what happened in the past, but rather experiencing very powerful, ongoing feelings in the present. The patient must learn that open, honest relationships are possible, that there is life after projective identification.

This is a worrisome time in therapy, not only for the patient but for the therapist. The intense emotions generated in this stage often leave the therapist wondering whether he has sabotaged all the hard work that has come before. Sometimes in an attempt to right things, the therapist may try to convince the patient that "things will get better," or ask the patient to "come for a couple of more times to see how things go." This only postpones the inevitable and makes things more difficult later on. If the therapy is to succeed, the patient needs to learn what it means to be in a close nonmanipulative relationship with another human being.

THE PATIENT RESPONSE

As one might expect, most patients do not react to confrontation with calm resolve. A rejection of sorts has taken place which is experienced at different levels and with varying degrees of intensity. On the most immediate level, the rejection is experienced as a simple refusal on the therapist's part to respond to a concrete request or demand. On a deeper level it is experienced as a direct challenge to the patient's way of structuring relationships. At the most profound level, it symbolizes rejection of part of the patient's inner world. As such, it is taken as a rejection of the patient's self.

Very often, the patient responds to the perceived rejection by becoming angry or withdrawn. The patient flies into a rage, becomes highly belligerent, or threatens to quit treatment. The therapist is accused of being hateful and of deliberately interfering with all the progress that has been made. Alternatively, the patient starts to sulk and to retreat into long periods of silence. The interaction appears to have come to a halt and a pall settles over the therapy.

This does not mean that the patient has abandoned the projective identification. Very rarely do patients give up their projective identifications without a struggle. After a brief respite, the patient tries to recoup and pick up where things left off. Sensing that there has been a direct assault on the projective identification, the patient takes certain countermeasures to defend against it.

These countermeasures can take a number of forms. Among the more common ones are intensification, blaming, secondary projective identification, and leavetaking. Examples of each will be considered separately although in practice they often blend into one another.

Intensification

One of the major ways in which patients respond to confrontation is by intensifying their demands. The ingratiating patient becomes more helpful, more sacrificing, more willing to do anything to solicit appreciation. Patients who use sexual projective identification become more daring and frank. They accuse the therapist of being conventional or of acting like a prude. Sometimes the patient intensifies the metacommunicative demand by sexually goading the therapist. One of my patients called me a "sissy" when I told her I would not sleep with her.

Patients sometimes will intensify the metacommunicative demand by "messing up." The patient precipitously resigns from work, fails out of school, or decides to end a marriage. Blatant demonstration of ineptitude and incompetency are paraded before the therapist to "prove" what denial of the metacommunication has wrought. Although one is tempted to interpret what is happening, the therapist's energy is better spent in continuing to counter the patient's demands than in making interpretations.

An instance of intensification in a projective identification of dependency can be seen in the case of Catherine. She was the patient, it may be recalled, who insisted that I help her deal with her employer as well as help her figure out how to deal with men once she began to date after a divorce. Catherine had become somewhat overwrought when I first confronted her. She claimed that I was driving her crazy by saying the kinds of things I said.

In the session that followed, Catherine told me that she was sure I said what I had said just to see how she would react. She called me her "lifeline" and insisted that she wouldn't give me any trouble if I simply would be there when she needed me. The more I refused to capitulate to her "request," the more desperate she became. Catherine then insisted that she would fall apart if I didn't take care of her. When I reiterated that I wasn't going to, she became quite somber and declared, "Then you will be personally responsible for what happens to me."

One of the ways that dependent patients intensify their dependency is by tapping into the therapist's sense of responsibility. One of my patients aroused a fair amount of concern by coming to the therapy with a can of beer soon after I confronted the demands in his projective identification of dependency. He spent the session sipping from the can and wondering aloud why I didn't tell him to stop. After all, he might get drunk and get into an accident. Although he did not drink more than one beer, I still worried that he might injure himself since I knew that he had been involved in some automobile mishaps.

My concern over his drinking was a replay of earlier countertransferential feelings that made me feel I had to constantly "watch over him." This time I held back and decided not to say anything. True to form, he got into a minor automobile accident one evening after leaving the therapy session. He returned the next session to tell me about it and to let me know that it was my fault. He insisted the accident occurred because I didn't stop him from drinking. He persisted in his accusation despite the fact that a breatha-lyzer test administered at the site of the accident indicated that he was sober.

Of course, the most drastic way of intensifying the metacommunicative demand and really raising the ante is by threatening suicide. Such threats conjure up strong countertransferential feelings of responsibility and create a great deal of apprehension in the therapist. It is at times like this that the therapist has to fend off the temptation to back off and tone down confron-tational efforts.

An example of this is demonstrated in a therapy containing a projective identification of dependency in which threats of suicide had become a prominent feature (Ogden, 1982). It involved a patient, Mrs. N., whose mother had killed herself when Mrs. N was 10 years old. Apparently the mother had come into the patient's room moments before shooting herself to give the patient a bedtime kiss. The child had turned her head away and later on was told she was to blame for her mother's death.

In the course of a protracted and intense therapy, Mrs. N. repeatedly threatened suicide and in the course of therapy took a moderately serious dose of antidepressant medication. The object relational character of what was going on is highlighted by Ogden, who writes:

From the perspective of the concept of projective identification, the second year of therapy could be seen as an interpersonal enactment of a specific internal object relationship, wherein the therapist was being forced to experience the unbearable responsibility felt by a 10-year-old girl for the life and death of her depressed, chronically suicidal mother. (p. 59)

The patient's suicide attempt was a turning point in the therapy for it was not long after that the therapist was able to deal with the patient's projective identification.

In his classic work on countertransference, Racker (1968) makes a dis-tinction between "concordant" countertransference and "complementary" countertransference. In the concordant version, the patient projects his child self onto the therapist so that the therapist enacts the role of child while the patient takes on the role of significant other. In the complementa-ry case, just the opposite occurs. The patient projects the parent role onto the therapist and reenacts the object relational counterpart of the child.

Most of the examples of projective identification and the countertrans-ferential responses to them in this chapter have been of the complementary type. My experience is that they are most prevalent and are the ones which crop up most often in treatment. There are instances, however, in which the concordant type predominates or in which the two fluctuate. The example of Mrs. N. is one in which the countertransference is more concordant in that the therapist is made to feel responsible for the patient's (and symbolically the mother's) suicide attempt.

The therapist, in any case, responded to the threat of suicide by telling Mrs. N. that he could not continue to work with her effectively if suicide threats continued to be a constant part of their relationship. What he essentially was saying to her was that he would not conform to her meta-communicative threat. He would not collude with her in the belief that he was responsible for whether she lived or died. By confronting the metacom-munication, the therapist signaled that he would not take on the "burden of responsibility (that the patient) forced upon him" (p. 59). Soon thereafter the threats declined dramatically.

The important consideration in cases like these is to communicate to patients that you are not going to spend your life worrying whether they will be alive from one moment to the next. You are going to be neither their guardian nor their savior. At the same time it is necessary to affirm the relationship. It is clinically irresponsible to tell patients that you will have nothing to do with them if they talk of killing themselves. I violated this dictum in the case of Isabel, the severely depressed suicidal patient discussed in Chapter 4 only because I felt it necessary to shock her into relational awareness. When I first met her, she hardly knew I was in the room.

By the same token, the therapist treating Mrs. N. did not tell her that he would not continue to work with her if she continued to threaten suicide. He told her that he could not continue to work with her *effectively* if she persevered in structuring the relationship in this manner. This may seem like a fine point but it is a critical one and underlies much of what happens in object relations treatment. Confrontation of the metacommunication, wherever it occurs, always needs to be accompanied by relational affirma-tion if the confrontation is to succeed.

Blaming

Another way that patients respond to confrontation is by blaming the therapist for the feelings they experience. Patients who structure their relationships by means of projective identifications of power insist that the therapist essentially has told them to take charge. Patients who use projec-tive identifications of sex insist that the therapist is the one who suggested the possibility of a sexual liaison. In what seems like a complete turnabout, the therapist is accused of some of the very responses that are induced by the patient's projective identification.

In the case of projective identifications of ingratiation, for example, patients may charge the therapist with using them for ulterior motives. They accuse the therapist of using their case for grand rounds presentations or for classroom material. One of my patients was sure I was writing a psychiatric novel in which she would be one of the major characters. There is, of course, a narcissistic element in accusations of this sort, but they also reflect the patient's way of disavowing responsibility for his projective fantasy. It is as if the patient tunes into the countertransference and uses this "information" to defend himself against what is taking place.

Use of the countertransference for defensive, i.e. blaming, purposes also can be seen in instances of sexual projective identifications. In cases such as these, patients accuse the therapist of being sexually interested in them or of acting in a provocative fashion. Pam, a patient whose father regaled her with his dirty jokes, showed up late for one session soon after I had begun to confront her sexual maneuvering. It was unusual for her to be late and I waited half an hour before deciding to leave. As I walked out the office, she ran up to the door out of breath and obviously quite upset.

It took her a while to compose herself and even longer to tell me what had happened. Apparently she had arrived in time for her appointment but was fearful of facing me. She returned to her car and began to head home. But before she had driven more than a block or two she made a U-turn and headed back. She confessed that she had driven back and forth at least a dozen times before finally deciding to park the car and "confront me." She was convinced that I had designs on her sexually and that sexual involvement was the price I would exact if she wanted to stay in treatment.

Blaming, finally, can be seen in cases of patients who projectively identify through dependency. Very often these patients accuse their therapist of not letting them grow up. In the course of working with such patients, I have been accused of giving too much advice, of being too directive, and of being "too much of a mother." Often the accusations border on the ludicrous considering the amount of help-seeking in which the patient engages. But such remarks are made with such intensity that one cannot but be convinced that the patient truly believes them.

Whether blaming occurs in the context of a projective identification of dependency, sexuality, power, or ingratiation, it arises out of the patient's awareness that the projective identification is in danger of being eradicated. The patient's defensive efforts signify an attempt to block the therapist's inroads into the interpersonal pathology. In an attempt to fend off imminent exposure, the patient settles upon what is perceived as a source of therapist vulnerability—the countertransference. It is as if the patient in desperation has decided that the best defense is a good offense.

Secondary Projective Identifications

There are some occasions where confrontation results in neither intensification of the metacommunicative demand nor blaming of the therapist. Instead the patient seems to abandon the projective identification. This, of course, is what one hopes will happen in this stage of treatment. The therapist wants to get beyond the projective fantasy and help the patient explore what it means to be in a relationship without projective identification.

Instead something quite different happens. In the midst of what seems to be a period of calm and reflection, another projective identification begins to emerge. Patients who were ingratiating suddenly react in accord with a projective identification of dependency. If they were behaving dependently before, they start to behave in ways that are more in line with a sexual projective identification. It is as if another projective identification were waiting in the wings as a backup in case anything went wrong. And now that it has, the secondary projective identification makes its appearance.

The theatrical metaphor perhaps misrepresents the speed at which this occurs. It is not simply a matter of one projective identification making its exit and the second one bursting on the scene to take its place. Rather, the second projective identification emerges slowly and makes itself known in subtle ways. But the impact it has is undeniable. It forces the therapy back into stage two and forces the therapist to deal with what is essentially a whole new set of communications and metacommunications.

The foregoing can be seen in a series of interchanges between a patient name Beth and myself which began with a confrontation of a projective identification of dependency (Cashdan, 1973). There had been a great deal of emotional turmoil associated with the confrontation, and toward the end of the session the patient indicated that she didn't think she would be coming back. Beth nevertheless showed up the next session to continue the therapy.

The neediness and help-seeking that had characterized our sessions up till then toned down considerably, but in the sessions that followed Beth began to bring in more and more material about her sexual involvements. During one of these she described a date with a man which ended in heavy petting. Beth's description included a highly detailed account of how the man brought her to orgasm.

The following sequence begins with my response to the sexual metacommunication:

THERAPIST Why all the details? Were they all really necessary?

BETH You never seemed bothered by details before.

THERAPIST But you could have just told me you petted with the guy and left it at that.

BETH (emphatically) I just thought you should know.

THERAPIST (after more questioning of this sort) I think you were just trying to get me hot.

BETH (in a half-surprised, half-joking tone) You dirty old lecher.

THERAPIST They're your stories.

BETH (now getting very serious) You're crazy!

THERAPIST They're your stories and they're very sexy.

BETH (angrily) Let's change the subject: I don't want to talk about it anymore. (Cashdan, 1973, pp. 89–90)

I did, however, continue to press the matter and in the next session the meta-communication came to the surface when Beth asked me to go drinking with her after the therapy session so that I could get to know her better.

A similar shift involving the same two projective identifications (dependency and sexuality) occurred with Mrs. N., the woman who as a 10-year-old was made to feel responsible for her mother's suicide. It will be recalled that Mrs. N. relied heavily on what was clearly a projective identification of dependency and put her therapist on the ropes by constantly threatening to kill herself. This did not diminish until the therapist confronted her with the manipulative nature of her suicide threats. But though the frequency of suicidal threats decreased and Mrs. N. began to speak more in the sessions, her attempts at manipulating the therapist did not. Some time thereafter, the therapy began to take on sexual overtones:

Over the next several months, the therapist noted that the patient seemed sexually attractive to him for the first time. The patient had made only fleeting references to sex during the first two years of the therapy but now began to complain that she hated the way her husband acted as if sex with her was his right. (Ogden, 1982, p. 61)

The introduction of sexual content into the therapy combined with what seems to be indications of a sexual countertransference suggests the beginning of a sexual projective identification. The fact that this comes so soon on the heels of a successful confrontation of another projective identification (dependency) indicates that sexuality probably existed as a secondary projective identification all along.

The appearance of secondary projective identifications often is discouraging because it seems to represent a therapeutic setback. But even though it technically is, it typically is not cause for dismay. Though one has to repeat much of what was enacted earlier so as to force the metacommunication associated with the new projective identification into the open, this is not as time-consuming or difficult as it is the first time.

To begin with, the dyadic nature of the therapy has already been established. One doesn't need to expend a great of energy moving the therapy into the "here-and-now." The therapist also is more attuned to his or her countertransferential reactions to the patient and so can more readily identify and use them. Finally, the simple fact that the secondary projection is secondary means that it is not as well entrenched or defended against. It thus is easier to coax the metacommunication associated with it to the surface.

The therapeutic response to the secondary projective identification is the same as the response to the first. The therapist needs to solicit a direct behavioral expression of the metacommunication and then confront it. There are no shortcuts, no interpretive "connections" that substitute for the confrontation that needs to occur. Regardless of whether the projective identification operating at the moment is primary or secondary, the patient needs to learn that it cannot be used as a legitimate means of relating to the therapist.

Leavetaking

If all else fails, patients very often threaten to leave. Having done everything in their power to keep the relationship intact, they feel there is nothing else they can do. The bottom has fallen out and they see only one alternative: terminating treatment. Whether in anger or resignation, the patient announces that there is no reason to continue. The therapist wants nothing to do with him and it seems that any future contact would prove futile if not painful.

This decision is based on the patient's shadowy but powerful belief that the therapist's rejection of the projective identification means that the therapist has "discovered" the split-off bad parts of the self. It needs to be kept in mind that projective identifications are a means of forming relationships, a defense against exposure of the bad self, and a way of righting archaic and painful object relationships. In failing to accomplish the first two, the patient sees no hope of ever accomplishing the third. There seems no alternative but to take leave of the therapy and the therapist.

[margin note:] Reasons for P.Id. / 2, 3

But it is not that easy to leave. Despite the anger and disappointment currently being felt, the patient feels a certain, somewhat inexplicable, connection with the very person who seems responsible for his predicament. This affinity is the residual effect of the emotional bonding that took place in the very beginning of therapy. This is why it was so important to expend energy engaging the patient in stage one. The emotional connections which formed the basis for engagement now reassert themselves and act as buffers against current feelings of loss and rejection.

The therapist uses this as a basis for reaffirming the relationship. It is at this critical juncture in the treatment process that the therapist needs to concretely demonstrate his ongoing commitment. The therapist needs to let the patient know in no uncertain terms that the therapy, far from being over, is as viable as ever. The more concrete one can be about it, the more effective it is. One way of doing this is by simply telling the patient that you still are his therapist and that the therapy hour belongs to him.

Thus, Beth responded to confrontation of the neediness and help-seeking in her primary projective identification by crying and accusing me of destroying her. After about ten minutes of sobbing, the following sequence ensued:

> BETH Does it pay for me to keep coming?
> THERAPIST I'll be here next week . . . same time, same place.
> BETH I'm not sure I'll be coming.
> THERAPIST You decide what's best. Just remember, this time is yours;
>   I'll be here no matter what you decide (Cashdan, 1973, p. 89).

It is noteworthy that Beth's initial leavetaking response ("Does it pay for me to keep coming?") was phrased in terms of a dependent communication, i.e., advice-seeking. In any case, she returned in the next session and resumed the therapy. It was not until some sessions later that the secondary projective identification (sexuality) emerged.

However the patient responds to therapist confrontation, the therapist must take care not to abandon his efforts prematurely for fear that the patient will get too upset or quit treatment. Doing so only allies the therapist with those inner relational forces that perpetuate the patient's pathological behavior. If patients are to free themselves from the forces that perpetuate their projective identifications, they must transcend their metacommunicative ways of dealing with people. They must confront the therapist as a human being in his own right, not as an extension of a projective fantasy.

THE RELATIONAL SHIFT

By the end of the third stage, patients begin to realize that their maladaptive ways of relating to the therapist are no longer viable. Their behavior takes on a less driven quality and they begin to interact with the therapist somewhat differently. Instances of projective identification crop up now and then but they become less frequent and less intense as time goes by. A calm settles over the relationship and the patient starts to wonder what comes next.

This shift in the therapist-patient relationship marks the beginning of the fourth and final stage. Something has changed but the patient still is not sure what it is. There still is no cognitive appreciation of what has happened or how it bears on past object relations. All the patient knows is that the relationship feels very different from the way it felt before. This signals a significant turning point in the treatment process.

One of the things I ask patients once therapy is over is whether they can identify a "turning point" in the therapy. More often than not, they point to something that occurred during the third stage of treatment. Beth told me that the turning point for her occurred when she "returned" to therapy and found I was waiting for her as I said I would. She said that from that moment on something changed in our relationship and she began to see herself differently.

Pam responded in a similar fashion. She had absolutely no doubt that things changed dramatically the night she drove back and forth outside my office, vacillating over whether or not to come up to see me. She said that her decision to come up and deal with the sexual nature of our relationship marked the beginning of significant changes in the therapy. In retrospect, she also thought it signaled important changes in her relationship with others.

The end of stage three brings a sense of relief not only for the patient but for the therapist as well. A series of difficult interchanges has been enacted and the participants have come through much together. There are still some important occurrences that loom ahead, not the least of which is termination, but the character of the therapy has definitely changed. Confrontation has cleared the air and patient and therapist sense that something different lies ahead. It is with this feeling that therapist and patient enter the final phase of treatment.

CHAPTER 7

Stage Four: Termination

The fourth and final stage of object relations therapy provides patients with an appreciation of the way their projective identifications affect others. It also provides them with some insight into the etiology of their maladaptive ways of relating and some understanding of how earlier relationships figure into these patterns. Finally, it addresses issues having to do with termination. Leaving the therapy means more than simply wrapping up loose ends and saying goodbye. It means dealing with issues of separation and the meaning it has for the way one functions as an autonomous human being.

The last stage of therapy tends to be a relatively subdued period in the treatment process. It is a time for reflection, a time for sober reconsideration of all that has gone before. The therapy becomes somewhat cerebral and directed to outside concerns. This also is a period in therapy during which more interpretive activity occurs. At the same time, the therapist must take care not to turn the therapy outward prematurely. To maximize the potential benefits of object relations treatment, the therapist needs to stay "in the room" just a bit longer and to continue to focus on the therapy relationship. The specific form this focus takes is feedback.

FEEDBACK

Most patients are relatively unaware of the kinds of messages they convey through their projective identifications. People who are self-sacrificing only rarely appreciate that their behavior is, in fact, manipulative. Patients who are seductive very often express legitimate surprise that they are sending out erotic signals. The behaviors and communications that make up projective identifications are a way of life, and persons who use them often are surprised to learn that they are acting in other than ordinary ways.

Most patients also are quite oblivious of the impact their projective identifications have on others. They are unaware that the people with whom they interact harbor strong feelings about how manipulative and constraining their behavior may be. They may acknowledge that people get frustrated with them and occasionally withdraw, but they are never really sure why. For them, the emotional behavior of others frequently is a mystery.

A major goal in the fourth and final stage of treatment is to provide patients with vital information about the way they are perceived by others. Patients need to learn in a very direct and immediate way how their interpersonal manipulations affect those about them. This is accomplished by providing patients with feedback about what it is like to be the recipient of their projective manipulations. The purpose of this is to furnish them with a "processed version" of the projection identification so that it can be assimilated (re-internalized) and used to modify internal self-object relationships (Ogden, 1982, p. 17).

To maximize the therapeutic effect of this "processed" feedback, the therapist needs to keep it on a personal plane. The therapist should avoid getting into long hypothetical explanations of how the patient's wife, husband, coworkers, and children are likely to perceive or respond to the patient. Instead of dealing in generalities or with the hypothetical reactions of others, the therapist draws upon his own experiences with the patient as a source of feedback.

It is in this stage of therapy that I tell patients who engage in projective identifications of dependency how their constant requests for direction and advice leave me feeling frustrated and annoyed. Rather than making me feel protective and solicitous, I feel put upon and taken advantage of. I pointed this out to Beth and enumerated the many times I felt this way, giving specific examples. One of them was the time she felt like walking out of therapy and virtually asked me for permission to do so.

Along similar lines, I tell patients who have expressed suicidal intentions at an earlier point in treatment that their suicidal threats frightened me at the time. I reveal that my first impulse was to wash my hands of them and thus eschew responsibility for what they might do. I tell these patients that my immediate impulse was to refer them to a psychiatrist for drug treatment or possible hospitalization. I let them know that whatever care and compassion I felt was overshadowed by an impulse to put distance between myself and them.

Once again, we see the countertransference utilized as a therapeutic tool. But now it is used for feedback. In relying on his personal response to the patient as a source of feedback, the therapist uses the countertransference in a new way. In the beginning of treatment, it was employed as a diagnostic aid to identify the projective identification. Later in treatment, it was used to pinpoint the precise character of the metacommunication. Now it is used as a means of providing valuable information to the patient about the impact his behavior has on others.

Whereas a great deal of the feedback that is provided is retroactive, in that it bears on incidents that took place in earlier stages, much of it also bears on what is happening at the moment. The behaviors that make up the patient's projective identification do not disappear overnight. Dependent patients tend to have a pleading or whiny quality in their voice. Often there is a pained expression on their face when they ask for help. Patients who use projective identifications of power continue to be critical and to make imperious remarks. There frequently is a belligerent quality in their utterances of which they are hardly aware. And patients who use projective identifications of sexuality color much of what they say and do in erotic ways.

My tendency in all these instances is to simply comment on what is going on. I may say something in the order of, "Do you know that whenever you ask me something, there is a pleading quality in your voice?" I may follow up by telling the patient that whenever this happens, I have the feeling that he will fall apart if I don't come up with the right answer. More importantly, I make it known that I feel uncomfortable when this happens and that it puts distance between the two of us. I indicate that I don't want to feel as if I have failed if the advice I offer doesn't improve matters.

In a similar vein, I point up the erotic connotations of what is currently said or done in patients who employ sexual projective identifications. I told one patient whom I had confronted over a projective identification of sexuality and who continued to adopt highly revealing postures that, while her behavior turned me on, it left me with the feeling that "she lived between her legs." I was quite explicit about the particular way she hiked up her skirt, about how she coquettishly cast her eyes downward while making suggestive remarks, and about the other ways in which her behavior had become habitually locked into erotic patterns.

Rather than getting upset at what I said, the patient responded with intense interest and was eager to learn more. It was as if I had revealed a part of herself of which she was relatively unaware. It is noteworthy that patients almost always respond positively to such feedback, especially when it occurs at this point in the treatment process. Although the patient said that "acting sexy" made her feel better about herself, she had no idea how much her sexual way of being in a relationship affected the way others responded to her.

As the projective identification recedes into the background, vestigial expressions of it can be addressed in a more relaxed and lighthearted way. The patient described above had made it a practice to attend therapy in stylish but revealing outfits. This changed somewhat once the metacommunicative aspects of her behavior were addressed, although she continued to dress quite fashionably. In one session, though, I was taken somewhat aback when she arrived in baggy pants and a draped and somewhat formless blouse. This was a rather dramatic turnabout. When I jokingly commented, "You'll soon look like a man," she laughed and replied, "I'm doing it for your own protection."

Aside from the purely informational value that feedback provides, its introduction into the therapy signifies a major shift in the nature of the relationship. The feedback—born as it were of the countertransference—is a gift of sorts, a part of the therapist that the therapist gives to the patient. Whereas earlier, only the therapist could "use the countertransference," now the patient can use it as well. The fact that another person is willing to share his personal experience, the fact that it is given as an offering rather than as an accusation, allows the patient to experience what it feels like to be in an open relationship with another human being.

This constitutes a very different kind of a relationship than the patient's previous relationships. For perhaps the first time in his life, the patient experiences what it is like to interact with another human being without having to be defensive or having to resort to manipulations. For perhaps the first time, the patient comes to experience what it means to have a friend in the profoundest sense of the word (Schofield, 1964, p. 109).

There is a passage in the film *Ordinary People* in which the protagonist, Conrad, asks his therapist, "Are you my friend?" It comes toward the end of the therapy after Conrad has been through a series of painful but powerful confrontations. His therapist, Dr. Berger, answers "yes" and embraces the boy. Soon thereafter the two are able to explore the circumstances underlying the death of Conrad's brother. Like Conrad, patients who reach this point in object relations therapy come to experience what it means to be in a relationship where openness and self-exposure do not imply danger and potential rejection.

What this connotes in object relations therapy is the subtle beginnings of an internalization process that in many ways acts to counterbalance the forces of projective identification. As the patient "releases" the therapist from the relational vise of the projective identification, the therapist comes to take on the characteristics of a "good object." The therapist ceases to be a transformed version of the bad mother who hopefully will reverse the painful inner scenarios of early life. Instead the therapist becomes for the patient a significant positive introject in his or her own right.

It is difficult to convey the depth of this experience without getting maudlin or sentimental. But it is fair to say that patients who go through the process find it very powerful. They describe it as "freeing" and even exhilarating. Patients who relinquish their projective ways of being in the world feel as if a millstone has been lifted from their necks. They begin to see human relationships in a different light and are able to consider options which they have never before thought possible.

INTERPRETATION

It was pointed out earlier that interpretation does not play a major part in object relations therapy. But this does not mean that interpretation has no place in the treatment process. It is simply that the emphasis on projective identifications and their modification favors the use of confrontation and other reactive techniques as the therapeutic interventions of choice. Although the therapist may interpret and communicate information, it is the restructuring of the relationship that is essential to lasting change.

The reason that object relations therapy emphasizes relational restructuring as opposed to cognitive restructuring is that the theory upon which object relations formulations are based focuses on events that are essentially prelinguistic in nature. Phenomena such as splitting and the development of self-object representations occur so early that they are not linguistically codified. It is difficult for the patient to comprehend the meaning of what occurred very early in life if the tools of comprehension, i.e. words, were not as yet conceived.

This poses a paradox. How does one explore events that are linguistically inaccessible? How does one come to understand and give meaning to events that occurred before the linguistic foundations of memory were set? One way is to simply acknowledge that something pathogenic occurred very early in life. While its precise nature may never be accessed, the very fact that it did occur is something that can be shared. This in itself may be therapeutic.

Bearing this limitation in mind, one still can explore later interactions with significant figures in the patient's life by viewing them as sequelae of early pathogenic interactions. Though years may pass and relationships change, pathological relationships retain a core of similarity. The woman who used her one-year-old to masturbate still regarded him as a penis seven years later. And a parent who forms a dependent object relation with a child at six months is more than likely to instill helplessness in the child at six years. One can get at the core of the patient's pathogenic object relations without having to delve into irrecoverable events of infancy.

How, then, do interpretations in an object relations therapy differ from interpretations in more traditional approaches? The answer lies in the nature of the issues that are highlighted. Within more traditional approaches, i.e., those that are more oedipally directed, interpretive activities are apt to focus on issues of parental dominance, parent-child rivalries, and the discharge of libidinal tensions. In object relations therapy, the significant issues have more to do with threats of abandonment, rejection, and "good" and "bad" internalizations.

Ogden provides an example of the foregoing in his description of a therapy with a patient whose history was punctuated by unfulfilling relationships with men (1982, pp. 91–102). The patient, Miss R., sought therapy after a breakup with her most recent boyfriend left her feeling that life had become "unbearable." Her relationship with him had been very intense and dependent, and represented the fourth time in 12 years that a close relationship had ended in shambles.

In the course of treatment, the patient revealed that her relationships with men generally left her feeling tormented, embarrassed and humiliated. The tormented nature of these relationships surfaced in the interaction with the therapist. In the course of treatment, the patient would do things that seemed designed to goad the therapist into attacking her. When he pointed this out to her, she became very distant and removed. It was almost as if she ceased to be in the room.

The patient's reaction and her feelings about it eventually were linked to a tormenting-tormented relationship with her mother, a powerful, angry woman who constantly demeaned her daughter and subjected her to ruthless attacks. The patient remembered her childhood as consisting of a "barrage of verbal attacks from a mother whose venom seemed to increase instead of subside with each assault." She was told by her mother that she was incorrigibly stupid, unlikable and exceedingly ugly.

In a particularly intense session, the therapist made the following interpretation: "You must have struggled desperately to be a child your mother could despise and torment, because you must have been afraid that if you weren't, you would have ceased to exist for her at all" (p. 99). By calling attention to issues of abandonment, acceptability, and even existence, the therapist used interpretation to highlight a relational dynamic that was at the core of the patient's feelings of goodness and badness.

A similar intervention can be seen in my work with Pam, although the interpretations centered on her relationship with her father. This took place some time after the rainy evening in which Pam drove back and forth past my office, frightened of coming up to see me. Discussing her fearfulness and the role that sexual feelings played in it enabled us to explore the role that sexuality played in relationships with men in general, including her father who constantly subjected her to salacious stories.

In the course of one of our discussions, I said to her, "Your feeling that I only value you for sexual reasons don't seem that different from the kinds of feelings that make you feign interest in your father's dirty jokes." Pam responded to this somewhat sadly but agreed that this was the case. This led to further examination of other episodes involving interactions with her father in which her physical attractiveness was a focal point. As we dis-cussed these, Pam came to recognize how her sense of worth had become almost exclusively tied up with providing sexual satisfaction.

The more that the interactions between father and daughter were exam-ined, the more evident it was that the father's needs rather than Pam's fantasies were the driving force behind the relationship. This was not a case of a young child whose oedipal (or electral) longings led to the repression of libidinal urges. It was a case of a child who had been "relationally abused" by a man who taught her that she was valued only for her looks. The interpretations made in this phase of treatment focused on this and the implications it had for Pam's feelings of self-worth and acceptability.

Though interpretations are not a major part of object relations therapy, they can help the patient translate one type of experience—a feeling about oneself—into another type of experience—interaction with another person. In some ways, this constitutes a developmental reversal of the process in which interactions with others were transformed into a sense of self. What this does is allow the patient to construe feelings of goodness and badness in terms of good and bad experiences with specific individuals. This ulti-mately functions as a basis for "letting go."

LETTING GO

In order to be able to successfully terminate treatment, patients need to be able to let go of pathological object relations. To be more specific, patients need to be able to break loose from figures in the past with whom patho-logical bonds have been formed. This has been impossible until now be-cause the figures who were instrumental in formation of the bad self are the same ones responsible for whatever feelings of goodness (desirability) exist. To "let go" is tantamount to relinquishing the good parts of the self as well as the bad.

For the patient to let go of a significant object relation, there needs to be a restitutive object to take its place. For most of the patient's life, such an object did not exist. There was no inner object that communicated, "You are good; you are worthwhile; you are valued." Whenever a relationship that contained this kind of potential came into being, the corrupting effect of the patient's projective identification undermined it. There consequently was no lasting relationship in which the patient could feel loved and accepted apart from his ability to fulfill another person's needs.

The therapy dramatically changes this. Now there is the relationship with the therapist. In object relations therapy the therapist does more than just help the patient deal with inner objects. In the course of treatment, *he becomes one of these objects*. By allowing himself to become part of the patient's projective fantasy and rearranging the outcome of the relational scenario that ensues, the therapist becomes a powerful new presence in the patient's inner world. The therapist thus functions as an internal counter-force that enables the patient to combat—and ultimately let go of—the destructive object relations that existed beforehand.

Practically speaking, patients never totally relinquish their inner objects. Miss R.'s mother and Pam's father are a part of them and will be to the day they die. But internalization of the therapist and the security it creates enable the patient to experience parts of early objects that previously were split off. Inner objects earlier experienced as all good *or* all bad now are experienced as good *and* bad. What the patient needs to let go of is the restrictive view that has been nurtured by highly polarized inner representations.

What does it mean to "let go"? It means to forgive. It means being able to experience one's inner objects as fallible and to absolve them of their shortcomings. The patient needs to see his early caretaker(s) as flawed human beings who were incapable of engaging the patient in a nonmanipulative relationship because of their own shortcomings (Hope, 1987). Unless the patient forgives his inner objects, the patient will find it impossible to forgive himself.

Therapists nowadays are devoting increasing attention to the role that forgiveness plays in releasing residual feelings of bitterness. Johnson (1985) suggests that, "The final, necessary step [in therapy] is *forgiveness*: forgiveness of what happened, forgiveness for what is happening, forgiveness of what may still happen" (p. 298). The therapist needs to point the patient in this direction, so that by the time the fourth stage in therapy is near completion the patient is capable of absolving early objects. The patient does not have to forgive these object for what they did, but rather for their inability to appreciate the devastating psychological legacy it would leave behind.

At the end of my therapy with Pam, she was able to transcend her bitterness and to see her father as the somewhat limited individual he was. As we talked about their relationship, she was able to appreciate that he not only deprived Pam of the kind of relationship she deserved but in many ways deprived himself of Pam. With me as an inner ally, Pam finally could confront the "bad father" in her and say no to it. At the end of therapy, Pam had a "different" father. She was sad about what she had lost, but she was able to forgive him for what he was.

Forgiveness is not always easy. Often it needs to be preceded by anger or other intense feelings that have been stored up for years. An instance of this was graphically demonstrated in a group therapy led by myself and a cotherapist, Ruth. The group, designed to deal with relational issues associated with divorce and separation, consisted of six women.

One of the members, a somewhat depressed woman in her early twenties, had recently separated from her husband after being married a little more than a year. Although shy and somewhat withdrawn in the beginning, Celia revealed that the reason for the separation was that she and her husband had drifted apart, and that she felt responsible for it. For some unfathomable reason, she had become increasingly cold and distant from him. In addition, lovemaking had become unpleasant, even repugnant, for her, and in the end the two had decided to separate.

As the group began to gel and the members became more intimate with one another, it became clear that something traumatic had occurred early in Celia's life. It was difficult to get her to talk about her childhood. When she did, she painted an obscure picture, particularly with regard to her father, who came across as a vague and shadowy figure. In addition, she tended to react to me in a peculiar way. At times she seemed to be very compliant, almost as if she wanted me to see her as a "good little girl." At other times she made me feel as if my questions constituted a personal violation of sorts.

In one session somewhere well along in the group's existence, Celia began to refer to an incident that occurred when she was eight or nine. It involved her father and had frightened her enormously. Even though she tried to talk about it, she had a lot of difficulty doing so. Sensing that Celia's story probably had incestuous overtones, and feeling that she needed to confront what had happened, I encouraged her to tell the group about it.

Celia began by telling about going to bed one evening and waking up to find her father standing at the side of the bed. I asked her to go on:

CELIA He sat down on the bed and stroked my hair.
THERAPIST And then . . .
CELIA He told me that he loved me.
THERAPIST And you told him that you loved him.
CELIA Uh huh.
THERAPIST And what did he do then?
CELIA (after much hesitation) He put his hand under my nightie.
THERAPIST And . . .
CELIA (after more hesitation) He put his hand between my legs.
THERAPIST And . . .
CELIA And he did things to me (crying).
THERAPIST And he did it more than once.
CELIA (Nodding)
THERAPIST And again and again.
CELIA Yes.

There was a long pause, after which I said, "And you were the little cockteaser that led him on."

For a moment there was silence. Then pandemonium broke loose in the room. Celia began to shout hysterically, "I didn't mean to. I didn't mean to." She screamed and cried at the top of her lungs while repeating the same phrase over and over. The group members, first shocked, turned their attention to me and began to denounce and condemn me.

Some of the women rose from their seats to comfort Celia and tried to calm her down. I told them to let her be; I insisted she had to confront what happened and to deal with the guilt surrounding it. I even pried their hands away from her shoulders, which only enraged them more. Fortunately, Ruth was in the room. It was perhaps even more fortunate that she was a woman. She asked the group to back off and to let Celia go through whatever she was going through. I am convinced her presence saved the day.

The next 15 minutes were perhaps the longest 15 minutes I ever spent as a therapist. I felt as if I had pushed the Celia over the edge. She seemed unable to stop crying and gulped for air in paroxysmal fashion. Finally, she began to quiet down. When she finally stopped crying, she described in painstaking fashion how she had lived with her terrible secret and how for most of her life she felt responsible for what had happened.

Once things calmed down, the members of the group addressed the issue of culpability. As they did, the anger and depression that had been stored up in Celia for years began to surface. In the process, she began to see that her love for her father was so great that it prevented her from believing that he was to blame for what had happened. Loving him as she did, she concluded that she somehow must have led him on.

The members of the group continued to support Celia and helped her get in touch with the feelings of anger and betrayal associated with her trauma. When the group came to an end, she thanked me and the other members for helping her come to grips with what had happened to her as a child. She indicated as she left that she planned to pursue individual therapy. I do not know whether she ever did or whether she was able to forgive her father for what had happened. Perhaps forgiveness in such instances is too much to expect, but it at least should be explored. Otherwise relationships with abusive inner objects, though understood, are apt to be experienced as self-punishment (guilt) and self-hate.

But it may be that forgiveness for some patients may be impossible. Roy, the black child who suffered from pica and whose parents had deserted him, had constructed an idealized picture of his parents that was virtually impregnable. According to Roy, his father was a preacher and was traveling around the country spreading the word of the Lord. His mother was a gospel singer and accompanied him in his mission. The reason they did not come to visit him was that they were so busy spreading the word of God. I was not able to challenge Roy's vision in any meaningful way and finally decided that it probably was wiser not to. It may be that at the age of 10, forgiveness is just too much to ask.

Where forgiveness of past objects is possible, it fosters the relationship-enhancing experiences that were set into motion by the events of the previous stages. The therapist's acceptance of the patient in the face of the patient's projective onslaughts is a form of forgiveness in its own right. In optimal circumstances, it comes to be internalized as self-forgiveness. Forgiveness of past objects strengthens this but is not absolutely necessary for successful therapy to occur.

SEPARATION

Separation is a difficult process under any circumstance. It is especially difficult in a therapy where the relationship with the therapist is the central ingredient. It therefore follows that separation of the patient from the therapist needs to be regarded as a salient feature of the therapeutic experience rather than as something simply tacked on at the end of treatment.

The act of separating entails more than just shaking hands and wishing the patient well. It constitutes the culmination of a powerful internalization process that begins with the patient's incorporation of the therapist into a projective fantasy and ends with the patient's developing the capacity for forgiveness. In the course of therapy, the therapist is incorporated within the patient's inner world and integrated into the patient's self as a significant object.

The process by which this takes place in some ways mirrors earlier interactions in which significant relationships with others also were transformed into a sense of self. One of my patients, an accountant in his thirties who typically would become extremely anxious in social situations and then become depressed over "being a failure," described his experience of the process to me in this way:

In the beginning of therapy, I was completely confused about how to respond to others when they were critical. For that matter, I didn't know how to act when they were nice. I would wonder, "What should I say?" or "What should I do?" No matter what I decided, I always felt as if I had made the wrong choice. But somewhere toward the middle of therapy, I began to hear myself ask, "What would you [referring to the therapist] do in this situation?" And then I would talk to you about it in my head. At the end of therapy, I found I wasn't doing this anymore. I simply would ask myself, "What would be the best way to handle this?" and I just did whatever seemed right.

The progression from an inner dialogue with the therapist to an inner dialogue with oneself ("I simply would ask myself") reflects the progression from interaction with inner objects to interaction with the self that was described in Chapter 2.

But the significance of all this is not simply that the therapist is internalized. It is that he is internalized as a "good object." In the course of treatment, the therapist is, in the words of Kohut, "internally transmuted" into a source of worth and self-esteem. The growing sense that one is desirable and worthwhile forms the basis for the patient's restructuring of his inner world and of relationships in the external world. A fortified self, strengthened by the incorporation of a good inner object, constitutes the means by which object relations therapy is "transported" into the world at large.

As the therapist becomes more and more a part of the patient's inner world, the patient needs to rely less and less on the therapist's physical presence to feel secure. One could say the therapist has functioned as a transitional object of sorts. Just as the young child needs a transitional object to provide solace and security until he can physically and perceptually let go of the mother, so the patient needs the therapist to smooth the transition between letting go of bad objects and incorporation of good ones. But unlike a transitional object, the therapist is not relegated to a dark corner of a closet or a box in a musty attic. Though therapist and patient must part, the therapist remains a part of the patient's inner world.

To ensure that separation is not experienced by the patient as a catastrophic loss or as abandonment, the therapist needs to actively engage the patient in the separation experience. The therapist does this by making the feelings and thoughts associated with termination explicit. His job is to enable the patient to talk about the apprehension and sadness, as well as the exhilaration, that the patient feels. There is joy *and* sadness in parting, which gives it the potential of being a very meaningful interpersonal event in the patient's life.

To make this work, the therapist needs to acknowledge that he also harbors feelings about separation. The end of therapy is not a sad event only for the patient; if the therapist has truly been "with the patient" in the way that object relations therapy suggests is necessary, there is a sense of loss on the therapist's part as well. I think it is very important to share some of this with one's patients. I almost always do. I make it a point to let my patients know that I am gratified that they have reached this juncture in their lives and saddened by the fact that they no longer will be an active part of mine.

It is difficult to capture the depth of feelings that often characterizes the end of therapy. Therapists tend to avoid talking about the loss and emptiness they feel after separating from patients with whom they have worked for long periods of time and on whom they have expended great amounts of emotional energy. It almost seems unprofessional. Chances are that feelings of this sort touch on experiences of personal loss or are a reminder of the therapist's own early experiences of separation (Beitman, 1987, p. 264). Acknowledging these feelings can lead to separation experiences that are growth-producing for patient and therapist alike.

Taking all this into consideration, it perhaps is appropriate to return to the place where I began—to my work with Roy and the pictures he drew in the course of therapy (see Chapter 2). It may be recalled that one of the last pictures Roy painted depicted a number of spaceships departing the moon. It also may be remembered that the picture showed a single figure stranded on the moon's surface. Roy produced the drawing shortly after he learned that I would be leaving the institution.

The sessions that followed this drawing were stormy to say the least. They included intense expressions of anger as well as periods of withdrawal. On a couple of occasions, Roy refused to come to therapy and I had to go to the ward to fetch him. It was abundantly clear that he felt I was leaving him because he was bad. My departure was an abandonment—incontrovertible proof that he could not be loved.

It took a while to get beyond this and for Roy to share his feelings of sadness and loss with me. I shared similar feelings of my own with him. Though I admittedly felt bad about having to leave him (I think I still do to this day), our relationship began to take on a different flavor. This is reflected in the last picture that Roy produced. As can be seen in Figure 4, Roy is sailing on a ship with me standing on the deck beside him (in those days, I smoked and wore horn-rimmed glasses). The sea is serene and a sense of calm, even optimism, pervades the scene. With only a bit of imagination, one can view it in its original colors. The sun is bright yellow as it peeps from behind the clouds and the sea is azure blue.

Like the first picture that Roy drew (see Figure 1, p. 31), this one also is set on the open sea. But the two are vastly different in emotional tone. The first picture showed planes and submarines attacking a boat and trying to sink it. It was a picture of chaos and imminent destruction. This is a picture of tranquility and integration. Rather than flying apart, things are coming together.

FIGURE 4

The truly gratifying aspect of Roy's drawing came out of our discussion of the work. When I asked Roy to tell me about the picture, he said that it showed the two of us going for a sail. I pressed him about the two small figures in the dinghy at the side of the boat. I asked him to tell me who they were. He thought for a short while and then replied, "They are other little kids looking for help."

Roy's ability to view me outside the context of our immediate relationship was, I think, a indication of his ability to separate. He was able to see me not just as *his* therapist, but as someone capable of giving help to others. What's more, he felt good about it. Responses of this sort—in adults as well as children—are a measure of the patient's ability to part from the therapist in a healthy way and a reflection of the therapy's success.

In the end, the fact of the matter is that our patients become a part of us just as we become a part of them. In the relational dialect of object relations theory, the therapist's identity as a therapist cannot be separated from his relationship with the patient. If "we are our others," then not only is the patient us, but we are our patients.

As the therapy comes to a close, some of this feeling can be shared by something as simple as thanking the patient for putting up with some of the therapist's idiosyncrasies or occasional lapses. The therapist might want to acknowledge the patient's forbearance in the face of trying episodes that occurred during the course of treatment. For a brief moment, patient and therapist have an opportunity to relate not as patient to therapist but as human being to human being. And in the best of all therapeutic worlds, this is how things should be when the therapy comes to a close.

SECTION III

The Therapist

CHAPTER 8

The Personal Side of Object Relations Therapy

There are many factors that come into play in a therapist's decision to pursue a particular therapy as a basis for working with people. Some of these have to do with theoretical considerations. A therapist has to believe that the premises upon which the therapy is based are conceptually sound. The basic principles that govern what takes place in therapy somehow must be consistent with broader principles of human functioning, including principles of human development and human motivation.

A therapist who decides to do object relations work accordingly needs to be convinced of the motivational significance of early object relationships and their influence on later relationships. There also needs to be some appreciation for the way that splitting and projective identification figure in the development and expression of psychopathology. Most important, a clinician who adopts object relations therapy as a means of working with people needs to be committed to the proposition that the therapist-client relationship forms the basis for therapeutic change.

Even if these theoretical and cognitive prerequisites are satisfied, the therapist still needs to feel comfortable carrying out the therapy. There needs to be a fit between the personality of the therapist and the demands of the system. The same could be said for any treatment process. Many of the techniques of Gestalt therapy such as "hot seat" exercises and "top dog-underdog" scenarios require that the therapist feel at ease leading patients through these procedures. Not all therapists do. I suspect that one probably has to be a bit of Fritz Perls or Erving Polster in order to be an effective Gestalt therapist.

Object relations work places its own demands on a therapist. To begin with, there is the matter of what it means to be the target of the patient's projective identification. What does it signify for a therapist's psychological well-being when he or she is "used" in this way? How does the therapist deal with personal feelings of frustration, anger, or depression that are bound to crop up as part of the treatment process?

Salient questions also arise regarding the countertransference. How does the therapist distinguish feelings prompted by the patient's projective identifications from similar feelings that are unrelated to them? How does one discriminate sexual feelings induced by a projective identification of sexuality from sexual feelings that derive from other sources, i.e., from factors in the therapist's life that have little if anything to do with the therapy relationship. Feelings don't come neatly packaged with "Therapy" and "Extratherapy" labels attached to them.

Questions such as these transcend work with particular patients and strike at the core of what it means to do object relations work. Because therapists who do object relations therapy must use themselves as therapeutic instruments, such issues have a direct bearing on the therapist's ability to function effectively. Addressing these issues leads to a keener understanding of one's identity as a therapist and ultimately to more effective treatment.

THE THERAPIST AS TARGET

Allowing oneself to become a focus for the patient's projective identification is not entirely a conscious decision. It is not even entirely up to the therapist. The evolution of a projective identification in the therapy is something that develops primarily out of patients' needs to satisfy their projective fantasies. In fact, the discovery that one has become the target of a projective identification often is made only after the fact. Ogden, for example, states that the recognition that one has become the recipient of a projective identification is "to some extent a retrospective judgment, since the therapist's unconscious participation in [the patient's] interpersonal construction must precede its recognition" (1982, p. 43).

There nevertheless needs to be an understanding on the part of the therapist that projective identifications are going to emerge and that the therapist is going to be a prime target for them. The therapist's initial "willingness" to allow himself to become a recipient of the patient's projective identification interacts with the patient's needs and allows the therapy to take on its object relational character. Still, the therapist's de facto decision to let himself be used in this manner means that he is going to be subjected to unpleasant emotional experiences.

One of these is guilt. I have on numerous occasions, for example, felt very bad about not being able to give a patient what seemed to be demanded of me. One patient asked if I would agree to be a cosigner on a car loan. She said that I knew her best and that unless I cosigned she wouldn't be able to go through with the purchase. Her request was, of course, inappropriate and I felt annoyed at being put in the position of having to say no. At the same time, I felt guilty over having to refuse her. It made me feel like a parent denying his child something he desperately wants or needs. Though I later could appreciate that I had been the target of a projective identification of dependency, it was not that apparent when the request was made.

Strong feelings also are generated when the patient makes thinly veiled suicidal threats. What is the therapist supposed to feel when the patient states that he "can't stand the futility of it all"? What is the therapist to do when a patient makes statements such as this just as he is leaving the office? Should the therapist follow the patient home to make sure he doesn't take a drug overdose or slash his wrists? Obviously not. But that doesn't mean you aren't left with nagging doubts about whether you've done the right thing. To allow oneself to be "used" in this fashion means that you often are going to feel frustrated, put upon, and worried.

Allowing oneself to become the target of projective identifications can also result in strong feelings of anger. Patients who employ projective identifications of power, for example, constantly let the therapist know that they aren't being helped. Some threaten to switch to another therapist (they rarely do), while others make it a point to criticize whatever the therapist does. It is difficult not to become annoyed when this happens, especially when it becomes a regular feature of the therapy.

Some patients make it a point to compare the therapist with a previous therapist (if they have been in treatment before) or with a guru-like figure in their lives. Nothing that the therapist says or does seems to satisfy them or fulfill their expectations. One of my patients responded to practically everything I said with, "That's not the way my last therapist saw it." I recall getting very annoyed and thinking to myself, "Then why don't you go back to him?" If there is one thing that is sure to arouse a therapist's ire, it is a patient who makes you feel as if you don't know what you are doing.

Finally, there is the matter of sex and sexual projective identifications. No one likes to be sexually manipulated. No one enjoys having to deal with sexual matters in contexts where sex seems inappropriate and out of place. The presence of sexual manipulations in therapy seems to violate basic understandings about what is to take place in a professional relation-ship. Therapists often deal with feelings of an erotic nature by either withdrawing or blaming them on the patient. But as can be imagined, this is not conducive to effective therapy.

The upshot of all this is that doing object relations work invariably entails uncomfortable feelings and disquieting thoughts. This is part and parcel of the work. One of the things I tell my supervisees, particularly those who are just starting out, is that somewhere down the line they are going to become the subjects of "therapist abuse." Most fail to take me seriously. Their vision of therapy is one in which the patient, if anyone, goes through emotional turmoil. It is not until they actually do the work and experience what it means to be the target of a projective identification that they seriously begin to appreciate what I mean.

The problems generated in becoming the target of the patient's projec-tive identifications are compounded by the fact that the feelings produced often extend beyond the therapy session. Emotional interchanges with one patient may spill over into a session with another and produce unwanted results. The therapist may be preoccupied, worried, or even upset and not be fully aware that these feeling originate elsewhere. Even if this doesn't happen, the therapist may "store up" his feelings until the end of the day and "take the patient home with him."

There is no simple way of dealing with this dilemma unless one decides to completely dissociate one's feelings from one's experience. On the one hand, the therapist has to guard against becoming so enmeshed in the projective identification that he becomes angry at being manipulated and vents his annoyance at the patient. On the other hand, the therapist doesn't want to become so emotionally distant from what takes place that the countertransference is essentially blocked. The therapist committed to ob-ject relations work is forced to walk a thin emotional line.

There are several ways of dealing with the conflicting feelings that being a target arouses. One is to view the therapy experience as an opportunity for self-exploration and to consider the negative feelings one experiences as the "price" one pays for this learning. Although object relations therapy focuses on the various projective identifications of patients, all of us have dependency, sexuality, ingratiating, and power components within us. In-teractions with patients along these dimensions may allow the therapist to get in touch with and explore parts of himself that otherwise might remain hidden.

Another way is to immerse oneself in the projection and make the best of it, perhaps even revel in it. If a patient engages me in a projective identification of ingratiation, I sometimes let the appreciative part of me enjoy what is happening. I think to myself, "What a nice person (the patient) is. Who else would go out of their way to be so thoughtful and considerate?" In other words, I go along for the ride, convincing myself that I deserve all the consideration and attention I get.

If the patient uses a projective identification of sexuality, I let the sexual part of myself get caught up in the proceedings. I may say to myself, "This isn't bad. What other profession would offer an opportunity not only to get sexually aroused, but to get paid for it as well?" I silently consider how much money *I* should pay the patient for providing me with this sort of pleasure.

And if the patient uses a projective identification of power, I sit back and muse over the possibility that all the criticism being directed my way is well deserved. I listen carefully to what the patient has to say and consider the possibility that his "evaluation" may indeed prove beneficial. If nothing else, taking this stance introduces a measure of humility into the way one approaches one's work.

Sometimes the humor and playfulness of the therapist's inner world can become part of the therapy itself and further the therapeutic interaction. A female patient who used a projective identification of sexuality said to me in the course of describing her sexual exploits, "I'm a regular pistol in bed." I laughed, having never heard that expression before, and responded with, "I can appreciate that by the number of guys you've mowed down." She laughed also and it became easier to discuss the deeper motives that lay behind her sexual behavior. Sometimes a bit of levity helps to counteract some of the negative feelings that arise from being drawn into the patient's pathology.

But not always. The pull of a projective identification often is so strong that the therapist cannot help but become irritated and angry. I think that some of this is unavoidable and is the natural outcome of a successful projective induction. When subjected to these feelings, I try to remind myself that I chose to do this work of my own free will and that responses of this sort go with the territory. This usually does the job and allows me to once again immerse myself in the proceedings. However one goes about it, the important thing is not to take out one's feelings on one's patients. To do so is tantamount to punishing patients for the very reason they are in therapy.

Once the therapist is reconciled to his role as a target, it becomes necessary to deal with the feelings this arouses. To successfully conduct therapy, the therapist needs to be able to use these feelings for therapeutic ends. This raises questions about the character and scope of the countertransference.

COUNTERTRANSFERENCE:
THERAPEUTIC AND OTHERWISE

The one method or procedure that object relations therapy relies upon most is the use of the countertransference. The countertransference enables the therapist to diagnose the nature of the patient's projective identification and also provides clues on how to combat it. It functions as a relational litmus paper of sorts, yielding the critical information upon which feedback to the patient is ultimately based. Most object relations therapists probably would consider a therapy devoid of countertransference incomplete and lacking in substance.

The question arises as to how the therapist knows that countertransference is, in fact, countertransference. How does the therapist know whether feelings experienced during the therapy hour are generated by the patient's projective identification or by events extraneous to it? Is the therapist's impulse to "take care" of a needy patient prompted by a projective identification of dependency or is it prompted by circumstances in the therapist's life that have nothing to do with the patient?

These questions bear on the very nature of what is meant by countertransference. Brief mention was made earlier of the way that the term is construed in traditional psychoanalysis. In psychoanalysis, countertransference is used to describe undesirable, psychogenetically derived responses on the part of the analyst which interfere with the treatment process. Object relations countertransference, in contrast, is generated by the therapy relationship and facilitates rather than impedes what takes place in treatment. Clearly the two are not one and the same.

Once again we have a situation in which the same term is used to describe very different phenomena. Spotnitz (1985) has tried to clarify the situation by making a distinction between the "objective countertransference" and its counterpart, the "subjective countertransference." According to Spotnitz, the objective countertransference describes what the therapist experiences as a result of the "emotional contagion" from the patient. The subjective countertransference refers to everything else and is "equivalent to Freud's description of the countertransference" (Kirman, 1980, p. 133).

While well intentioned, this distinction tends to cloud matters. Both sets of countertransference responses are subjectively felt and felt very intensely. To call one set objective and the other subjective suggests that the therapist is able to distinguish the quality of the emotions felt at any given moment and to identify their source. This rarely is achieved in practice and is at best an ambitious undertaking.

Rather than talk about different categories of countertransference, it might be better to restrict the use of the term to *the emotional reactions of the therapist in response to the patient's behavior in the therapy relationship*. This is how Greenberg and Mitchell define the term: "Countertransference is an inevitable product of the interaction between the patient and the analyst rather than a simple interference stemming from the analyst's infantile drive-related conflicts" (1983, p. 389). This way of defining countertransference is fast becoming the standard in the profession (Kernberg, 1984; Masterson, 1976, 1978; Ogden, 1982; Rinsley, 1982; Searles, 1979). If the term is used in this way, other emotional influences could then be interpreted in light of the way that they affect and possibly interfere with the countertransferential response.

One set of these influences might indeed be psychogenetic (historical) in nature and conform to what traditionally is labeled countertransference in psychoanalytic writings. If this is the case, one could legitimately consider whether a therapist's sexual countertransference is truly a response to the patient's projective identification or a byproduct of an unresolved oedipal conflict. While it may not be possible to completely separate the two, the relative influence of the latter might be gauged by how pervasive and persistent the countertransference is, and how difficult it is for the therapist to address it.

Another set of influences is more contemporary in nature and derives from stresses and strains in the therapist's ongoing relationships. As we interact with our own family members, friends, and colleagues, tensions associated with these interactions may produce emotional responses which can color the patient-induced countertransference. It is quite likely that historical influences have been overexaggerated and that contemporary ones affect the countertransference more than has been previously recognized.

An example of this can be seen in an informal consultation I held with a colleague of mine who was also a personal friend. An experienced therapist, she had become bogged down in a therapy with a patient she had been treating for problems that essentially had to do with separation-individuation. The patient, a grown woman, was infantilized by her mother and had little faith in breaking away from her and leading her own life. Although the patient had come a long way, it seemed that the therapy had reached a plateau. The sessions, filled with aimless rehashing of material that had already been covered, were becoming highly repetitious.

After listening to my friend describe the case and some of the more recent sessions, several things became apparent. One was that the patient seemed to be in pretty good shape. Many of the problems that brought her into treatment had been successfully dealt with and she was beginning to function like an autonomous adult. The other was that my friend and the patient were totally avoiding talk of termination. The more I listened to her describe the case, the more I became convinced that the therapy had achieved its goals and needed to be ended. In terms of object relations therapy, the therapy was mired somewhere in the fourth stage.

Though my friend was not an object relations therapist in the strict sense of the word, her work closely approximated what object relations therapists do. In describing her work with the patient, it was evident that the two had spent much time focusing on their relationship. It was also evident that the manipulations (mostly of a dependent nature) which earlier characterized their relationship had been dealt with therapeutically and now were a thing of the past. The problem was that my colleague still was feeling solicitous and somewhat protective. She interpreted this as a countertransferential indication that the patient still needed to be in treatment.

Since my colleague was also a friend, I happened to know that she recently had been divorced. I also knew that she had been very close to her husband and that he had relied heavily on her over the span of a marriage which had lasted close to 20 years. I asked her whether perhaps the divorce was related to what was taking place in treatment. Perhaps her sense of being needed was affecting her more than she thought and was influencing her work with this particular patient. She seemed somewhat skeptical but said she would give it some thought.

When I ran into her some time later, she told me that the therapy was going well and that she and her patient were very close to terminating. She said that she had considered what I had said and taken a close look at what was happening in the sessions. After examining her behavior, she realized that her feelings about the patient's neediness was, in fact, a function of her own need to be needed and not a function of the patient's dependency. Once she acknowledged this, she was able to broach the subject of termination and the therapy moved off center.

There are other emotionally charged events in a therapist's life in addition to divorce that can affect the nature of the countertransference. One is death or terminal illness in a member of the therapist's immediate family. Shapiro (1985) writes of the prolonged illness and death of her mother and the way it affected her work with one of her patients. She tells of how her own feelings of impending loss interacted with the patient's threat to leave treatment, and how the patient's threat of abandoning her was heightened by what was going on with her mother. Others have written of similar experiences and of their impact on the countertransference (Balsam and Balsam, 1974; Rodman, 1977).

Because of the personal nature of object relations therapy, it is necessary to ensure that the feelings that comprise the countertransference are indeed derivatives of the therapeutic interaction. It is easy for therapists who feel unappreciated by colleagues or family members to see their patients as more ingratiating than they really are. It is common for therapists who are experiencing sexual difficulties in their marriages or other romantic involvements to suddenly become sensitized to sexual cues that weren't evident earlier. And it is not that unusual for therapists who feel unneeded to see their clients as more needy than they really are.

With all these potentially confounding influences, the therapist needs to regularly scrutinize feelings that are considered countertransferential. Sometimes it is possible to call upon someone with whom you work to help in this regard. Ogden, for example, writes, "An ongoing dialogue with a supervisor, consultant, or colleague is often an indispensable adjunct to work with very disturbed patients because of the difficulty [entailed in] recognizing one's unconscious participation in a patient's projective identification" (1982, p. 44). Even if the patient isn't very disturbed, the availability of a sounding board to help sort out countertransferential feelings from other kinds of feelings often makes the difference between a therapy that is relatively lucid and one that is hopelessly confounded.

Failing this, or in addition to it, the therapist must rely on himself. I regularly monitor countertransferential reactions, questioning their origin and wondering whether they can be depended upon. Even though this is time-consuming and often bothersome, I view this as a kind of fine tuning that is necessary if I hope to rely on myself as a "therapeutic instrument" (Ernsberger, 1979). Patients normally resist the confrontations to which they are subjected; unless I am convinced I am on firm ground, I know that I am likely to run into trouble.

One indication that extratherapeutic feelings may be interfering with the countertransference is a caseload in which the same projective diagnosis appears with monotonous regularity. If a therapist diagnoses the projective identification of sexuality in one patient after another, the chances are that something sexually significant is taking place in the therapist's life that is affecting therapeutic perceptions. Though most or even all of a therapist's patients may exhibit projective identifications of sexuality, it is not very likely. If they do, the therapist has a very unique patient pool or a highly selective referral network.

Dealing with the countertransference means that the therapist must, in a sense, do therapy on himself as well as on the patient. This ensures that what happens in the therapy is in the best interest of the patient and of the therapy process. It also contributes to the therapist's personal and professional growth. Rather than being buffeted about by unfathomable forces, the therapist is able to draw upon his total experience to enhance his identity as a therapist and to maximize the chances of successful therapeutic outcomes.

CONFRONTING CONFRONTATION

There are two places in object relations work where the demands of the treatment process place a great deal of pressure on the therapist. One occurs at the end of stage two and centers about the therapist's efforts to elicit a frank expression of the patient's projective identification. This requires a high degree of determination on the part of the therapist as he actively "pursues" the pathological metacommunication until it becomes a palpable part of the relationship.

The other occurs in stage three and involves confrontation. As indicated earlier, confrontation entails more than just pointing out the maladaptive aspects of the patient's projective identification. It involves attacking the premise upon which the patient constructs relationships. If the therapist does not address the metacommunicative basis of the projective identification in a forthright manner, the patient's maladaptive behavior is apt to persist in derivative ways.

Though the need to confront is theoretically persuasive, putting it into practice is another matter. As indicated in an earlier chapter, it is not that easy to say "no" to people who stand before you emotionally bared. Unless a therapist is totally divorced from his feelings, it is hard not to experience guilt when confronting patients who are needy and forlorn. If there is one place in therapy in which the therapist's resolve is put to the test, it typically is in stage three, where confrontation is called for.

There are a number of reasons for this. A very basic one is that confrontation simply does not square with the way most therapists view themselves. As helping professionals, we tend to see ourselves as caring, empathic human beings dedicated to helping others sort out their lives and construct a meaningful existence for themselves. In the process we may resort to various psychological interventions to ensure success. But the reason we resort to these interventions in the first place stems from a sincere desire to reduce suffering.

Confrontation conjures up images of rejection, of denial, of doing something that is contrary to the empathic sensitivity we feel we possess as therapists and human beings. We worry about the negative implications of what we are doing. We wonder whether confrontation might do emotional harm, whether we might cause more suffering than good. If the patient's difficulties are lodged in defective relationships, might not confrontation lead him to construe the ongoing relationship as defective and undermine all that has been accomplished to this point?

I think many of these concerns derive from the therapist's own inner splits and the need to preserve an inner sense of goodness. The necessity for confrontation is at one level a part of doing effective therapy. One needs to confront in order to see the therapy process to its conclusion and be a "good" therapist. But at another level confrontation taps into feelings of badness. To confront connotes rejection and potential harm. In order to deal with these contradictory pulls, the therapist modifies or transforms the confrontation so that the patient does not view the therapist in a bad light.

Some of the inner messages that may accompany or precede efforts at confrontation may take the form of "I have to do this but I don't want you to dislike me" or "I have to do this but I don't want you to get angry at me." In subtle and sometimes not so subtle ways, the therapist qualifies the confrontation to ensure that the patient does not regard him as malevolent. Through the logic of splitting and the inner world, the therapist tries to turn bad into good as a means of keeping an important relationship intact.

The fear that triggers the therapist's efforts in this regard most often has to do with loss. I think that most therapists have a heightened sensitivity about loss either because of personal experiences having to do with abandonment (Semel, 1985) or because they share experiences of this sort with so many of their patients. But even if the history of the therapist does not include profound loss, and even if current loss is not an issue, confrontation still contains risks. Although the groundwork for emotional bonding may have been laid in the early stages of treatment, there is always the possibility that the patient may bolt and quit the therapy for good.

It is not surprising, therefore, that therapists find ways of sidestepping or even avoiding confrontation. Therapists are, in the words of Harry Stack Sullivan, "more human than otherwise." All of us have a stake in seeing the work we do reach a successful conclusion. To ensure that it does, we may unwittingly circumvent the confrontational process in the mistaken belief that such avoidance will lead to positive results.

One way therapists sometimes avoid confrontation is by falling back on relationships outside the therapy. External involvements are used as excuses to soften the confrontation and ostensibly sidestep it. This occurred with a supervisee of mine named Mark who was treating a patient whose major way of relating to people was through a projective identification of sexuality.

The patient, a woman in her late twenties, drank heavily as a means of avoiding recurrent depressions. Her history indicated that her life was composed of a series of superficial and somewhat promiscuous relationships. As a result, she was raising a three-year-old child without benefit of child support because she was unable to identify the father.

In the course of therapy, the nature of the patient's projective identification emerged as she increasingly sexualized the therapy relationship. The patient repeatedly made highly suggestive remarks, struck provocative poses, and expressed an intense interest in Mark's relationships with people outside of therapy. She was particularly interested in his involvements with other women.

Mark was married but did not reveal this to the patient. On a number of occasions, he deflected the patient's questions about his personal life by turning them back on her. He would say things like, "You seem to have a strong interest in me. I wonder whether this is a way of not talking about yourself." Other times, he would simply turn the conversation in the direction of the patient's current romantic involvements.

But as the therapy progressed, the therapy relationship became more the focus of the hour. The character of the patient's projective identification became more evident as she became increasingly provocative and sexually emboldened. This culminated in a request on her part that she and Mark meet someplace apart from the clinic setting. She wanted Mark to see her as a person, not just a patient, so as to "broaden and enrich" their relationship.

Mark was quite aware of the scenario that was being enacted. We had discussed the patient's projective identification at length during supervision and the ways in which it was being played out. He also knew that he would have to confront the patient sooner or later. But when the moment finally arrived, he became somewhat flustered. He hemmed and hawed, mumbling something about the rules of therapist-patient contacts and how submitting to her request would only undermine the therapy process.

This did not dissuade the patient. She persisted in her effort to get Mark to meet with her after hours. She teased him and cajoled him about being old fashioned and about him needing to become less uptight. The more she teased him, the more tense he became. Finally, in an attempt to put an end to what obviously had become a very uncomfortable situation, Mark blurted out, "I can't. I'm married."

Later in supervision we discussed what had happened. It obviously was difficult for Mark to say to his patient what he needed to say—that he didn't want to sleep with her and that he wasn't going to. His reluctance had less to do with the sexual nature of her demands and more with his fear of damaging her sexual self-esteem. He felt that saying no to her would make her feel like an undesirable woman or, worse, an undesirable human being. So he "softened the blow" by using his wife as a shield. By couching his response in this way, he communicated that it was some other relationship, not *theirs*, that constituted the stumbling block.

Another way in which therapists commonly avoid confrontation is through interpretation. Instead of challenging the interpersonal use of the projective identification, the therapist demonstrates to the patient how current feelings are related to feelings about other figures in the patient's life. I think that this is one of the major devices to which therapists resort when difficult confrontations are called for. I find myself sometime adopting this "confrontational retreat" when I am working with patients who are particularly needy and helpless. Rather than confront the projective identification, I am apt to look for "reasons" as to why the patient relates in such dependent ways.

I am not entirely sure why I do this. I think it has something to do with seeing myself as a "good Sam." I tend to come to people's assistance when they need help, whether it involves helping a neighbor fix a broken lock or my children cope with a difficult task. For most of my life, I have seen this in a positive light ("It's nice to help out"), but I am beginning to wonder whether it has its negative side. Sometimes I am so "quick to help" that people tend to view me as intrusive. I therefore have begun to consider that perhaps my "helpfulness" is motivated not so much by a desire to help as by a desire to control.

Regardless of what motivates my behavior, I have become sensitized to my "proclivity to assist" and am able to see more clearly how it interferes with the treatment process. The place it is most likely to crop up is early in treatment (offering too much advice) and in the latter stages of treatment when it comes time to confront. When I find myself worrying about the fragility of the patient and spending a great deal of time "exploring" what went wrong in the patient's early life, I question whether I am, in fact, using interpretation as a defense against confrontation.

There is no way to really get around confrontation if one is to successfully pursue object relations therapy as a treatment modality. One needs to recognize that confrontation is one of the more difficult features of object relations work and that there is a natural tendency to avoid it. Keeping this in mind, it is possible to take precautions to ensure that one doesn't spend more time protecting oneself under the guise of protecting the patient. Knowledge of the pitfalls may not entirely eliminate the therapist's tendencies towards avoidance but may at least minimize the extent to which it interferes with the therapy process.

ON THE OTHER HAND

A therapist considering doing object relations therapy might conceivably wonder whether doing this kind of therapy is worth the effort. The necessity of considering what it means to be a target, of constantly examining the basis for the one's countertransference, and of making sure one doesn't unwittingly sidestep confrontation seems to place a burden on the therapist that other therapies do not. There is some truth to this, but there are compensations nonetheless. Doing object relations therapy has rewarding aspects which may not be immediately apparent but which make the work worth the demands it places on the therapist.

One is these is that therapy is rarely boring. When the relationship in the room is the medium through which meaningful change occurs, there is a creative tension in the air. I have worked with patients in a more interpretive-analytic context and recall spending session after session going over the same material and feeling I was getting nowhere. I often felt as if I were on a treadmill. This rarely occurs in object relations work. If I find myself getting bored, I examine the countertransferential aspects of the boredom and introduce it as part of the therapy.

Another rewarding feature of object relations work is that change, when it occurs, is palpable. The changes that occur in the relationship are perceptible and are there for both therapist and patient to experience. I have on numerous occasions commented to patients, "Look at how you are reacting to me now. Can you feel how different it is from when we first began?" The changes that take place are not inferential or assumed. They are part of the ongoing therapeutic transaction.

Of course, it is not the relationship with the therapist that is of ultimate importance. It is the way the patient feels about himself and the impact this has on his relationships at large. But this is true for all therapies. It is simply that in object relations work the therapist is offered the opportunity to judge on a firsthand experiential basis whether changes in the patient are merely "in the head" or have a basis in the ongoing relationship.

Along these lines, I have had more than a few patients contact me some time after therapy has ended to tell me about changes in their lives that paralleled the kinds of changes that had taken place in therapy. A patient whose projective identification of sexuality had been confronted and dealt with in therapy wrote to me some months after we concluded treatment to tell me about some significant changes in her life. One of these had to do with a geographical move. She had relocated from New England to New Mexico and was eager to tell me about an exciting new job opportunity that had materialized.

What she really wanted to tell me, however, was how she was handling a relationship with a new man in her life. Before coming to therapy, she would sexually bind men into relationships and then become manipulated by them. The men with whom she got involved typically would insist on moving in with her and then invade her space in ways that were intrusive and overbearing. The result was that she became upset, depressed, and was constantly getting into bitter struggles with her live-in boyfriends.

Though her most recent involvement was not devoid of sexual components, she felt sex was a part of the relationship and not the whole relationship. More important to her was the way she had handled her new boyfriend when he too suggested they move in together. Whereas earlier in her life she would have simply acquiesced, she told her new boyfriend that she wasn't ready or willing to make that kind of commitment. The simple fact that she was able to assert herself in this way and still feel secure about the relationship (and herself) was a tremendous source of pride to her, and it came through in her letter.

Another patient, a building contractor, initially had contracted for therapy to deal with what he termed self-defeating behavior. He admittedly had sabotaged one marriage, precipitated a bitter falling out with his elderly parents, and had driven a successful business into the ground. He was depressed, debt-ridden, and confused about where to turn next.

The major part of therapy was spent dealing with his projective identification of power and how it undermined many of his efforts at success. It was quite evident that much of his pathology was related to his attempts to control people and that this eventually was the basis for his self-defeating behavior. It was also clear that this same behavior was exhibited in our relationship and in the way he tried to control what went on in therapy.

The therapy was long and protracted and was characterized by many heated exchanges, but in the end the power struggle was resolved. By the end of therapy, his fortunes had changed dramatically. His business had begun to flourish, and he had reconciled with his parents. Both he and I agreed that his attempts to destroy the therapy and my efforts to prevent him from doing so were critical in turning his life around.

Such experiences are rewarding. They are a part of the reason therapists do therapy. But experiences such as these are few and far between. Most patients do not get in touch with their therapists after treatment is concluded and few provide testimonials attesting to a therapy's success. I think that a sustaining reason that therapists do object relations work—aside from making a living—is the opportunity it provides for personal growth.

Doing object relations therapy stretches one as a therapist and as a human being. It forces you to explore parts of yourself (your self) that might not otherwise be explored. Experiencing the patient's projective identifications and the splitting that underlies them forces us to examine our own inner splits. We are not that different from our patients, and dealing with the goodness-badness divisions in others gives us the opportunity to look at goodness-badness divisions within ourselves. Our patients hold up mirrors to us. If we are willing to look into them, we sometimes can get a clearer picture of who we are as human beings.

CHAPTER 9

Beyond the Therapy Room

Most therapists typically spend a good part of their day doing therapy, and a fair amount of time digesting and processing what they do. But therapists, like everyone else, have lives that extend beyond their work. In other professions, the line between the world of work and the world outside of it is clearly drawn. This is not always the case for psychotherapy. Whereas a plumber is unlikely to see elbows and tees in a Woody Allen movie, a therapist is likely to see instances of splitting and projective identification.

This is not surprising since the "stuff" of which therapy is constructed— interpersonal relationships—is the stuff of which the rest of the world is constructed. If, as suggested in the beginning of this book, considerations regarding psychotherapy derive from more general considerations regarding human development and the basic nature of human beings, then most of the events that surround us will contain many of the same elements that are found in therapy. Although this can at times be disconcerting, it sometimes can lead to valuable insights.

One's appreciation of drama may be enhanced, for example, by viewing the works of O'Neill, Albee, and even Shakespeare through object relations lenses. By the same token, the insights that certain artistic endeavors offer can reveal nuances of interaction that are often overshadowed in therapy by the umbrella of pathology. To say that psychotherapy informs life and vice versa only accentuates the powerful and pervasive influence of object relations in people's lives.

One of the places where a synergistic interplay between art and object relations can be observed is in fairy tales—both children's versions and those designed for adults. Because of their ability to tap into symbolic processes, fairy tales constitute an important means by which human beings address conflicts of an object relational nature. In this chapter an effort is made to demonstrate how one important object relations dynamic—splitting—enriches our understanding of fairy tales and how fairy tales, in turn, can be used in therapy to gain insight into representational processes which might otherwise prove inaccessible.

WICKED WITCHES AND OTHER MOTHERS

Fairy tales are time honored forms of entertainment for children which stimulate the imagination and provide endless delight. But they are much more. Fairy tales are written records of deeply held beliefs about the nature of the world. The fairy tales of Jacob and Wilhelm Grimm, for example, are based on legends and myths that had been circulating in central Europe for centuries. In fact, the stories that make up *The Grimm Brothers House-hold Tales* did not originate in the imagination of the Grimm brothers but were dictated to them by a 92-year-old peasant woman with a phenomenal memory.

Fairy tales consequently contain some of the deepest convictions children (and adults) harbor about the nature of the world and the people who inhabit it. As such, they include themes which bear on critical aspects of emotional development, themes having to do with greed (*Jack and the Beanstalk*), envy (*Snow White*), and deceit (*Rumpelstiltskin*) to name but a few.

Bettelheim (1976) argues that a major theme in fairy tales is mastery over sexual, i.e., oedipal concerns:

Whether openly stated or only hinted at, oedipal difficulties and how the individual solves them are central to the way his personality and human relations unfold. By camouflaging the oedipal preoccupations, or by only subtly intimating the entanglements, fairy stories permit us to draw our own conclusions when the time is propitious for our gaining a better understanding of these problems. (p. 201)

While an oedipal perspective on fairy tales makes sense in a few select stories, it leads to some strained conclusions in others. Bettelheim contends, for example, that the dwarfs in Snow White are really paternal derivatives and symbolically represent a sexual temptation for the child. The reason that Snow White is able to safely sleep in their house without fear that she will act on her unconscious sexual wishes is that dwarfs in fairy tales typically possess eunuch-like qualities and therefore pose no threat.

Bettelheim also suggests that the slipper in Cinderella constitutes a symbolic vagina. Cinderella's efforts to squeeze her foot into her slipper is nothing more than a disguised expression of her wish to get the prince into a slipper of another sort (pp. 268–270).

A careful examination of fairy tales suggests that a more powerful theme in these stories has to do with splitting. Weaving itself through practically every fairy story, the splitting dynamic highlights the primal struggle between good and bad. It therefore is not unusual to find most major fairy tales populated by good and bad maternal images. On the positive side we find good mothers and fairy godmothers. On the negative side we find witches, evil sorceresses, and malevolent stepmothers. To overcome badness, the child must confront and defeat the witch and her derivatives.

Snow White is a classic portrayal of this dynamic in action. As most readers will recall, the story begins before Snow White is even born. Her mother, the queen, accidentally pricks her finger while sewing by an open window, causing several drops of blood to fall on the snow outside. Upon seeing the red droplets outlined against the white expanse, she wishes for a daughter whose "lips will be red as blood and whose skin will be white as the snow." Soon thereafter, Snow White is born.

Shortly after the child's birth, however, the mother dies. The absence of the real, ostensibly good, mother is a prominent feature in fairy tales. Either she dies very early in the story or she simply is not mentioned. This acts to ensure that the "good mother" stays insulated from the "bad mother" (the witch) and guarantees that she will not be contaminated. It also ensures that she cannot be harmed. Witches are powerful figures and a confrontation with figures of this sort can lead to disastrous consequences.

Though Snow White survives the death of her mother, she finds herself increasingly at the mercy of a malevolent stepmother who envies her good looks. The new queen not only is jealous of Snow White but plots to get rid of her. But she is not content to merely banish her from the kingdom. She wants to dispose of her entirely. This is more than run-of-the-mill badness. This is evil incarnate.

To make things worse, Snow White's father, the king, is of little help. This is characteristic of fathers in fairy tales, who typically are portrayed as weak and spineless creatures. The father in Hansel and Gretel, for example, meekly stands by while his wife plots the children's death. The fact that fathers are portrayed as useless and peripheral figures in fairy tales should not surprise us in light of the fact that the earliest experience of splitting is lodged in the child's relationship with the mother rather than with the father.

Without the king or anyone else to get in her way, the queen sets out to consummate the terrible deed. She summons her gamekeeper and commands him to kill Snow White. Fortunately, the gamekeeper feels compassion for the child and lets her escape into the forest, where she stumbles upon the house of the Seven Dwarfs. Most of the rest of the story centers on the stepmother's attempt to do in Snow White through various means (asphyxiation, poison, etc.) and Snow White's repeated rescue by the dwarfs.

In the end, Snow White is claimed by the prince and the queen gets her just desserts. Invited to the wedding nuptials by the prince and Snow White, she decides to attend to satisfy her narcissistic curiosity. Once there, the queen is forced to put on red hot shoes and condemned to dance to her death. Snow White and the prince live happily ever after, no longer threatened by her deadly presence. Evil is vanquished and goodness prevails.

Snow White is a prototypical fairy tale in that it encapsulates badness within a single figure. By doing so, it portrays evil forcefully and unambiguously. Once this is accomplished, justice in the fairy tale is swift and certain. There is no redemption, no bargains struck. If goodness is to prevail, the queen must be destroyed. What's more, her destruction must be complete and irrevocable. Only in this way can badness totally be overcome.

BALANCING BADNESS:
THE FAIRY GODMOTHER

Snow White and stories like it depict only one side of the goodness-badness spectrum. The witch and her counterparts radiate evil and clearly represent all that is bad. But where are the forces of good? Where is the shining presence that might conceivably help the child in the struggle against badness? It obviously would help matters if the story contained a figure who could do this, someone who could represent goodness forcefully and unequivocally.

There is another group of fairy tales in which figures of this sort occur. These are the tales that contain enchantresses, fairy godmothers and other benevolent mother figures. Such stories differ from stories like *Snow White* in that they contain at least one dominant individual who is unambiguously and irrevocably good. It is within such stories that the concrete expression of the splitting dynamic is realized. Perhaps the best known example of this type of story is *Cinderella*.

The story of Cinderella starts off in similar fashion to most fairy tales— with the real mother absent. She is nowhere in sight and there is no mention of what might have happened to her. All we are told is that the father has taken a second wife and that she doesn't seem to be a very pleasant person. In fact, she is described by those who know her as "the proudest and most disagreeable woman in the whole country."

The first part of the story describes Cinderella's attempt to cope with the stepmother and her two obnoxious daughters, who are virtual extensions of their mother. The stepsisters are favored by their mother and assigned a life of luxury while Cinderella is compelled to wash the floors and clean the grates. Cinderella suffers in silence, not daring to complain to her father, who we are told is "entirely ruled by his wife." Once again, we find a father who is virtually useless.

The central part of the story deals with Cinderella's desire to attend the ball thrown by the king in honor of his son. While she renounces any desire to attend and cheerfully helps her stepsisters prepare for their departure, she secretly envies them. But even if she could go, she does not have the wherewithal to attend. What would she wear and how could she get there? These questions are answered by the magic appearance of the fairy godmother.

The fairy godmother is everything the stepmother is not. She is loving and caring. She wants Cinderella to look pretty. She wishes her to have a good time. She wants her to have a life beyond that of a lowly scullery maid. She even arranges for Cinderella to be personally greeted by the prince when she arrives at the ball. Who else but a "good mother" would go to such lengths?

The rest of the story is familiar to all who ever had to be home before midnight. The prince falls in love with Cinderella, pursues her, but loses her at the last moment when the clock strikes 12. A kingdom-wide search is rewarded when his servants fit the glass slipper left at the ball to the foot of the scullery maid. The prince takes Cinderella as his bride and the two run off to live happily ever after, but not before Cinderella forgives her stepsisters. In an act of pure benevolence, she marries them off to two noblemen.

But where is the evil in the story? Where is the unremitting badness we have come to expect of stepmothers and witches? The stepmother is obnoxious, as are her daughters, but they aren't *that* bad. Where is the brutality? Where is the lethal pursuit? Where is the retribution that plays so large a part in other fairy tales?

The answers, paradoxically, are in another story. The one recounted above, with which most people are familiar, is a "refined" version of the original *Cinderella*. It was not written by the Grimm brothers but rather by Charles Perrault for Louis XIV and the court at Versailles (Carter, 1977). Perrault's version, written in 1697, stripped the original of unnecessary vulgarities so as not to offend the king and his entourage. The Grimm brothers version (*Aschenputtel*) stays faithful to the story's original intent and presents the splitting dynamic in full force.

In the version transcribed by the Grimm brothers, the stepmother is more than just an unpleasant woman who happens to favor her own daughters over her stepdaughter. She teases and deceives Cinderella by making promises she does not intend to keep. She also promises the young girl that she can go to the dance if she performs certain tasks. When Cinderella faithfully does what she is told, the stepmother goes back on her word.

The stepmother's witch-like qualities, however, are depicted most saliently in her relation to her own daughters and the lengths to which she will go to ensure that one of them will win the prince's hand. When the first daughter fails to force her foot into the glass slipper, the mother hands her a knife and instructs her to lop off her big toe. "When you are queen," she tells her, "you will have no more need to go on foot." When the other sister experiences similar difficulties, the mother passes the knife to her and tells her to slash off her heel. The stepmother is so eager to become queen mother that she will resort to any means, even mutilation of her own flesh and blood, to achieve her ends.

In contrast to the Perrault version, the Grimm version ends on a note that truly does justice to the splitting dynamic. On the day of Cinderella's wedding to the prince, the two sisters arrive at the palace to curry favor with their stepsister. Cinderella invites them to be her bridesmaids. As they take their place, however, they are attacked by two white pigeons. The birds, who have acted as Cinderella's protectors during the story, peck out the sisters' eyes as they walk down the aisle. By maiming her stepsisters, Cinderella exacts revenge on the stepmother and deals a blow to the badness she represents.

Though the Grimm brother's version of *Cinderella* is a fairly straightforward splitting tale, its ending differs from the other fairy tales that contain witches and witch derivatives. In *Snow White*, the queen is forced to dance to her death; in Hansel and Gretel, the witch is burned to death in an oven; and in Alyunuschka and Ivanuschka, a well-known Russian fairy tale, the witch is set on fire atop a funeral pyre.

In *Cinderella*, the witch, i.e., the stepmother, survives. She is not forced to dance to her death nor is she burned alive in an oven. Even her stand-ins, the stepsisters, are spared death. It is as if the concrete representation of goodness, the fairy godmother, acts as a buffer against the forces of evil in the story. This suggests that evil (badness) may be allowed to survive if there is something or someone around to counterbalance it.

The reconciliation of good and bad—and ultimate integration of the two—is a major goal of object relations treatment. If the patient is to cease splitting off bad parts of the self through pathological interactions, the patient first must come to terms with the fact that what is considered "bad" is not necessarily grounds for rejection or abandonment. The fact that good and bad can "live" side by side holds out the opportunity for the acceptance of badness as an integral part of the self.

THE FUSION OF GOOD AND BAD

The possibility that goodness and badness might coexist is realized in a Russian fairy tale entitled *Vasilisa the Beautiful* (Afanas'ev, 1945). Like other tales of splitting, the story centers about a confrontation with a witch. But in contrast to other witches who are bad through and through, the witch in *Vasilisa the Beautiful* is both good *and* bad. The story bears retelling because it is rich in references to object relations and because most readers may not be as familiar with it as they are with other fairy tales.

The story begins with young Vasilisa summoned to the bedside of her dying mother. Before the mother dies, she blesses her daughter and gives her a doll. "Keep it with you wherever you go," she tells her only child as she hands her the doll. "When you are in trouble, give her some food and ask her advice. As soon as she is finished, she'll tell you what to do." With these words, the mother passes away.

The doll clearly is a transitional object and *Vasilisa the Beautiful* is one of the few fairy tales that contains one. Not only does the doll safeguard the child from some of the danger she faces in the story, but it gives her comfort when she is frightened and alone. To the extent that the mother literally offers it as a substitute for herself, the doll fulfills the surrogate function that transitional objects are meant to satisfy.

The story follows the general outline of *Cinderella* in that the father, a rich merchant, subsequently marries a domineering woman with two daughters. As in the case of Cinderella, the stepmother and daughters burden Vasilisa with all sorts of unpleasant housework. But Vasilisa has something Cinderella does not: the doll. Every night when the household is asleep, Vasilisa asks the doll for help. The doll comforts her and, in the wee hours of the morning, performs all the household chores.

Things go along this way for years, with Vasilisa becoming more beautiful with every passing day. She is courted by all the eligible bachelors in the village, none of whom expresses any interest in the stepsisters. This naturally frustrates the stepmother and stepsisters, who scheme to get rid of her. One day when the father is away on business, they tell Vasilisa that all the candles in the house have gone out and cannot be relit. The stepmother orders Vasilisa to venture into the forest and seek a light from the dreaded witch Baba Yaga who lives deep within, knowing full well that an errand of this sort means Vailisa's death.

The story follows Vasilisa into the forest, where she stumbles across the hut of Baba Yaga. The hut is surrounded by a fence made of human bones, each of which supports a human skull. The hut itself has doors with "human legs for door posts, human hands for bolts, and a mouth with sharp teeth in place of a lock." As Vasilisa stares at the spectacle before her, the eyes in the skulls begin to glow and Baba Yaga appears.

The witch asks her what she wants. Vasilisa explains and the witch agrees to give her the light she seeks, but not before she performs a series of chores. Baba Yaga tells Vasilisa that she wants her to sweep the yard, clean the hut, and cook dinner the next day. The witch also orders the frightened child to wash the linens and sort out some bushels of wheat. To show Vasilisa that she means business, the witch warns her that she will kill her unless everything is done by the time she returns.

Knowing full well that she cannot accomplish all this in one day, Vasilisa retreats into the corner of the hut and begins to weep. But the doll calms her. "Fear not, Vasilisa the Beautiful," the doll tells her. "Eat your supper, say your prayers, and go to sleep; the morning is wiser than the evening." Vasilisa is calmed. She goes to sleep and wakes in the morning to find that all the work has been done.

This scenario is repeated for three days in a row, with Baba Yaga each day threatening to kill Vasilisa if her demands are not met. Finally, in frustration, the witch asks Vasilisa how she manages to get all the work done. Vasilisa says nothing about the doll, but instead answers, "I am helped by the blessing of my mother." This infuriates Baba Yaga and sends her into a rage. "I want no blessed ones in my house," she bellows and orders Vasilisa to leave. But before she sends her off, she gives her one of the fiery skulls and tells her, "Here is a light for your stepsisters. Take it; that is what they sent you for."

The fire from the burning skull lights the forest path and guides Vasilisa back home. The stepmother and stepsisters, despite their hatred for Vasilisa, are delighted to see her. They apparently have been unable to strike a fire in the house since she has been gone, and the cottage has been in perpetual darkness. The three take the skull and bring it inside, but as they do the eyes stare at them. They try to hide but the eyes track them down, burning them wherever they go. In the morning they are reduced to ashes. Only Vasilisa remains, freed at last from the clutches of her stepmother and stepsisters.

Many features of *Vasilisa the Beautiful* parallel those found in Western fairy tales. There is a stepmother intent on getting rid of the heroine, a father who isn't much help, and a witch who threatens to destroy the heroine if she doesn't complete a series of difficult tasks. But the witch in this story is unlike most witches encountered in other tales. Though she is evil, she is also compassionate and caring (von Franz, 1967). Baba Yaga not only allows Vasilisa to live but also provides her with the means by which to destroy her enemies.

This is a developmental advance over the monolithic badness presented in other fairy tales. It signifies a growing awareness in children that good and bad can exist in the same individual. Until children come to acknowledge this, their feelings about themselves continue to be rooted in the primitive notion that badness must be destroyed for goodness to survive. This belief must be transcended if children – and adults – hope to eventually tolerate the badness that exists within themselves.

The fact that fairy tales do not fully accomplish what they set out to do – eradicate badness once and for all – is one of the important learning experiences of childhood. Bad feelings about the self tend to persist even though the witch in the fairy tale is destroyed. As human beings mature, they consequently turn to other forms of fantasy to symbolically reconcile the split between good and bad. One manifestation this takes is a series of "adult fairy tales" which center around a phenomenon called doubling.

FAIRY TALES FOR ADULTS

The notion of doubling has its roots in the German myth of a *doppelgänger*, a folkloric belief which presupposes that every human being possesses a replica self (Keppler, 1972; Tymms, 1955). In some instances, the doppelgänger, literally "double walker," takes the form of its owner's shadow (Rank, 1971). In other versions of the myth, it consists of a person's image. An individual wakes up one morning, looks in the mirror, and finds that his reflection is gone. In most versions, though, the doppelgänger simply is a flesh and blood double who leads a separate existence (Guerard, 1967).

Although the purest form of the myth portrays the double as a precise duplicate of its counterpart, variations do exist. In some tales of doubling, the double is physically distorted. In other stories, it differs along psychological lines. But whatever form it takes, the double is intimately bound to the story's protagonist in a profound way. What's more, it is always diametrically opposed to the protagonist insofar as issues of goodness and badness are concerned.

Perhaps the most famous tale of doubling is Stevenson's *Dr. Jekyll and Mr. Hyde* (1886). The story of a English physician who cleaves his body into two separate but diametrically opposed components, Stevenson's story is in many ways an adult counterpart of a children's fairy tale. There is the division between good and bad, the ongoing struggle between the two, and the inevitable climax in which good triumphs over evil. Only now, the two sides of the split are portrayed as parts of a single character. Instead of fairy godmothers and witches, we have two figures who seem to be separate parts of the same person.

Most people's familiarity with Stevenson's story comes from the many movies it has spawned. In these, Dr. Jekyll usually is portrayed as a somewhat curious scientist who accidentally gives birth to the criminal Hyde in the course of scientific experimentation. In the book, however, it is clear that Jekyll's efforts are prompted less by scientific curiosity than by a need to deal with an inherent split in his own personality (Sanford, 1981, p. 102). What Jekyll really wants to do is give physical expression to his bad side so that he will not have to constantly deal with the psychological consequences.

In one passage of the book, Jekyll reflects on these two parts of himself:

If each . . . could be housed in separate identities, life would be relieved of all that was unbearable; the unjust might go his way, delivered from the aspirations and remorse of his more upright twin; and the just could walk steadfastly and securely on his upward path, doing the good thing in which he found his pleasure, and no longer exposed to disgrace and penitence by the hands of this extraneous evil. (p. 80)

Jekyll's remarks are nothing less than the phenomenon of splitting expressed in existential terms: How does one maintain a sense of oneself as a worthwhile human being in light of this elemental division in the human psyche? If personality is by its very nature split into good and bad, and this split is deep and pervasive, how do we go about maintaining a unified picture of who we really are? The question is not whether evil exists, but rather how one goes about leading a reasonable existence in light of the fact that it does.

It is this dilemma that motivates Jekyll to invent some way of coping with his inner split. His solution is to separate the good and the bad into two physically separate beings. He accomplishes this by chemically creating the mysterious Edward Hyde. A shrivelled, misshapen creature, Hyde takes on all the characteristics of which Jekyll would like to divest himself.

Hyde is, of course, Jekyll's "doppelgänger," his double. A murderer and thief, he is not only psychologically reprehensible but physically repugnant as well. But as repugnant as Hyde is, Jekyll nonetheless is drawn to him. He writes, "I was conscious of no repugnance, rather a leap of welcome. This,

too, was myself" (p. 83). It is clear that at some level of primal consciousness Jekyll truly *knows* Hyde. This self-revelation is nothing less than the
adult experience of early childhood splitting.

Though Jekyll succeeds in what he sets out to do—splitting his good self
off from his bad self—he is unprepared for what ensues. One day he
awakens to find that he spontaneously has changed into Hyde. Changes
which heretofore had been brought about by drugs were now taking place
on their own. Jekyll realizes that he is losing control, and in his confession
writes, " . . . I began to spy a danger that, if this were much prolonged, the
balance of my nature might be permanently overthrown . . . " (p. 90).

Jekyll tries to revoke the process but finds he cannot. Try as he might, he
finds that Hyde cannot be denied. As a last resort, he barricades himself in
his laboratory to try to find the right combination of ingredients that will
turn things around. But the various drugs at his disposal prove to no avail.
Jekyll faces the inevitable: he soon will turn into Hyde and never return
again. At the last moment, he takes poison. By killing himself, he puts an
end to the despicable Hyde, but at the same time he destroys himself.

Stevenson's story of Henry Jekyll's tragic efforts to reconcile the split
within himself gives external form to the splitting dynamic. Like its childhood fairy tale counterpart, the story accomplishes this by depositing
goodness and badness in separate characters and then considering the consequences. What makes the doppelgänger version of splitting uniquely
adult is the way it resolves the split.

In children's fairy tales, badness is destroyed without attempts at reconciliation or concern for the consequences. The goal of the fairy tale, simply
put, is to get rid of the witch. Once the witch is eliminated, the evil queen
punished, or the stepmother driven out of town, everyone can live happily
ever after. To rid oneself of badness, though scary, is not much more
complicated than the removal of a wart—at least in the eyes of the very
young.

Adults are not fooled this easily. If nothing else, they realize that life is
not as simple as it is made out to be in fairy tales. If life teaches nothing
else, it teaches that badness cannot be totally eradicated and that efforts to
do so are futile and ill conceived. The message contained in the doubling
tale is that wholesale efforts to eliminate badness are likely to end in self-
destruction. This is a very different message from that found in children's
fairy tales. To be adult requires one to face the fact that goodness and
badness may be opposite sides of the same coin.

The doppelgänger theme weaves itself through a number of adult fairy
tales. Among them are Oscar Wilde's *The Picture of Dorian Gray* (1891) and
Henry James' *The Jolly Corner* (1947). In these stories and others like them,

the doppelgänger is portrayed as physically different from the protagonist. A distinguishing feature of these tales is that badness and evil take on bodily characteristics.

This, of course, is the way it is in children's fairy tales where the witch is ugly and repulsive. Just as the witch is small, misshapen and ugly, so Mr. Hyde and the portrait of Dorian Gray also are loathsome and unsightly. But this is not always the case. In other doppelgänger stories the double is an exact replica of the protagonist (Rogers, 1970, pp. 18–39). In these tales, he is neither disfigured nor particularly evil looking. Instead he is a precise mirror image of the story's central character. The only way one can tell the two apart is by a subtle but nevertheless telltale difference in their personalities.

THE CLONING OF GOODNESS

A vivid example of this type of doubling is contained in Edgar Allen Poe's *William Wilson* (1839). Published in roughly the same period as *Jekyll and Hyde* and *Dorian Gray*, *William Wilson* tells the story of a young Englishman who encounters his double early in life and spends the rest of his life trying to evade him. The story inverts the usual doppelgänger relationship, in that the double in Poe's tale is good while the protagonist is bad. But the central dynamic—that of a split between good and bad—is unaltered.

The story of *William Wilson* begins in a boarding school nestled in the English countryside. There William Wilson happens across another student with the same name who is very much like him in physical ways: his double not only is the same height but also has a similar build. The only physical difference that Wilson can detect (and a minor one at that) is in their voices. The other William Wilson always speaks in a low whisper.

As the story unfolds, additional similarities emerge. The other Wilson not only dresses the same way as William Wilson, but copies his gait and even begins to use the same phrases. There is, however, one significant psychological difference. The doppelgänger seems to possess what William Wilson terms "a moral sense." Through innuendo, or sarcastic remarks made at just the right moment, he lets William Wilson know that he possesses a far keener sense regarding what is good and what is bad.

Because the doppelgänger bears such an uncanny resemblance to him, William Wilson wonders whether the two might be related. Early in the story, he muses over the possibility that they might be twins. He dismisses the possibility but speculates about some other kind of connection:

I discovered, or fancied I discovered, in his air, and general appearance, a something which first startled, and then deeply interested me, by bringing to mind dim visions of my earliest infancy—wild, confused and thronging memories of a time when memory herself was yet unborn. I cannot better describe the sensation which oppressed me than by saying that I could with difficulty shake off the belief of my having been acquainted with the being who stood before me, at some epoch very long ago—some point of the past even infinitely remote. (p. 68)

Here, in a rare moment, we see the author of a doppelgänger tale make a direct reference to early infantile splitting. Wilson intuitively feels he knows his double in a way that precedes logical (cognitive) knowing. Through his protagonist, Poe takes us to an era when "memory herself was yet unborn." For a brief moment we are transported back to a time in life when feelings overshadowed thought, to a time when one's experience of the world was encapsulated in a primitive dichotomy of good and bad.

The story follows William Wilson through Eton and Oxford, where he engages in "protracted debaucheries." In both schools the doppelgänger materializes every time Wilson cheats or takes advantage of someone. Every time Wilson misbehaves, the doppelgänger appears, face shrouded, and whispers "William Wilson" in his ear.

In the years that follow, William Wilson travels throughout Europe, to Vienna, Paris, Berlin, even to Moscow, to evade his pursuer. But try as he may, he cannot shake his shadowy nemesis. In desperation, he resolves to put an end to the unholy alliance that binds the two together. The fateful confrontation takes place in Rome at the palazzo of the aging Duke Di Broglio.

Wilson has been invited to a masked ball by the Duke and has accepted the invitation, not to dance as much as to seduce the beautiful young wife of his host. Upon arriving at the palace, he spies the Duke's wife in the milling throng and eagerly sets out in her direction. He is about to call out to her when he feels a light touch on his shoulder. Before he has a chance to turn around, he hears the familiar low voice whisper his name.

Enraged, Wilson whirls to confront his tormentor, noting as he does that the intruder's costume is identical to his own. He goes into a frenzy and drags his counterpart into a nearby antechamber, where he challenges him to a duel. The contest lasts but a few moments. After a brief scuffle, Wilson forces his opponent against a wall and with brute ferocity plunges his sword into his chest.

There is a knock at the door and William Wilson shifts his attention momentarily to see who is there. Finding no one, he turns back into the room. He is surprised to find that his double is gone. Instead, he spies a large mirror on the wall that he had not noticed before. Wilson peers into the mirror and is terror stricken to see himself, all bloodied, approaching with a sword in his chest. As he stares at his reflection, the full enormity of what he has done finally dawns upon him. In his attempt to destroy his double, William Wilson has succeeded only in destroying himself.

One of the revealing characteristics of stories that contain doubles is that they contain strong autobiographical elements. The figures of Hyde and Jekyll, for example, mirror conflicts in the childhood of Robert Louis Stevenson in which disdain for sterile social convention was pitted against the demands of a strong-willed father (Calder, 1980). Stevenson's father wanted his son to be an engineer while Stevenson opted for the life of an "outlaw" writer. And Oscar Wilde, in a letter to a close friend, wrote about *The Picture of Dorian Gray*, "It contains much of me in it" (Hart-Davis, 1963, p. 352).

Similar autobiographical links are evident in the writings of other authors whose works contain doubling themes. Joseph Conrad's novel *The Secret Sharer*, the story of a ship captain's attempt to deal with a crime committed by his double, follows Conrad's own troubled command of the *Otago* in 1888. And it is telling that Dostoevsky, who suffered from bouts of depression and panic attacks throughout his life, ends his novella, *The Double*, with the protagonist being taken away to a mental hospital.

But the personal significance of the doppelgänger tale is perhaps nowhere more striking than in *William Wilson*. There is a passage early in the narrative in which the young Wilson first learns the precise day of his counterpart's birth. When it turns out to be the same date as his, he wonders whether the two might be brothers:

But assuredly if we had been brothers, we must have been twins: for after leaving Dr. Bransby [the headmaster], I casually learned that my namesake was born on the nineteenth of January, 1809 — and this is a remarkable coincidence; for the day is precisely that of my own nativity. (p. 64)

William Wilson attributes this to coincidence. It may well be. But one wonders how coincidental it is that Edgar Allen Poe himself was born in Boston, Massachusetts, on precisely January 19th, 1809?

Doubling stories, in short, are fairy tales for adults. But whereas in children's fairy tales it is possible to destroy badness so that everyone lives happily ever after, this rarely is accomplished in the adult version. The moral contained in tales of doubling is that it is not only impossible but foolhardy to try to destroy badness. If human beings hope to nurture and sustain mature interpersonal relationships, they somehow must learn to integrate the good and the bad that is their interpersonal legacy.

SPLITTING IN CINEMA

The same splitting themes contained in classical fairy tales and tales of doubling can also be found in cinema. Otto Rank was one of the first to call attention to this is his analysis of a well-known film of his time called *The Student of Prague* (Rank, 1971). Directed by Hans Heinz Ewers, the film tells the story of a dashing young student named Balduin who mysteriously is separated from his "other self" and spends the rest of his days ruing the consequences.

The film begins with Balduin, the best fencer at the University of Prague, having dissipated all his money. Alienated from his studies and friends, he wanders through a forest, where he rescues the young daughter of the Baron Waldis-Schwarzenberg from drowning. Balduin is invited to her castle to meet the Baron and while there learns that Margit, the girl he rescued, is engaged to be married. He has in this short period of time become enchanted with Margit and is quite disconsolate over this revelation.

Sometime later in the story, Balduin is visited by a sinister old man named Scapinelli, whom he came across earlier in the film. The old man offers him wealth if he signs a contract agreeing to let him take anything from his room. Balduin looks around at the sparse furnishings and bare walls and happily signs the contract. He is amused to see that Scapinelli, after carefully examining everything there is in the room, settles on Balduin's image in the mirror. Balduin goes along with the joke but is astonished when his image detaches itself from the mirror and follows Scapinelli through the door.

From this point on, the story roughly follows the lines of *William Wilson*. Balduin, no longer a poor student, pursues Margit but is always interrupted by his double. Margit's fiance eventually becomes so exasperated by Balduin's unwanted intrusions that he challenges him to a duel. Margit's father, however, intercedes, for he knows of Balduin's skill with a sword. The Baron asks him to spare the life of his intended son-in-law and future heir. Balduin agrees. But on his way to the site of the duel to tell Margit's fiance that the duel is off, he spies his double coming from the opposite direction. He despairs when he sees his doppelgänger wiping the blood from a bloody saber he holds in his hand.

Barred from the Baron's house because of the fiance's death and unable to realize a future with Margit, Balduin sits despondently in his room. As he gloomily contemplates his future, he suddenly sees his double standing in front of him, grinning. Balduin grabs a gun and fires at him, only to find that the phantom has disappeared. He laughs in relief, believing that he finally had rid himself of his tormentor. His joy is short-lived as he senses sharp pain in his chest and realizes that his shirt is soaked with blood. Balduin collapses on the floor, at which point Scapinelli reappears and tears up the contract, scattering the pieces over the lifeless corpse.

The Student of Prague is a film version of a traditional doppelgänger tale in which the doubling is expressed through two characters, each representing one side of the split (Schlappner, 1967, p. 129). In more contemporary cinematic renditions of splitting, the division of good and bad is portrayed psychologically rather than physically. One example of this is Bertolucci's *The Partner*; another is Judith Rossner's *Looking for Mr. Goodbar*. There is, however, one contemporary piece of cinema which stays faithful to the classical two-person portrayal of doubling. It is Woody Allen's *The Purple Rose of Cairo*.

In Allen's film within a film, Tom Baxter, a celluloid character, steps off the screen to enter the life of the beleaguered heroine, Celia. Tom is everything a woman could ask for, and Celia sees him as the answer to her dreams, a ticket out of the life of drudgery and abuse to which she has been subjected. Film analysts Gabbard and Gabbard use the following words to describe Tom: "He is unfettered by human selfishness and greed, by the baser instincts characteristic of the dark side of man" (1987, p. 222). One is hard pressed to find a more persuasive description of "goodness."

Tom's real life counterpart, Gil Shephard, the actor who plays Tom on the screen, seems at first very much like Tom. Arriving in town to right matters, he accidently bumps into Celia and overwhelms her with his sincerity and down-to-earth qualities. But Gil is extraordinarily vain and self-serving, interested only in himself and his career. He promises Celia the stars if only she can persuade Tom to return to his movie. Celia helps Gil, believing that he loves her. In the end, though, he deserts her, leaving her to her lonely existence and cinematic fantasies.

The Purple Rose of Cairo pits goodness against badness by playing Tom Baxter off against Gil Shephard and questioning whether pure goodness is at best a celluloid fantasy. At the same time it gives us a modern depiction of what is interpersonally meant by "badness." Were we to construct a list of the qualities that might fall under the rubric of "relational badness," the personal characteristics of Gil Shephard—selfishness, exploitation and deceit—would likely head the top of the list. For this reason alone, *The Purple Rose of Cairo* provides us with a vivid modern-day cinematic rendition of splitting.

But of all the splitting stories that have come to the screen, perhaps the most powerful is *The Wizard of Oz*. The cinema version, based on Frank Baum's book, contains a highly sophisticated depiction of splitting, one that is much more contemporary than that presented in classical fairy tales and even some adult splitting tales. Like its classical counterparts, *The Wizard of Oz* contains many of the elements found in a splitting fantasy—an absent mother, a witch (two, in fact), a fairy godmother (Glenda), and a struggle to the death. But contained in *Oz* are messages about goodness and badness that are deeper and more trenchant than any of the ones we have encountered so far.

One of these occurs very early in the story, when the house that transports Dorothy to Oz falls on the Wicked Witch of the East and kills her outright. If this were an ordinary fairy tale, the story might have ended right there. All Dorothy would need to do is find a means of getting home. It is not long though before the Wicked Witch of the West arrives on scene. Sister of the dead witch, she is determined to exact revenge on the person responsible for her sister's death.

The lesson contained in this beginning episode is that evil is not that easily dispensed with. Not only is it ubiquitous, but it can pop up in different guises. It may not be enough to get rid of one witch; another may be lurking in the wings to take her place. Just as the Munchkins are only temporarily freed by the death of the Wicked Witch of the East, so Dorothy is only temporarily freed of the evil in her life.

But before the Wicked Witch of the West can harm Dorothy and her friends, Glenda, the Good Witch of the North, appears. A benevolent witch, Glenda is an enchantress very much like the fairy godmother in Cinderella. She too has special powers and demonstrates them by presenting Dorothy with magic red slippers that the witch claims are hers. Her benefactor tells her that the slippers will take her to the Emerald City where a Wizard lives and that he can help her get back to Kansas.

From an object relations perspective, it is evident that the red slippers are transitional objects. Like the doll in Vasilisa, they provide Dorothy with security as she sets out into the world. Vasilisa's mother gives Vasilisa the doll just before she dies; Glenda gives Dorothy the slippers moments before she disappears. In both instances, the objects are designed to safeguard the child when the maternal protector is not around.

To this point, *The Wizard of Oz* is a relatively straightforward splitting tale. Although we get a double dose of badness early on, the forces of good and evil are clearly delineated. The story becomes more complex as Dorothy travels along the path of life (the yellow brick road) and meets the three figures who ultimately accompany her on her journey to the Emerald City.

The first figure she encounters is the Scarecrow. Devoid of a brain, the

Scarecrow feels rather useless because he is unable to think. If only he had a brain, he would be smart. The next figure encountered is the Tin Man. His problem is that he lacks a heart. But it isn't the physical organ he is missing as much as the ability to experience feelings. "I'd be tender and be gentle, and slightly sentimental," he crows, "If I only had heart." The third and final character is the cowardly Lion. What he lacks is courage.

The characters that Dorothy meets along the yellow brick road are more than mere figments of her imagination. They are parts of her inner world. Examining them in detail, we find that each represents a form of "badness" that Dorothy—and presumably most children—would like to overcome. Children want to be smart, to be able to feel, to be brave. A child who feels stupid, who cannot feel, and who believes he is a coward is a child who invariably feels that he is bad and undesirable. In journeying to the Emerald City to help the Scarecrow, the Tin Man, and the Lion come to terms with their "deficiencies," Dorothy is really trying to come to terms with her own.

Once the foursome arrive at the Emerald City, they find that the Wizard is not as receptive as they were led to believe. He tells Dorothy that she must steal the witch's broom and return it to him before he can share any of his secrets with her. Though frustrated, she and her three friends set off once more, this time in the direction of the witch's castle. The stage is once again set for the climactic battle between good and evil. But with a little help from her friends, Dorothy manages to destroy the witch. Badness is vanquished and the forces of goodness once more prevail.

But the battle is anticlimactic. The real victory has yet to be won. Dorothy's friends still do not have what they have come for. They return to Wizard, who presents the Scarecrow with an academic diploma (Doctor of Thinkology), the Tin Man with a heart-shaped clock (a new "ticker"), and the Lion a medal with the word "Courage" emblazoned on it. But as he delivers their awards, the Wizard points out that these are merely superficial manifestations of what they really seek. The qualities for which they have been searching lie within each of them and have been there all along.

This is the lesson that Dorothy learns in Oz and the knowledge she takes back with her to Kansas. Her journey has led to the realization that she must search within herself if she hopes to overcome her own personal shortcomings. The source of badness lies not without but within, and one needs to come to terms with this if life is to proceed. In the end, the victory that Dorothy wins is a victory over herself. This, of course, is the message that all of us—children and adults alike—must accept if we ever hope to successfully negotiate the yellow brick roads of our own lives.

FAIRY TALES, DOUBLING, AND PSYCHOTHERAPY

Literature and cinema offer psychotherapists a rich source of interpersonal material for examining object relations in action. There are levels upon levels of meaning in novels and films that bear on the nature of the representational world. The phenomenon of splitting is just one object relations concept that offers evidence of the way object relations affect our world and thus are reflected in cinema, literature and other creative enterprises.

But movies and literature that speak to object relations are of more than just passing intellectual interest. They have a potential for furthering the psychotherapeutic process. In an exhaustive review of psychiatry in cinema, Gabbard and Gabbard (1987) suggest that, "The cinema is the great store-house for the intrapsychic images of our time, and movies touch on fundamental human psychological processes with which patients and therapists alike identify" (p. 163). Rank (1971) echoes these sentiments when he writes, "It may perhaps turn out that cinematography, which in numerous ways reminds us of the dream-work, can also express certain psychological facts and relationships . . . in such clear and conspicuous imagery that it facilitates our understanding of them" (p. 4). A similar argument can, of course, be made for literary images.

The question is: How can these images be used to further the psychotherapeutic process? What is the relevance of these images for object relations work? The answer lies in the realm of metaphor. Literary and cinematic images, particularly those having to do with splitting, have the ability to function as symbolic links to object relational processes that may not be accessible through normal channels.

In Chapter 7, I argued that object relations therapy is not an interpretive therapy, not because there is anything inherently wrong with interpretation, but because most object relations experiences of significance are pre-verbal in nature. This is where metaphors can come into play. Because of their ability to leapfrog the constraints of verbal interpretation, metaphors offer the patient a means of getting in touch with splitting processes which may have been encoded only in nonverbal ways. As such they act as conduits to early splitting experiences that are literally "beyond words."

This is not to suggest that the therapy be turned into a book or film seminar. However, patients often bring into the therapy examples of movies they have seen or novels they are reading in the same way they bring in dreams or other material. On these occasions, the object relations therapist can subtly direct the patient to the metaphoric qualities of these works.

This provides the patient with the opportunity to access some of the polarities that lie behind early splitting.

Thus, one of my patients began a session by telling me that she had taken her daughter to see a re-release of Disney's *Snow White*. While she enjoyed the experience of seeing the film with her daughter, who was the same age as the patient when the patient first saw the film, she was greatly disappointed in the film the second time around. The patient remembered being enchanted with the figure of Snow White, whom she remembered as brave and self-reliant. Now she saw her as a wimp, as someone who sacrificed her sense of self by becoming the Seven Dwarfs' housekeeper and lackey.

Obviously the film was being seen through different eyes and by a person whose perspective had changed over the years. In the course of discussing this, I called her attention to the struggle of good and evil in the story and how Snow White had to constantly withstand her stepmother's efforts to destroy her. The film version does not include the sequences in the fairy tale in which the queen, disguised as an old woman, combs Snow White's tresses with a poison comb and tries to suffocate her by tightening a corset around her waist.

The patient was familiar only with the Disney version of *Snow White* and expressed interest in reading the Grimm Brothers' version. What the latter clearly depicts and which is not made clear in the film is that the stepmother's narcissism ("Mirror, mirror on the wall . . . ") reflects Snow White's own narcissistic tendencies. This is seen in Snow White's desire for the comb (to enhance her looks) and for the corset (to accentuate her bosom). I do not think it was mere coincidence that issues of physical attractiveness and desirability were central issues in the patient's life and that much of her problems centered about the use of a projective identification of sexuality.

Along similar lines, Ogden (1982, p. 101) tells of a patient who reported being very moved after viewing *The Wizard of Oz* the evening before a therapy session. The particular sequence that affected her most occurs at the end of the film when Dorothy discovers that the Wizard is not magical after all. Once his disguise falls away, Dorothy sees him for what he is: an unimpressive, bald-headed little man.

In fit of anger and disappointment, Dorothy shouts, "You're a very wicked man." The Wizard replies, "No, Dorothy, I'm not a very *good* wizard, but I'm not a *bad* man." The patient burst into tears and began to talk about how she had to be something special—a wizard—in order to exist for her mother. "If I wasn't a wizard, I was nothing to her," the patient sobbed. Though the patient was responding to the wizard metaphor in the story, it also was evident that at some level she also was responding to the good-bad distinction in the wizard's remark.

Another instance in which *The Wizard of Oz* proved useful in therapy occurred in the case of a highly narcissistic and somewhat overcontrolled patient of mine. The patient, a professional musician, entered therapy to deal with intense bouts of anxiety. These typically occurred in social situations of a non-musical nature in which he nevertheless felt he had to "perform."

In the course of therapy, he began to let his guard down and to tell of his feelings of being stupid, of not taking stands on issues he believed he should, and of being concerned over the lack of feelings he had for others. I pointed out to him that the deficiencies he experienced were almost identical to the deficiencies experienced by the figures in *The Wizard of Oz*. At first he seemed mildly surprised by my remark. But after giving it some thought, he began to consider that there might, in fact, be something in the analogy. From there we went on to talk about the "bad" parts of himself and how his efforts to deny them was a negation of a very real part of who he was.

The examples given in this chapter only sample the many literary and cinematic sources that touch on object relations theory. There are literally dozens of fairy tales and doubling stories that speak to issues of splitting and the relational nature of the inner world. One could devote pages, for example, to the work of Ingmar Bergman. Even the Star Wars trilogy with its epic struggle between Darth Vader and The Force is rich in object relations themes. Whereas literary and cinematic material is not essential to the success of object relations treatment, it affords therapist and patient an opportunity to interact along lines that are less pathologically tinged. Perhaps this is reason enough to bring material that is "beyond the therapy room" into the therapy room and make it a part of the treatment process.

References

Afanas'ev, A. (1945). *Russian fairy tales*. New York: Random House, 1973.

Balsam, R.M., & Balsam, A. (1974). *Becoming a psychotherapist. A clinical primer*. Boston: Little, Brown.

Beitman, B.D. (1979). Engagement techniques for individual psychotherapy. *Social Casework, 60*(5), 306–309.

Beitman, B.D. (1983). Comparing psychotherapies by the stages in the process. *J. Operational Psychiatry, 14*(1), 20–27.

Beitman, B.D. (1987). *The structure of individual psychotherapy*. New York: Guilford.

Benjamin, J. (1986). A desire of one's own: Psychoanalytic feminism and intersubjective space. In DeLauretis, T. (Ed.), *Feminist studies: Critical studies* (pp. 78–101). Bloomington, IN: Indiana University Press.

Berger, P.L., & Kellner, H. (1964). Marriage and the construction of reality. *Diogenes, 46*(3), 1–20.

Bettelheim, B. (1976). *The uses of enchantment*. New York: Knopf.

Bicknell, D.J. (1975). *Pica: A childhood symptom*. London: Butterworth.

Blumer, H. (1969). *Symbolic interactionism*. Englewood Cliffs, NJ: Prentice-Hall.

Bollas, C. (1983). Expressive uses of the countertransference. *Contemporary Psychoanalysis, 19*, 1–34.

Boszormenyi-Nagy, I., & Spark, G.M. (1984). *Invisible loyalties: Reciprocity in intergenerational family therapy*. New York: Brunner/Mazel.

Bretherton, I., & Beeghly, M. (1982). Talking about internal states: The acquisition of an explicit theory of mind. *Developmental Psychology, 18*, 906–921.

Breuer, J., & Freud, S. (1895). Studies in hysteria. *The standard edition of the complete psychological works of Sigmund Freud*. Vol. 2. New York: Norton.

Calder, J. (1980). *Robert Louis Stevenson: A life study*. New York: Oxford University Press.

Cameron, N., & Magaret, A. (1951). *Behavior pathology*. Boston: Houghton Mifflin.

Carter, A. (Trans.) (1977). *The fairy tales of Charles Perrault*. London: Victor Gollancz, Ltd.

Cashdan, S. (1967). The use of drawings in child psychotherapy: A process analysis of a case study. *Psychotherapy: Theory, Research, and Practice, 4*(2), 81–86.

Cashdan, S. (1973). *Interactional psychotherapy: Stages and strategies in behavioral change*. New York: Grune and Stratton.

Cicchetti, D. (1987). Developmental psychopathology in infancy: Illustration from the study of maltreated youngsters. *Journal of Consulting and Clinical Psychology, 55*, 837–845.

Conrad, J. (1910). *The secret sharer*. New York: New American Library, 1983.

Cooper, M.M. (1957). *Pica*. Springfield, IL: Thomas.

Cottrell, L.S. (1969). Interpersonal interaction and the development of the self. In D.S. Goslin (Ed.), *Handbook of socialization theory and research*. Chicago: Rand McNally.

Crane, L. (Ed.) (1963). *Household stories of the Brothers Grimm*. New York: Dover.

Dostoevsky, F. (1945). *The double*. In *The short novels of Dostoevsky*. New York: Dial Press.

Epstein, L., & Feiner, A.H. (Eds.) (1979). *Countertransference: The therapist's contribution to the therapeutic situation*. New York: Jason Aronson.

Ernsberger, C. (1979). The concept of countertransference as therapeutic instrument: Its early history. *Modern Psychoanalysis, 4*(2), 141–164.

Fairbairn, W.R.D. (1954). *An object relations theory of the personality*. New York: Basic Books.

Flavell, J. (1963). *The developmental psychology of Jean Piaget*. Princeton, NJ: Van Nostrand.

Forward, S., & Torres, J. (1986). *Men who hate women and the women who love them*. New York: Bantam.

Freud, S. (1917). Mourning and melancholia. *The standard edition of the complete psychological works of Sigmund Freud*. Vol. 14. New York: Norton.

Gabbard, K., & Gabbard, G.O. (1987). *Psychiatry and the cinema*. Chicago: University of Chicago Press.

Greenberg, J.R., & Mitchell, S.A. (1983). *Object relations in psychoanalytic theory*. New York: Basic Books.

Grotstein, J. S. (1981). *Splitting and projective identification*. New York: Jason Aronson.

Guerard, A. (1967). *Stories of the double*. Philadephia: Lippincott.

Guntrip, H. (1971). *Psychoanalytic theory, therapy, and the self*. New York: Basic Books.

Hart-Davis, R. (Ed.) (1963). *The letters of Oscar Wilde*. London: Rupert Hart-Davis.

Hoffman, J.J. (1985). Client factors related to premature termination of psychotherapy. *Psychotherapy, 22*, 83–85.

Hope, D. (1987). The healing paradox of forgiveness. *Psychotherapy, 24*, 240–244.

Horney, K. (1939). *New ways in psychoanalysis*. New York: Norton.

Horowitz, M. (1976). Cognitive and interactive aspects of splitting. *Amer. J. Psychiatry, 134*, 549–623.

Horton, C. (1981). *Solace*. Chicago: University of Chicago Press.

Hunt, M. (1944). *The complete Grimm's fairy tales*. New York: Random House, 1972.

James, H. (1947). *The jolly corner*. In F.O. Matthiessen, (Ed.). *The American novels and stories of Henry James*. New York: Knopf.

Johnson, S.M. (1985). *Characterological transformation: The hard work miracle*. New York: Norton.

Kaiser, H. (1965). *Effective psychotherapy*. (L. Fierman, Ed.). New York: Free Press.

Kaplan, L. (1978). *Oneness and separateness: From infant to individual*. New York: Simon and Schuster (Touchstone Books).

Karpel, M.A., & Strauss, E.S. (1983). *Family evaluation*. New York: Gardner Press.

Keppler, C.F. (1972). *The literature of the second self*. Tucson: University of Arizona Press.

Kernberg, O. (1975). *Borderline conditions and pathological narcissism*. New York: Jason Aronson.

Kernberg, O. (1976). *Object relations theory and clinical psychoanalysis*. New York: Jason Aronson.

Kernberg, O. (1982). Self, ego, affects, and drives. *Journal of American Psychoanalytic Association, 30*, 893–917.

Kernberg, O. (1984) *Severe personality disorders*. New Haven: Yale University Press.

Kirman, W.J. (1980). Countertransference in facilitating intimacy and communication. *Modern Psychoanalysis, 5*(2), 131–145.

Klein, M. (1952). Some theoretical conclusions regarding the emotional life of the infant. In M. Klein (Ed.), (1975). *Envy and gratitude and other works, 1946–1963*. New York: Delacorte Press.

Klein, M., & Tribich, D. (1981). Kernberg's object-relations theory: A critical evaluation. *Int. J. Psychoanalysis, 62*, 27–43.

Kohut, H. (1971). *The analysis of the self*. New York: International Universities Press.

Kohut, H. (1977). *The restoration of the self*. New York: International Universities Press.

Langs, R. (1973). *The technique of psychoanalytic psychotherapy*. New York: Jason Aronson.

Langs, R. (1982). Countertransference and the process of cure. In Slipp, S. (Ed.) *Curative factors in dynamic psychotherapy*. New York: McGraw-Hill.

Lichtenberg, J.D. (1983). *Psychoanalysis and infant research*. Hillsdale, NJ: The Analytic Press.

Mahler, M. (1952). On child psychosis and schizophrenia: Autistic and symbiotic infantile psychoses. *Psychoanalytic Study of the Child, 7*, 206–305.

Mahler, M., Pine, F., & Bergman, A. (1975). *The psychological birth of the human infant*. New York: Basic Books.

Malin, A., & Grotstein, J. (1966). Projective identification in the therapeutic process. *International Journal Psycho-Analysis, 47*, 26–31.

Mann, J. (1973). Confrontation as a mode of teaching. In G. Adler & P.G. Myerson (Eds.), *Confrontation in psychotherapy*. New York: Science House.

Massie, H.N. (1975). The early natural history of childhood psychosis. *J. Amer. Acad. of Child Psychiatry, 14,* 683–707.

Massie, H.N. (1978a). Blind ratings of mother-child interaction in home movies of prepsychotic and normal infants. *Amer. J. Psychiatry, 135*(11), 1371–1374.

Massie, H.N. (1978b). The early natural history of childhood psychosis. Ten cases studied by analysis of family home movies of the infancies of the children. *J. Amer. Acad. Child Psychiatry, 17,* 29–45.

Massie, H.N. (1982). Affective development and the organization of mother-infant behavior from the perspective of pychopathology. In E.Z. Tronick (Ed.), *Social interchange in infancy: Affect, cognition, and communication* (pp. 161–182). Baltimore: University Park Press.

Masterson, J.F. (1976). *Psychotherapy of the borderline adult: A developmental approach.* New York: Brunner/Mazel.

Masterson, J.F. (1978). The borderline adult: Transference acting out and working through. In J.F. Masterson (Ed.), *New perspectives on psychotherapy of the borderline adult.* New York: Brunner/Mazel.

Mead, G.H. (1934). *Mind, self and society.* Chicago: University of Chicago Press.

Meyers, H.C. (Ed.) (1986). *Between analyst and patient: New dimensions in countertransference and transference.* Hillsdale, NJ: Analytic Press.

Minuchin, S. (1974). *Families and family therapy.* Cambridge: Harvard University Press.

Myers, N.A., Clifton, R.K., & Clarkson, M. (1987). When they were very young: Almost-threes remember two years ago. *Infant behavior and development, 10,* 123–132.

Ogden, T. (1982). *Projective identification and psychotherapeutic technique.* New York: Jason Aronson.

Poe, E.A. (1839). *William Wilson.* In *The portable Poe.* New York: Viking Press, 1957.

Racker, H. (1968). *Transference and countertransference.* New York: International Universities Press.

Rank, O. (1971). *The double: A psychoanalytic study.* Chapel Hill: University of North Carolina Press.

Rinsley, D.B. (1982). *Borderline and other self disorders.* New York: Jason Aronson.

Rodman, F.R. (1977). *Not dying.* New York: Random House.

Rogers, R. (1970). *The double in literature.* Detroit: Wayne State University Press.

Sandler, J. (Ed.) (1987). *Projection, identification, projective identification.* Madison, CT: International Universities Press.

Sanford, J.A. (1981). *Evil: The shadow side of reality.* New York: Crossroad.

Schaefer, C.E., & Millman, H.L. (Eds.) (1977). *Therapies for children.* San Francisco: Jossey-Bass.

Schlappner, M. (1967). Evil in the cinema. In C.G. Jung Institute, Zurich (Ed.). *Evil.* Evanston: Northwestern University Press.

Schofield, W. (1964). *Psychotherapy: The purchase of friendship.* Englewood Cliffs, NJ: Prentice-Hall.

Searles, H. (1979). *Countertransference and related subjects.* New York: International Universities Press.

Semel, V.G. (1985). Countertransference and the continual fantasy of patient terminations: A modern psychoanalytic study of one therapist's resistance. *Modern Psychoanalysis, 10*(1), 47–63.

Shapiro, R. (1985). A case study: The terminal illness and death of the analyst's mother—Its effects on her treatment of a severely regressed patient. *Modern Psychoanalysis, 10*(1), 31–46.

Spotnitz, H. (1985). *Modern psychoanalysis of the schizophrenic patient.* New York: Human Sciences Press.

Stern, D. (1977). *The first relationship: Infant and mother.* Cambridge: Harvard University Press.

Stern, D.N. (1985). *The interpersonal world of the infant.* New York: Basic Books.

Stevenson, R.L. (1886). *Dr. Jekyll and Mr. Hyde.* New York: Bantam Books, 1981.

Strauss, A. (1956). *The social psychology of George Herbert Mead.* Chicago: University of Chicago Press.

Sullivan, H.S. (1953). *The interpersonal theory of psychiatry.* New York: Norton.

Thompson, C.L., & Rudolph, L.B. (1983). *Couseling children.* Monterey: Brooks/Cole.

Tronick, E.Z. (Ed.) (1982). *Social interchange in infancy: Affect, cognition, and communication.* Baltimore: University Park Press.

Tymms, R. (1955). *German romantic literature.* London: Methuen.

von Franz, M. (1967). The problem of evil in fairy tales. In C.G. Jung Institute, Zurich (Ed.), *Evil.* Evanston: Northwestern University Press.

Vygotsky, L. (1986). *Thought and language.* A. Kosulin (Ed.), Cambridge: MIT Press.

Wilde, O. (1891). *The picture of Dorian Gray.* New York: Dell, 1968.

Winnicott, D.W. (1971). *Playing and reality.* London: Tavistock Publications.

Ziajka, A. (1981). *Prelinguistic communication in infancy.* New York: Praeger.

Index